THE COURT OF APPEAL

Civil justice has been undergoing a massive transformation. There have been big changes in the management of judicial business; the Human Rights Act 1988 has had a pervasive impact; the Constitutional Reform Act 2005 has effected many changes—notably, the prospective transfer of the appellate jurisdiction of the House of Lords to a new Supreme Court. Against this backcloth of radical change, this book looks at the recent history and the present-day operation of the civil division of the Court of Appeal—a court that, despite its pivotal position, has attracted surprisingly little scholarly attention. It examines the impact of the permission to appeal requirements, and the way in which applications—particularly those by litigants in person—are handled; it looks at the working methods of the Lords Justices and at the leadership of the Court by recent Masters of the Rolls; it considers the relationship between the Court and the House of Lords—looking at high-profile cases in which the Court has been reversed by the Lords. Notwithstanding the impending arrival of the Supreme Court, it concludes that 'the Court of Appeal will remain firmly in place, occupying its crucial position as, to all intents and purposes, the court of last resort—indeed, a supreme court—for most civil appellants.'

The Court of Appeal

Gavin Drewry
Louis Blom-Cooper
Charles Blake

with the assistance of
Suzanne Fullbrook

·HART·
PUBLISHING

OXFORD AND PORTLAND, OREGON
2007

Published in North America (US and Canada)
by Hart Publishing
c/o International Specialized Book Services
920 NE 58th Avenue, Suite 300
Portland, OR 97213-3786
USA
Tel: +1 503 287 3093 or toll-free: (1) 800 944 6190
Fax: +1 503 280 8832
E-mail: orders@isbs.com
Website: www.isbs.com

Hart Publishing, 16C Worcester Place, OX1 2JW
Telephone: +44 (0)1865 517530 Fax: +44 (0)1865 510710
E-mail: mail@hartpub.co.uk
Website: http://www.hartpub.co.uk

British Library Cataloguing in Publication Data
Data Available

ISBN-13: 978-1-84113-387-4 (hardback)
ISBN-10: 1-84113-387-6 (hardback)

Typeset by Compuscript Ltd, Shannon
Printed and bound in Great Britain by
TJ International Ltd, Padstow, Cornwall

Foreword
by
The Lord Chief Justice, Lord Phillips of Worth Matravers

I am delighted to have been asked to introduce this new work on the Civil Division of the Court of Appeal by Gavin Drewry, Louis Blom-Cooper QC, and Charles Blake. In their introduction the authors identify a lacuna in the literature on the judicial system: there was, until recently at least, the lack of a systematic study of the theory and practice of the Civil Division of the Court of Appeal, in contrast to the attention paid to the Criminal Division of the same Court. They acknowledge, of course, the reports commissioned by the (then) Lord Chancellor's Department in the area, in particular those by Sir Jeffery Bowman and by Lord Woolf, my predecessor as both Master of the Rolls and Lord Chief Justice, (the latter examining civil procedure as a whole). These reports have heralded radical changes to the approach to civil appeals. This study is thus timely and important. Timely because the civil procedure reforms have now had the chance to 'bed in', and the authors have therefore been able to subject them to meaningful scrutiny. Important because, as is demonstrated in the chapters which follow, the Civil Division of the Court of Appeal is in the vast majority of civil cases the court of last resort. It is perhaps therefore surprising that an independent study of this kind has not previously been published.

The book is more than a simple history and description of the work of the Civil Division. It addresses broader questions as to the nature of the appellate jurisdiction and the relationship of the division with both the lower courts and the House of Lords. These aspects of the examination are particularly welcome in the light of further changes on the horizon. The government is proposing wholesale reforms in relation to tribunals, with the introduction of an upper-tier appellate tribunal. We are also on the verge of the replacement of the House of Lords by the Supreme Court, which will complete the measures enacted by the Constitutional Reform Act 2005. It is to be hoped that those responsible for policy and implementation in these areas are as rigorous as the authors of this work in their thinking about the requirements of an efficient and effective appellate system.

It is written in chapter two that:

A measure of detachment from the dust of forensic combat is the hallmark of the appellate court.

There is a need for a similar measure of detachment in any analysis of the raft of recent reforms which have come to bear both on the appellate court and on the judiciary as a whole. Messrs Drewry, Blom-Cooper, and Blake have succeeded in detaching themselves from the dust, and for that those of us charged with finding our way through it are indebted to them.

Acknowledgements

For various reasons—some of them very much down to the authors, others less so—this book had a longer period of gestation than could reasonably have been expected. Some of the authors' expressions of thanks must therefore be flavoured with a considerable dash of contrite embarrassment. This ingredient is particularly apposite in respect of our gratitude both to our publisher and to the Nuffield Foundation, which so generously funded the project. Richard Hart, the Managing Director of Hart Publishing, has been ever generous with support and advice, and has regularly turned a diplomatic blind eye to our chronic over-optimism about producing the manuscript of our book. The Nuffield Foundation, and, in particular, Sharon Witherspoon, have also been immensely supportive; they have kindly allowed us several extensions of time on the grant expiry date to enable us to bring the project to completion. We are greatly indebted to both Richard and Sharon for their continuing faith in us, which must, at times, have entailed considerable exertion on their part to achieve the requisite suspension of disbelief.

We gratefully acknowledge the support given to us by the Department of Social and Political Science (now Politics and International Relations) at Royal Holloway, University of London, where the project has been based.

We have received a great deal of invaluable professional advice along the way. During the main period of our research activity we benefited greatly from the support of a distinguished advisory group, chaired by Sir John Laws, the other members being Presiley Baxendale QC, Professor Andrew Le Sueur, and Master Roger Venne. We also owe a great debt to Roger Venne, to his successor as head of the Civil Appeals Office, David Gladwell, and to their colleagues—too numerous to mention individually—not only for providing us with so much invaluable information and advice, but also for putting up with our physical invasion of their working space. Peter Thompson, the general editor of the *Civil Court Practice* (the 'Green Book'), was very helpful in unravelling some troublesome points about Part 52 of the Civil Procedure Rules. We are very grateful for having been given such generous access to the Office and its records, without which the project would not have been feasible. Brendan Keith, head of the Judicial Office of the House of Lords, and his colleague, Christine Salmon, gave us very helpful information about recent and continuing developments in the appellate jurisdiction of the House.

In addition, we interviewed the Master of the Rolls (then Lord Phillips) and ten of the 37 Lords Justices. Our interviews were conducted on a non-attributable basis but, even though we do not name names, we have very much appreciated their giving us the benefit of their time and sharing with us their opinions and experiences. Needless to say, none of those acknowledged here, whether named or unnamed, bears any responsibility for the opinions expressed in this book, or for any errors of fact.

Several other names also deserve a grateful mention. Joyce Plotnikoff and Richard Woolfson undertook a consultancy project on the workings of the Court of Appeal on behalf of the Lord Chancellor's Department (as it then was) just as we were beginning our own research. They generously gave us access to their very useful report and we had several helpful conversations with them about matters of common interest. At the writing-up stage, Ruth Massey joined the team as our editorial adviser. She played an invaluable role in helping to convert our imperfect drafts into a state fit for submission to the publisher, and we have greatly appreciated her excellent advice and perceptive comments.

Finally, we must say a very special thank you to Suzanne Fullbrook, our valued research assistant. Suzy's hard work and loyal commitment have made a very significant contribution to the project, signalled by the inclusion of her name on the title page of this book.

Gavin Drewry, Louis Blom-Cooper and Charles Blake

Royal Holloway, University of London
July 2006

Contents

Foreword by the Lord Chief Justice, Lord Phillips of Worth Matravers v
Acknowledgements vii
About the Authors xiii
Table of Cases xv
Tables of Legislation xvii

1 Introduction 1

    The Research Agenda 5
    A Note on Methodology 6
    Plan of the Book 8
    Annex A: Data Collected for Each Case in the Data-Set 9
    Annex B: Researchers' Informal Aide-Mémoire for the Conduct of
        Semi-Structured Interviews With Judges in the Court of Appeal 10

2 The Nature of the Appellate Process 13

    Appeals in Historical Perspective 15
    Species of Appeal 16
    The Rationale of English Civil Appeals 20
    Appeal and the Trial Process 22

3 Origins and Development of the Court of Appeal 31

    The Position Before 1875 31
    A New Home for the New Court 34
    Rights of Appeal: From Hanworth to Evershed 34
    A Transatlantic Lesson? Slow Moves Towards Modernisation
        Since the 1960s 37
    Insights from Within 39
    The Woolf Reforms 43
    A View from the 1880s—Plus Ça Change? 45

4 New Public Management in the Court of Appeal:
  The Woolf and Bowman Reforms 47

    Thatcherism and the New Public Management 48
    Thatcherism Catches Up with the Judiciary 49
    New Public Management and the Courts—The Rising Tide 52
    The Woolf Reports on Civil Justice 54
    The Court of Appeal: From Woolf to Bowman 55

Implementing Woolf and Bowman: The *Tanfern* Direction 58
Judges as Case Managers? 61

5 A Right of Appeal? 67

The New Procedure in Outline 67
The Requirement for Permission to Appeal.........................69
Dealing With an Application for Permission to Appeal................69
Second Appeals..71
Restrictions on Appeals about Case Management 73
Appeals from Specialist Tribunals 74
Reform of Permission to Appeal 74
Alternative Dispute Resolution: Mediation, Costs, and
    Lower Courts 76
After Permission to Appeal has been Granted: Review or
    Rehearing? 78
The Outcome of an Appeal...81

6 The Court of Appeal at Work—Some Facts and Figures 83

The Official Statistics..83
Permission to Appeal: The Procedure in Practice 84
The Human Rights Act 1998 90
Where was PTA Applied for?...91
Represented and Unrepresented Applicants 93
Time Taken for Applications to be Processed.........................94
Determination on the Papers, and Oral Hearings......................96
Judicial Time Taken to Hear PTA Applications........................97
Permission to Appeal Granted by the Court Below 99
The Journey of an Application: an Applicant's Eye View of the
    Court of Appeal 100

7 The Judges 105

Leading the Court: Masters of the Rolls 105
The Court Today 109
Who Goes Upstairs? 111
Annex A: Masters of the Rolls, 1873–2006 113
Annex B: The Judges of the Court of Appeal(Civil Division) 114

8 Judgments 123

Individuality and Collegiality......................................123
Judgments: Single, Multiple or Composite 126
Prolixity of Judgments 129

9 Unrepresented Applicants 133

   A Litigant's View 138
   The *Taylor v Lawrence* Effect 140
   The Case for Abolition of the Right to an Oral Hearing in
   Seeking Permission to Appeal 140

10 Who has the Last Word? the Court of Appeal
    and the House of Lords.. 143

   Review and Supervision...145
   Appeals in the Abstract..147
   Appealing to the Lords 148
   The Near-Extinction of Orally Argued Petitions for Leave..........150
   The Final Court of Appeal in Parliament 153

11 Reversal by the Lords: *Polanski, Porter, Roma*, and *Begum* 159

   Polanski v Vanity Fair...159
   Appeal and Audit—The Dame Shirley Porter Case 162
   The Roma at Prague Airport...169
   Begum: Another Approach to Discrimination and Human Rights....176

12 The Court in the Twenty-first Century—Some Reflections.......... 181

Bibliography 187

Index 191

About the Authors

Gavin Drewry is Professor of Public Administration at Royal Holloway, University of London. He is an honorary professor in the Law Faculty of UCL and is an elected member of the Executive Committee of the International Institute of Administrative Sciences. Among the first of his many publications was *Final Appeal: A Study of the House of Lords in its Judicial Capacity* (1972), co-authored with Louis Blom-Cooper.

Sir Louis Blom-Cooper QC has had a long and distinguished career as a practising barrister. Between 1989 and 1996 he served as a Judge of the Court of Appeal of Jersey and of Guernsey and was a Deputy High Court Judge in the Crown Office List (1992-1996). Among his many other public appointments, he was the last Chairman of the Press Council (1989-1990) and was Chairman of the Mental Health Act Commission (1987-1994).

Charles Blake is a practising solicitor and serves as a part-time Immigration Judge. He has been a lecturer in law and is a former senior member of the Government Legal Service.

Table of Cases

AUSTRALIA

Collins (alias Hass) v The Queen (1975) 133 CLR 120, 122 .... 141, 142

EUROPEAN

McGonnell v United Kingdom 39 (2000) 30 EHRR 289 155
Procola v Luxembourg (1995) 22 EHRR 193 155

UNITED KINGDOM

A v Secretary of State for the Home Department [2005] 3
    All ER 169 147
A and others v Secretary of State for the Home Department [2005]
    UKHL 71 59
Aerotel Ltd v Telco Holdings Ltd and others [2006] EWCA Civ
    1371 2006 130
Aoun v Bahri [2002] EWCA Civ 1141 72
Assicurazioni Generali SpA v Arab Insurance Group
    [2003] 1 WLR 577; (BSC) [2002] EWCA Civ 1642 .... 22, 23, 27, 79
Associated Provincial Picture Houses Ltd v Wednesbury
    Corporation [1948] 1 KB 223 107
Attorney General v Covey [2001] EWCA Civ 254; (2001)
    The Times 2 March 91, 93
Audergon v La Baguette Ltd [2002] EWCA Civ 10 79
Biogen Inc v Medera plc [1997] RPC 1 28
Broome v Cassell [1972] AC 1027 128
Burchell v Bullard [2005] EWCA Civ 538 77
Compaq Computer Corporation and another v Dell Computer
    Corporation Ltd [2005] UKHL 10 25
Cooke v Secretary of State for Social Security [2001] EWCA Civ 734 ... 74
Ebert v Venvil [2000] Ch 484 99
EI Du Pont Nemours & Co v ST Du Pont [2003] EWCA Civ 1638 79
Fowler de Pledge (a firm) v Smith [2003] EWCA Civ 703 80
G v G [1985] 2 All ER 225, 229; [1985] 1 WLR 647, 652 61
Gregory v Turner [2003] EWCA Civ 183 133
Grepe v Loam [1887] Ch 168 98
Hackney London Borough Council v Driscoll (No 1) [2003] EWCA
    Civ 614 79

Hall v Simmons [1999] 3 WLR 873 140
Halsey v Milton Keynes General NHS Trust [2004] EWCA
    Civ 576 .... 76, 77
HM Customs & Excise and Another v MCA and Another
    [2002] EWCA Civ 1039 .... 126, 129
IRC v Church Commissioners for England [1975] 1 WLR 251 152
Jaffray v Society of Lloyds [2002] EWCA Civ 1101 23
Jolly v Jay [2002] EWCA Civ 277 .... 70, 73
Jones and Others v Ceredigion County Council (No 2) [2005]
    1 WLR 3626 153
Lane v Esdaile [1891] AC 210 .... 146, 151
Lloyd Jones v T Mobile (UK) Ltd [2003] EWCA Civ 1162 74
McKenzie v McKenzie [1971] P 33 134
Meadow v General Medical Council, Attorney-General Intervening [2006]
    EWCA Civ 1390 22
Morris v Bank of India [2004] EWCA Civ 1286 70
The Ocean Frost: Armagas Ltd v Mundogas SA [1986] AC 717;
    [1985] 1 Lloyd's Rep 1, 57 26
Polanski v Condé Nast Publications Ltd [2005] UKHL 10 .... 25, 160
R v London County Justices [1894] 1 QB 543 105
R v Secretary of State for Trade and Industry ex p Eastaway [2001]
    1 All ER 27, 33 146
R (on the application of Begum by her litigation friend, Rahman) v
    Head Teacher and Governors of Denbigh High School, the
    Secretary of State for Education and Skills intervening [2006]
    UKHL 1 176
R (on the application of Jackson and others) v Attorney General
    [2005] 4 All ER 1253 147
Rondel v Worsley [1969] 1 AC 191, 257 .... 140, 141
Royal & Sun Alliance v T & N Limited [2002] EWCA Civ 1964 73
Southern & District Finance plc v Turner [2003] EWCA Civ 1574 80
Swain v Hillman [2001] 1 All ER 91 .... 59, 70
Re T (A Child) 2002] EWCA Civ 1736 69
Tanfern Ltd v Cameron-MacDonald [2000]
    1 WLR 1311 ....22, 58, 68, 72, 81, 91
Taylor v Lawrence 2002] EWCA Civ 90 140
Todd v Adam [2002] 2 All ER (Comm) 1 27

UNITED STATES OF AMERICA

Alleghany Corp v Breswick and Co, 353 US 151, 170 (1957) 83
Dick v New York Life Insurance Co, 359 US 437, 458–59 (1959) 150
Sale, Acting Comr, Immigration and Naturalisation Service v
    Haitian Centers Council Inc (1993) 509 US 155 175

Table of Legislation

Access to Justice Act 1999 45
    Part IV 58
    s 54 67
    s 54(1) 91
    s 54(4) 101
    s 55 .... 67, 80
    s 55(1) 59, 71
    s 56 67
    s 57 67
    s 57(1) 59
    ss 58–59 67
    s 70 53
Administration of Justice Act 1969 .... 2, 6, 36
    s 12(3)(a) 152
Administration of Justice (Appeals) Act 1934 .... 11, 35, 39, 148
Appellate Jurisdiction Act 1876 .... 32, 154
Arbitration Act 1996 18
Children Act 1989, s 25 58
Constitutional Reform Act 2005 .... i, v, 54, 62, 110, 152, 156, 183
Courts and Legal Services Act 1990 133
    ss 27–28 133
Crime and Security Act 2001 147
Criminal Appeal Act 1907 17
Crown Proceedings Act 1947 149
Drug Trafficking Act 1994, s 31 131
Human Rights Act 1988 .... i, 5, 7, 9, 90, 138, 142, 155,
                             167, 176, 178, 183, 184
Hunting Act 2004 147
Judicature Act 1873 .... 8, 16, 31, 33, 34
Judicature Act 1875 .... 8, 31, 33, 34
Judicature Act 1925 35
Local Government Act 2000, s 90 163
Local Government Finance Act 1982 165
    s 20 164
    s 20(3) 165
Matrimonial Causes Act 1973
    s 24 131
    s 25 131

Parliament Act 1949 147
Public Records Act 1958 105
Rent Acts 40
Supreme Court Act 1981 52
    s 58 52
    s 59 183
    ss 88–89 52
    Sch 2 52
Supreme Court Act 2005 105
Supreme Court (Offices) Act 1997 53

AUSTRALIA

Federal Judiciary Act 1903–73
    s 78 141
    s 86 141

INTERNATIONAL

European Convention on Human Rights 5, 90, 142, 167, 168,
                                               176, 177, 178, 183
    art 6 .... 23, 152, 168, 183
    art 6(1) 90, 155
    art 8 90
    art 9 178
Protocol 7 142
    art 2 142
Refugee Convention of 1951 .... 169, 170, 173, 174, 175, 176

SECONDARY LEGISLATION

Access to Justice Act 1999 (Destination of Appeals) Order 2000 58
Civil Procedure Rules 1998 (SI 1998/3132) 4, 7, 8, 27, 39, 58, 71,
                              75, 76, 83, 84, 91, 96, 97, 103, 104, 136, 160
    Part 1 81
        r 1.1(2) 76
        r 1.4(2)(e) 76
    Part 24, r 24.2 70
    Part 32
        r 32.3 160
        PD, Annex 3 161
    Part 35 17

Part 44, r 44.5 76
Part 52 .... vii, 67, 91, 101, 136, 142
    r 52 .... 80, 81
    r 52.3(4A) 75
    r 52.3(6) 70
    r 52.6 92
    r 52.6 92
    r 52.9 72
    r 52.9(2) 72
    r 52.11 .... 22, 23, 60
    r 52.11(1) 22, 23, 78, 79
    r 52.11(1)(a)–(b) 23
    r 52.11(2) 23
    r 52.11(3) 23, 79, 81
    r 52.11(3)(a)–(b) 23
    r 52.11(4)–(5) 23
    r 52.13 71
    r 52.14(1) 59
    PD 136
        para.9 79
Part 53, r 53.3(6) 70
Part 54 24
Civil Procedure Rules 1999 55
Immigration Rules 169, 174
Rules of the Supreme Court 27, 37
    Ord 53 24
    Ord 58, r 1 22
    Ord 59, r 3 22

AUSTRALIA

Rules of Court, Ord 70, r 2(6) 141

1

Introduction

THIS IS A study of an important legal institution, with a history that goes back some 130 years. The Court of Appeal is divided into a Criminal Division and a Civil Division, a bifurcation that was effected in 1968, when the Court of Criminal Appeal (set up in 1907) was merged into the Court of Appeal. The Civil Division—with which we are principally concerned—hears appeals mainly against decisions in the High Court and the county courts in England and Wales and from various specialised tribunals. (Scotland has its own courts of first instance and its own appellate system—but the final court of appeal across the whole of the UK is, at least for the time being, the House of Lords.) The Civil Division currently deals with about 3,000 applications each year (mostly applications for permission to appeal) and disposes of just over 1,000 substantive appeals.[1]

The main judicial manpower of the Court of Appeal (both divisions) consists, at the time of writing, of 37 Lords Justices of Appeal. They are sometimes assisted by High Court judges, drafted in for various purposes, and are joined occasionally by retired Lords Justices and, even more occasionally, by retired Law Lords. Heading the Court are the Lord Chief Justice (head of the judiciary, and of the Criminal Division of the Court) and the Master of the Rolls (who heads the Civil Division).

An outstanding feature of the English legal system is that appeals against decisions of courts and tribunals, whether made at first instance or by intermediate review bodies, are ultimately determinable by a single, highly centralised appeal court sitting almost exclusively in London.[2] The Court of Appeal, in its civil and criminal jurisdictions, thus stands, for almost all practical purposes, at the pinnacle of the hierarchy of judicial bodies in England and Wales.[3] Only a tiny fraction of the appeals heard in the Court of Appeal ends up in the House of Lords—the final appellate court at the time of writing (although, as noted in chapter ten, its jurisdiction is about to

---

[1] See ch 6 for tabulations of the relevant statistics.

[2] The Court now sits from time to time outside London, eg in Cardiff.

[3] Scotland and Northern Ireland have their own trial and appellate courts, with provision for further appeal to the House of Lords. The present study is concerned exclusively with arrangements in England and Wales.

be transferred to a new Supreme Court, scheduled to come into operation in October 2009).

Thus one might suppose that the pivotal nature of the Court of Appeal makes it a prime target for academic investigation—but, somewhat to the authors' surprise when they first embarked upon the research on which this book is based, this turned out not to be so. This is in sharp contrast to the comparatively large amount of academic attention that has been given to the judicial functions of the House of Lords, which handles only a tiny fraction of the number of cases—some 60 to 70 a year on average. Indeed, it was a study by two of the present authors in 1972[4] that was the first in a succession of books on the judicial functions of the House of Lords, followed soon afterwards by the studies by Robert Stevens[5] and by Alan Paterson[6]. Blom-Cooper and Drewry have subsequently, albeit briefly, revisited the subject.[7] Brice Dickson produced a useful overview of the work of the Lords during the period 1967–96.[8] Gavin Drewry also discussed some aspects of the relationship between the Court of Appeal and the House of Lords in the context of the 'leapfrogging' provisions of the Administration of Justice Act 1969.[9] Another recent book has analysed the use of discretion or creative choice by the Law Lords,[10] and there are various studies based on linguistic analysis of the reasoning in speeches;[11] two academics from, respectively, the universities of Haifa and Nottingham have applied economic modelling to test the possibility of political interference with judicial decision-making in public law decisions taken by the Court of Appeal, with reference to the pattern of promotions from that Court to the House of Lords.[12] Finally, there is a substantial study of the criminal jurisdiction of the Court of Appeal by Pattenden.[13]

---

[4] Louis Blom-Cooper and Gavin Drewry, *Final Appeal. A Study of the House of Lords in its Judicial Capacity* (Oxford, Clarendon Press, 1972).

[5] Robert Stevens, Law and Politics: *The House of Lords as a Judicial Body, 1800–1976* (London, Macmillan, 1982).

[6] Alan Paterson, *The Law Lords* (Basingstoke, Macmillan, 1982).

[7] Louis Blom-Cooper and Gavin Drewry, 'The Appellate Function' in Brice Dickson and Paul Carmichael (eds), *The House of Lords: Its Parliamentary and Judicial Roles* (Oxford, Hart Publishing, 1998) ch 6.

[8] Brice Dickson, 'The Lords of Appeal and their Work, 1967–96' in Dickson and Carmichael, *ibid*, ch 7.

[9] Gavin Drewry, 'Leapfrogging—And a Lords Justices' Eye View of the Final Appeal' (1973) 89 LQR 260.

[10] David Robertson, *Judicial Discretion in the House of Lords* (Oxford, Clarendon Press, 1999).

[11] Anthony Bradney, 'The Changing Face of the House of Lords' [1958] *Juridical Review* 178; WT Murphy and Rick Rawlings, 'After the Ancien Regime: The Writing of Judgments in the House of Lords, 1979–80' (1981) 44 *MLR* 617 and (1982) 45 *MLR* 34.

[12] Eli Salzberger and Paul Fenn, 'Judicial Independence: Some Evidence from the English Court of Appeal' (1999) xlii(2) *Journal of Law and Economics* 831–47. See also Eli Salzberger, 'A Positive Analysis of the Doctrine of Separation of Powers, or: Why do we have an Independent Judiciary?' (1993) 13 *International Review of Law and Economics* 349–79.

[13] Rosemary Pattenden, *English Criminal Appeals 1844–1994* (Oxford, Oxford University Press, 1996).

Further focus on the role of the Lords has been prompted both by the seemingly endless debate about the future composition and powers of the Second Chamber and by the proposal, announced in 2004, to transfer the appellate functions of the House of Lords to a new Supreme Court (see chapter ten). This led to the publication of a substantial collection of essays, to which some of the present authors have contributed.[14] However, until recently,[15] there has never been any systematic study of the Civil Division of the Court of Appeal, either in theory or in practice.

We must, of course, acknowledge that a court situated at the pinnacle of the national judicial hierarchy, one whose decisions are binding on all the courts below, a tribunal whose rigorous leave requirements give it a small, hand-picked docket of particularly difficult and interesting cases raising issues of general public importance, is bound to hog a disproportionate share of the limelight. But the scant attention given to the Court of Appeal, a tribunal handling a huge amount of judicial business and dispensing decisions of high authority—and which is indeed, as we note later, de facto the court of last resort for the great majority of civil appeals—is both striking and surprising.

At the time of Blom-Cooper and Drewry's work in the 1960s on *Final Appeal*, and indeed for many years after that, the Court of Appeal was overbearingly dominated by Lord Denning, the Master of the Rolls from 1962 to 1982. Denning was famous for his bold—indeed sometimes wayward—approach to judicial law-making (he had moved from the House of Lords, a five-judge tribunal, in which he often found himself isolated in a dissenting minority of one, to be head of the three-judge Court of Appeal). In his court no Lord Justice ever gave the first judgment. His life and work have been punctuated by his considerable writing, both judicially and extrajudicially. But his idiosyncrasies, both in declaring the law and in his literary style,[16] were regarded with mixed feelings even while he was still on the Bench, and his influence on procedure was little noticed or studied.

After 1982—perhaps coinciding with the beginnings of a 'new public management' culture in public administration (see chapter four)—a more formal approach to the work of the Court was adopted by the Lord Chancellor's Department and the judiciary. Lord Denning retired and

[14] Charles Blake and Gavin Drewry, 'The Role of the Court of Appeal in England and Wales as an Intermediate Court' in Andrew Le Sueur (ed), *Building the UK's New Supreme Court* (Oxford, Oxford University Press, 2004) pp 221–35.
[15] The Lord Chancellor's Department and its successor, the Department for Constitutional Affairs, have from time to time, in recent years, commissioned research into aspects of the operation of the Court of Appeal. Particular mention should be made of the important study by J Plotnikoff and R Woolfson, *Evaluation of the Impact of the Reforms in the Court of Appeal (Civil Division)*, for the Lord Chancellor's Department, November 2002. Details of recent and current exercises of this kind can be found on the DCA's website (www.dca.gov.uk).
[16] See Louis Blom-Cooper, 'Judges Among the Literati', Howard Lecture, 2002.

Lord Donaldson of Lymington was appointed Master of the Rolls. The post of Registrar was created to provide administrative support to the Court. Legislation was introduced to create a more structured, systematised, and modern method of preparing cases for a hearing. The emphasis remained on an oral procedure for expounding the grounds of and opposition to an appeal. But the questions that lie at the heart of the present study remained both unasked and unanswered: what is the precise nature and rationale of, and for, an appeal? Is it a rehearing? If it is, does that mean taking the evidence again or is the procedure limited to a review of the testimony and the legal issues arising? How does the role of the Court of Appeal differ from, and relate to, that of the House of Lords?

When our research began, there was not even a standard practitioners' text treating the Civil Division of the Court as a whole and unravelling the complexities of law and procedure relating to its functions. The notes to what used to be the Supreme Court Practice (the 'White Book') were never easy to follow and, having been built up from myriad case-law over the years, were not in a suitable form to be regarded as a comprehensive guide to the law and practice of appeals. An invaluable Manual of Civil Appeals—a professional commentary on the new Civil Procedure Rules—was first published around the time that our project started.[17]

The need to fill such a glaring lacuna in the literature on the judicial system has assumed greater urgency in the light of three recent developments. First, as noted above, the prospective establishment of a new Supreme Court has raised fresh questions about the rationale and operational dynamics of the appellate system and, in particular, about the relationships between appellate tribunals at different levels of the court hierarchy. The big questions that lay at the heart of Final Appeal—about the rationale of retaining a multi-level appellate hierarchy, and the nature of the relationships between the different levels—have been very much in the minds of the authors of the present study, more than three decades later.

Secondly, since 26 April 1999—in the wake of major reviews by Lord Woolf and Sir Jeffrey Bowman—the process of civil litigation and civil appeals has been undergoing a radical overhaul. Judges have been required to take on a much more proactive role in the management of litigation. The system of appeals has increasingly been curtailed by restrictions and limitations on the right of a losing party to appeal. The intended effect of these restrictions and limitations is, in their aggregate, to reduce the number of appeals to a manageable caseload with which the Court of Appeal can adequately cope, commensurate with expeditious and efficient disposal of business for all prospective appellants and respondents. It was an interest in

---

[17] Roger Venne, David Di Mambro, Phillipe Sands, Louise Di Mambro and Ian Joseph, *Manual of Civil Appeals* (London, Butterworths, 2000).

the impact of these management reforms on the structure and the working culture of the Court of Appeal (discussed in greater detail in chapters four, seven, and eight) that probably did most to prompt the authors to undertake the present study at this time.

But a third development also influenced our decision, and its timing. In October 2000, the Human Rights Act 1998 came into force. This legislation, giving statutory effect to the fundamental freedoms in the European Convention on Human Rights and enabling it to be applied in domestic litigation, has impacted on every UK court and tribunal, including, of course, the Court of Appeal. The impact has been greatest in the various fields of public law, particularly judicial review—areas of law in which the authors have a keen interest. So the impact of the 1998 Act has been an important part of the background to our research agenda.

The core of the projected study is thus the Court of Appeal in its civil jurisdiction—but with some attention also given to its overseer, the Appellate Committee of the House of Lords. In undertaking this study, we have not confined ourselves to a purely descriptive account of the operation of the Court of Appeal. The theory and philosophy of the appellate process are considered at length in chapter two, and intermittently in most other chapters, and are revisited—in the light of our research findings—in our concluding chapter. But the core of this book, and the focus of our research, is concerned with the day-to-day functioning of the Court of Appeal and the contribution of the Court to the administration of justice.

THE RESEARCH AGENDA

Much of the work has essentially been a mapping exercise: using both primary and secondary sources to compile a large amount of qualitative and quantitative factual information about the Court, the way it goes about its work, the time taken to process appeals and applications at different stages, and the extent and subject distribution of its caseload. This information (much of which is to be found in chapter six) includes basic data about the types and origins of cases coming forward, the throughput of applications and appeals, and their 'success rate' in terms of the proportion of these that are allowed. However, we have ventured beyond the raw data to consider a number of issues in greater depth.

We have looked in particular at the significance and implications of the requirement to obtain permission to appeal—one of the main products of the reviews by Lord Woolf and Sir Jeffrey Bowman, mentioned above. Later chapters examine the procedures for handling applications for permission and consider the impact of applications on the workload of the Court. We have looked at the operation of the permission filter, and the criteria applied in considering applications.

Along the way, we have also considered the decision-making process in the Court, including the use of legal assistants. We discuss the phenomenon of multiple/dissenting judgments and, equally, the strength of a unanimous decision said to be 'of the court'. There is also the use of lawyers in the Court, who are permanent members of the Department for Constitutional Affairs, spending a part of their career in the Court. They are very much a hidden resource: they rarely speak to the parties' lawyers yet perform a vital function in making sure that cases are properly prepared, that the documents are in order, and that the case is fit to be heard.

Another issue is the treatment of cases that eventually pass to the House of Lords. Which cases are these? When is leave to appeal given by the Court and when do litigants have to apply to be allowed to take their cases further? Are the leapfrogging provisions, introduced in the Administration of Justice Act 1969, now to all intents and purposes defunct? Above all, what is the relationship between the respective functions of the Court of Appeal and of the House of Lords?

The work and achievements of any court are the sum—more or less—of the contributions made by the judges who sit in it and, in particular, of those who lead it. In chapter seven we consider the recent membership of the Court of Appeal—and in particular the pivotal contributions of Masters of the Rolls. The history of the Court over the last 20 years could be written in terms of the forceful personalities of Lords Denning, Donaldson, Bingham, and Woolf. Lord Denning made the Court his own. But substantial arrears of work had built up at his retirement, and a new system consisting of a Registrar and computerised case management was introduced (the post of Registrar has now been replaced by that of Head of the Civil Appeals Office). Lord Donaldson brought new working methods and an interventionist style to the Court. Lord Bingham was in post for only a short period but brought an enormous intellectual weight to the task. Apart from his position as presiding judge, Lord Woolf has been responsible for changing the face of civil litigation. We have considered how far individual presiding judges can influence the entire form and style of decision-making of the Court.

A NOTE ON METHODOLOGY

The essence of our research method has been direct and indirect observation of the Court of Appeal at work. We wanted first to understand the procedures by which applications for permission to appeal (PTA) are received by the Court, and then to follow the progress of a defined group of applications through to their final determination, which is often no further than the refusal of permission, but may eventually culminate in the hearing and determination of a full appeal—and then, in a small number of cases, a further journey to the House of Lords.

Using Civil Appeals Office records we constructed a data-set of 800 cases, divided into four groups of 200 PTA cases. Four time periods were identified—June 2000, October 2000, January 2001, and May 2001—and the first 200 cases lodged at the Registry in each of those periods constituted the sample group. Choosing these dates as our starting points for data collection ensured that we included within our sample cases which were regulated by the new Civil Procedure Rules (and ones which would reflect the impact of the Human Rights Act). Looking at the progress of 800 cases over a 12-month period generated a substantial working sample from which patterns of activity could be identified. We also made grateful use of the published statistics produced by the Court itself.

Many applications did not in fact reach a final determination by a judge, but were settled, dismissed, or withdrawn for various reasons. In a proportion of those that were judicially decided, permission to appeal was granted. We then followed these cases through to the final determination, asking similar questions, although many were settled or withdrawn before appeal.

The information recorded for each of the 800 cases in our sample is listed as an annex to this chapter (Annex A). When answers to our list of questions had been obtained for each PTA data-set, we undertook an analysis of these answers to try to identify trends, and any problems encountered during the process. The issues we addressed fell into three main areas:

— The characteristics of each application: this included the subject-matter, the identities of the court(s) a quo, whether or not applicants sought to obtain permission to appeal from the court a quo, and whether the application was a first- or second-tier appeal application (the latter being subject to much tougher criteria of eligibility than those applicable to the former).
— The processes that an application goes through before being passed to a judge for consideration. This set of questions included such matters as time taken from the lodging of the application to final determination, including reasons for any delay, the internal workings of different groups within the Civil Appeals Office and, in the case of applications that were settled or withdrawn, the reasons for this outcome.
— The outcomes of PTA applications following judicial determination, both on the papers and at an oral hearing. The subsequent progress of cases granted PTA was then followed.

In addition to gathering statistical and other factual material from the Court of Appeal records, the researchers attended and observed a variety of court hearings.

We needed to identify those cases where a substantive appeal was unsuccessful and the applicant asked for leave to appeal to the House of Lords. This proved somewhat difficult because the Court of Appeal does not keep a record of these cases in a computerised form, so we had to identify them manually, by obtaining all of the court orders made within a six-month period, and recording those where leave was asked for. Following that, we consulted the records of the Judicial Office of the House of Lords to identify those cases involving petitions for leave to appeal following the refusal of leave by the Court of Appeal.

Semi-structured, non-attributable interviews were conducted with ten of the Lords Justices (including the Master of the Rolls); the researchers' aide-mémoire for the conduct of these interviews is annexed to this chapter as Annex B. We also consulted regularly with the successive heads of the Civil Appeals Office.

PLAN OF THE BOOK

We begin, in chapter two, by considering the nature of the appellate process, highlighting, in particular, the important distinction between 'supervision' (correcting errors and maintaining consistency in the decisions of the courts below) and 'review' (resolving difficult and important legal issues and enunciating authoritative jurisprudential principles in cases that have general public significance). In chapter three, we outline the origins and historical development of the Court of Appeal, from the passing of the Judicature Act in the 1870s to the Woolf–Bowman reforms that began in the 1990s. We then turn, in chapter four, to the impact of 'new public management' thinking, reflected in the Woolf–Bowman reviews, on the administration of justice in general, and the Court of Appeal in particular. Chapter five looks at the practical implications of the post-Woolf Civil Procedure Rules for the work of the Court and for those who appear before it.

In chapter six, we provide a statistical overview of the recent work of the Court, along with a narrative commentary on the progress of an application for permission to appeal from the point at which it is lodged to the point of final resolution. Chapter seven gives an overview of the judicial personnel of the Court, focusing, in particular, on the contribution of recent holders of the office of Master of the Rolls. Chapter eight examines the style and 'collegiality' of judicial decision-making, including the incidence of dissenting and assenting multiple judgments. In Chapter nine we look at a specific issue—one with major implications for the cost-effective use of scarce judicial resources: the time-consuming consideration of unrepresented applicants for permission to appeal, whose cases turn out, all too often, to be hopelessly ill founded. Chapter ten looks at the appellate functions of the House of Lords (soon to be superseded by the establishment of the Supreme Court) and the relationship (complementary or overlapping?) between its functions and those of the Court of Appeal. This account is complemented, in Chapter eleven, by studies of four important recent cases in which the Court of Appeal has been reversed by the House of Lords. The book ends with a short chapter summarising our main findings, and offering some reflections on the role and future of the Court of Appeal in the twenty-first century.

ANNEX A: DATA COLLECTED FOR EACH CASE IN THE DATA-SET

Name of case.

Whether or not the applicant was a litigant in person, or was legally represented.

The name and location of the court below.

The name of the Lord Justice who finally determined the application.

The name of the judge in the court below.

The subject-area of the case.

Whether or not a bench me morandum was prepared.

The time taken for the application for permission to be heard, at the oral hearing.

Whether or not the case involved Human Rights Act issues, and if so, what those issues were.

Whether or not the application was for a judicial review.

Whether or not the application was at any time threatened with dismissal by the Court.

Whether or not a paper application was made.

Whether or not an oral hearing took place.

Whether or not the court below gave permission to appeal, and whether or not the outcome of any such application to the court below in the form of an order was recorded by the Court of Appeal Office.

The result of all paper applications.

The result of an oral hearing.

Whether or not the case was dismissed by consent.

Whether or not it was allowed by consent.

Whether or not it was dismissed by the court office.

Whether permission to appeal was granted or refused.

Any ruling that the case was outside the Court's jurisdiction.

Whether the application was allowed on paper, therefore not needing to progress to an oral hearing.

Whether this was a case where the application, having been refused 'on paper', was renewed for determination at an oral hearing and, if so, whether an oral hearing took place.

Whether this was a case in which, having considered the application on paper, the Lord Justice adjourned the case for a full hearing.

Whether the parties enquired about Alternative Dispute Resolution.

Whether the application was a 'first-tier' or a 'second-tier' application.

The time taken from the date of lodging the application in the Registry to the date of a final determination of the case.

ANNEX B: RESEARCHERS' INFORMAL AIDE-MÉMOIRE FOR THE CONDUCT OF SEMI-STRUCTURED INTERVIEWS WITH JUDGES IN THE COURT OF APPEAL

Permission Stage

How far is it necessary to refer to the criteria for the grant of permission?

When do you move directly to an oral hearing of an application (litigants in person apart)?

In cases of oral applications for permission, when do you fix a hearing before yourself alone, two Lords Justices or three?

Do you think that the permission stage is operating as it should do? If not, how should the procedure or the criteria be modified?

Are the procedures for the preparation of papers/bundles for the permission stage working well?

Is there a need for more active management of the preparation of permission cases?

Is there any other modification you would like to see at the permission stage?

General Function of the Court

Does the removal of jurisdiction from the Court to hear some appeals (generally 'second appeals') reduce its function as an intermediate court?

Full Listing

Would the introduction of a Juge Rapporteur procedure assist the Court in full hearings or would it merely add an unnecessary layer of documentation and preparation?

In your experience how do dissenting judgments emerge?

How far does the Court engage in a full internal debate in such cases?

How does the Court decide whether to give one collegiate judgment or three separate judgments?

Leave to Appeal to the House of Lords

The Court seems to have adopted a policy of, in general, leaving such decisions to the House itself. This is not expressly supported by the 1934 Act [the Administration of Justice (Appeals) Act 1934]. Is this necessarily the best way of proceeding given that the House is not a Supreme Court as such?

If this is the policy, in which cases is an exception capable of being made?

2

The Nature of the Appellate Process[1]

The only ground upon which a suitor ought to be allowed to bring the judgment of one court for examination before the members of another is the certainty or extreme probability of finding in the latter tribunal more wisdom and learning, more maturity of deliberation, and a greater capacity of sound decisions than existed in the court from which the appeal is to proceed. But as every appeal is of necessity attended with the two great and positive evils of expense and delay, it is the bounden duty of every wise and good government to take all possible care that the court of appellate jurisdiction shall possess those advantages, and that superior capacity for wise and impartial adjudication, upon the presumption of possessing which, the public support and the confidence of individual suitors is given to the institution.[2]

I N THE COURSE of discussion and debate about aspects of the judicial process, extensive and somewhat indiscriminate use is made of the word 'appeal'. But what does 'appeal' really mean? Indeed, is it a meaningful term at all in any universal sense? The word is in fact merely a term of convenient usage, a piece of linguistic shorthand which accepts the existence of a penumbra of uncertainty in order to achieve universal comprehensibility at a very low level of exactitude. Thus, while 'appeal' is a generic term, broadly meaningful to all lawyers in describing a feature common to a wide range of legal systems, it would be misleading to impute a precise meaning to the term, or to assume, on the grounds that the word (or its translated equivalent) has some international currency, that the concept of an appeal means the same thing in a wide range of systems.

On any orthodox definition, an appeal includes three basic elements: a decision (usually the judgment of a court, or the ruling of an administrative tribunal) from which an appeal is made; a person or persons aggrieved by the decision; and a reviewing body empowered and willing to entertain the appeal. Thus the essence of an appeal is a request to a competent tribunal

---

[1] Parts of this chapter are adapted from ch 3 of Louis Blom–Cooper and Gavin Drewry's *Final Appeal* (Oxford, Clarendon Press, 1972).

[2] 1832 Tract: *Some Observations on the Necessity of Reforming the Judicial House of Lords, considered as the Court of Ultimate Appeal in the Administration of Civil Justice.*

to reconsider a decision arrived at by another body, or a request to the same body to review its own decision. This definition leaves much unsaid. How formal must the machinery for review be in order to fit the definition? Does, for example, a letter from someone under sentence for a crime to a head of state asking for executive clemency to be exercised count as an appeal? Does the consideration of an abstract point of law in isolation from the operation of that law in particular litigation (eg by 'Special Reference' to the Judicial Committee of the Privy Council) fit into the model? Probably it does not matter; our definition is stipulative and elastic. 'Appeals' can be arranged along a continuum of increasingly formalised procedure, ranging from a condemned man in supplication before his tribal chief, to something as jurisprudentially sophisticated as appeal by way of *certiorari* to the Supreme Court of the United States. Like Aneurin Bevan's elephant, an appeal can be described only as and when it walks through the courtroom door.

The nature of a particular appellate process—indeed, the character of an entire legal system-depends upon a multitude of interrelated (although largely imponderable) factors operating within the system: the structure of the courts; the status and role (both objectively and subjectively perceived) of judges and lawyers; the form of law itself—whether, for example, it is derived from a code or from judicial precedent modified by statute; the attitude of the courts to the authority of decided cases; the political and administrative structure of the country concerned—whether, for example, its internal sovereignty is limited by a federal structure, devolution of constitutional power, or (as in the case of the member countries of the European Union) adherence to a regional union of sovereign states. The list of possible factors is endless, and their weight and function in the social equation defy precise analysis. Indeed, we might as well attribute the character of the legal system at any given point in time to 'historical accident', a term whose use excuses the scholar from seeking more sophisticated answers.

Appeal covers a multitude of jurisprudential ideas. It means different things to different people, in different places at different times. The layman's expectation of an appeal is very often quite different from that of the lawyer, and many an aggrieved claimant denied his 'just' remedy by judge or jury has come upon the disturbing reality that, in England, until recent reforms, a disputed finding of fact seldom, if ever, formed the basis of an appeal. Similarly, a Frenchman, accustomed to a narrowly legalistic appeal in *cassation*, subject to subsequent re-argument in a court below, would find little familiarity in the ponderous finality of the judgments of the English Court of Appeal or the House of Lords. And a seventeenth-century lawyer, accustomed to a painstaking search for trivial mistakes in the court record, which formed the basis of the appeal by writ of error, would be bewildered by the greater flexibility and increased sophistication of jurisprudential argument that characterise a modern appeal.

APPEALS IN HISTORICAL PERSPECTIVE

In examining the development of appellate machinery in England since feudal times, we discover a chameleon–like judicial process which has blended into the landscape of changing social and constitutional conditions and which, even today, is still in a state of flux. Under the early feudal monarchy, before anything resembling a coherent legal system (in the modern sense) came into being, might was right. The mightiest sword was wielded by the King, who was able thereby to secure a virtual monopoly in dispensing justice. He strove to maintain this monopoly, not out of a sense of obligation stemming from a social contract, nor because of feelings of philanthropic paternalism towards his serfs, but for two more mundane reasons. First, the courts were a valuable source of revenue; secondly, the notion of the 'King's peace' was central to monarchical authority, the enforcement of justice by the King being a self–satisfying symptom of his power over his vassals. Appeal in this one–man judicial system meant little more than trying to catch the King in a more benign mood, or seeking the intercession of a favourite courtier. In invoking this ad hoc procedure the hapless suppliant might discover that further representation served only to aggravate the royal wrath, although not invariably so. A woman petitioned King Philip of Macedon for justice for her husband, and was refused. 'I will appeal against this judgment!' she exclaimed. The King-while still in his cups-roared back at her, 'And to whom will you appeal?' 'To Philip, sober,' the woman retorted. According to Valerius Maximus, who tells the Romanist story, the appeal succeeded.

The growing complexity of government made the differentiation of functions and delegation of authority essential; separate and increasingly formalised judicial institutions and procedures came into being. But, ultimately, the King remained the fountain of justice. It is here that we come upon the embryo of a modern appeal: a litigant dissatisfied with the decision of the courts petitioned the sovereign. Eventually, the busy (or bored) monarch came to delegate his powers of review to his Council (in which, at first, he retained a substantial voice), a body which soon split into two parts, Parliament and the Privy Council. Something akin to a 'judicial committee' of the Council came to deal with all appellate business, and a hierarchy of courts—fundamental to the modern notion of appeal—thus came into existence. In fact, there were several hierarchies as courts proliferated and fought for both increased jurisdiction and enhanced status; the situation was further complicated by the growth of a separate system of equity, administered by the courts of chancery to mitigate the rigidity of the common law. Decisions frequently oscillated for years between different courts administering different systems of law.

Appeal in those days, and until the mid-nineteenth century, was a very limited procedure; initially, a form of action had to be framed within one of the existing, rigidly stereotyped writs. If the facts were proved and the case correctly pleaded, then that was the end of the matter for the dissatisfied litigant. If, however, a technical error—no matter how small or incidental to the substance of the litigation—could be found on the face of the record of the proceedings, the decision would be reviewed on a writ of error in the superior courts, and quashed, regardless of the justice of such a result.

The modern English appellate system emerged from the need to rationalise a hotchpotch of conflicting jurisdictions. Elimination of the narrowly based appeal by writ of error also followed as a logical consequence of an increasing concern for substantive legal content rather than for procedural form in the judicial process. Once this step had been taken (and it was no more than a corollary of the growing acceptance of the law-making role of judges) the way was opened for the emergence of a supervisory role, alongside the more mundane function of correcting the errors of the trial court. This supervisory role, which encapsulated a second tier of appeal since 1876, in the form of the Judicial Committee of the House of Lords, became a part of the Court of Appeal's function, especially with the growth of judicial review, after 1977. (The modern history of the Court of Appeal is dealt with in chapter three.)

There are two, mutually complementary, ways in which we can explore the application of our general model of appeal to specific instances. First, we can set out a number of known procedures in paradigm form (or as Weberian 'ideal types') and discuss their relationship to each other and to the general notion of an appeal. Secondly, we can proceed geographically by examining appellate procedures in various overseas countries, paying particular attention to Anglo-Saxon legal systems.

SPECIES OF APPEAL

Appeal by Writ of Error

This archaic and unsatisfactory procedure (now mercifully living on only in attenuated form, and in recently modernised terminology, by virtue of the prerogative order, under the umbrella of judicial review) depended, as we have seen, upon the existence of an error on the face of the record of proceedings in the lower court. Points arising outside the narrow confines of the 'record' were unimpeachable, while many sensible decisions were quashed on a mere verbal quibble resulting from a slip of the clerk's pen. Historically, the procedure qualified as an 'appeal', albeit a very limited one. When the Court of Appeal was established by the Judicature Act 1873, the method of appeal prescribed was a 'rehearing', along the lines of the procedure adopted for the Court of Appeal in Chancery, and the same form of appeal was provided for by the reformed House of Lords in 1876. (In criminal appeals, writ of error was abolished by the Criminal Appeal Act 1907, which set up the Court of Criminal Appeal succeeding the Court for Crown Cases Reserved.)[3]

Appeal by Rehearing

This procedure is the essence of the modern British appellate system, perpetuated unhelpfully since 1999 in the wording of Part 35 of the Civil Procedure Rules (CPR), discussed below. Its name is ill conceived. The only true 'rehearings' are appeals to the Crown Court from a determination of a magistrates' court made on the hearing of an information or complaint, and on appeal in interlocutory civil proceedings from a Supreme Court Master to a High Court judge. In all other cases (for example in civil appeal from the High Court to the Court of Appeal, and to the House of Lords) the 'rehearing' is limited to an examination by the appeal court of transcripts of the proceedings below and other documents relating to the case, supplemented by the arguments of counsel. It is the rare exception rather than the rule, both in England and in Scotland, for fresh evidence to be heard on appeal, or for witnesses to be heard by the appeal court.

Appeal by Case Stated

This method of judicial review is provided by various statutes which require an inferior tribunal, at the request of one of the litigants, to 'state a case': this takes the form of a question upon a point of law. Thus a losing party to any proceedings (mainly criminal) before a magistrates' court may request the Bench to state a case for consideration by a Divisional Court of the Queen's Bench Division of the High Court. Argument is confined to the point of law raised in the case stated, and a successful appeal results in the case being sent back to the justices with a direction to convict (or to acquit, as the case may be).

The same procedure applies to some categories of civil proceeding, particularly in appeals to the courts from the ever-growing body of special tribunals. Thus an appeal by case stated lies from the Income Tax Commissioners (now subsumed in a general tribunal dealing with matters

---

[3] See Rosemary Pattenden, *English Criminal Appeals 1844-1994* (Oxford, Oxford University Press, 1996) pp 8–10.

of taxation) to a single Chancery judge in the High Court (although in some cases there is an intermediate appeal to the Board of Referees). Under the Arbitration Act 1996 an arbitrator or umpire could state an award in the form of a special case for decision of the High Court.

The procedure reflects the appellate tradition of maintaining as strict a separation as is realistically practicable between issues of 'fact' and issues of 'law'. This is particularly evident in appeals from statutory tribunals, set up with the intention that they will build up a body of expertise and experience in a narrow field which cannot be rivalled by the courts—particularly a 'generalist' generic appellate court; an appeal on a question of fact from such bodies would be otiose.

Appeal by way of Prerogative Order

It is here that we begin to encounter real difficulties in adapting our definition of 'appeal' to a procedure which certainly involves judicial review, but which questions the legality of proceedings while leaving the decision on the merits untouched. In other words, a person can *appeal* by stating a case to the Queen's Bench Divisional Court, following his conviction by a magistrates' court, on the ground that the decision was wrong in law. Alternatively, he or she can *appeal* to the Crown Court on a matter of fact. But if the real issue is, for example, whether or not the justices were acting within their jurisdiction in trying a particular type of case, then the appellant would apply to the Administrative Court for an order quashing the decision. So, too, in the civil jurisdiction.

The distinction may be a fine one, but it is more than a semantic quibble. The supervision of inferior tribunals, exercised by the courts through the prerogative orders, is of fundamental importance, particularly in administrative law. The orders of *certiorari*, *prohibition*, and *mandamus* (recently relabelled with the more modern and supposedly more user-friendly de-latinised names: quashing order, mandatory order, and prohibiting order) and the emergence of judicial review, encompassing the prerogative orders, enable the courts to supervise the decision-making process in numerous statutory bodies acting in a judicial or a quasi-judicial manner. Thus the work of local authorities, statutory tribunals, disciplinary bodies—even government departments, Ministers, and non-statutory bodies—is brought under the umbrella of the courts.

The prerogative order—formerly prerogative writ—dates back to the feudal days when the courts required a means of keeping a grip upon any possible rival centres of judicial power. In some respects, their ancestry is closely linked with the writ of error, at least as regards procedure. Thus *certiorari* may be issued for 'error of law on the face of the record' of the lower court's proceedings. Although in some contexts it is valuable to retain a distinction between 'appeal' and 'review', it is probably correct to consider the exercise of prerogative orders as a particular species of appeal, or not as an appeal at all. Judicial review itself might now be regarded as a species of appeal, although not against court decisions but against the decisions of Ministers and public authorities, and, strictly speaking, the court cannot substitute its own view of the ministerial decision. Hence judicial review is not an appeal other than in a restricted sense.

Cassation

We conclude this parade of appeal-types with a form of procedure that is totally alien (in theory at least) to common law systems—the continental process of *cassation*. Professor Jolowicz explains the relationship between 'appeal' and *cassation* as follows:

> In principle, as established in practice in the legislation of post-Revolutionary France, which provided the model for so many of the legal systems whose languages contain both appeal and cassation, the distinction of kind between the two is clear. On appeal the litigation as a whole—or so much of it as is the subject of the appeal-devolves upon the appellate jurisdiction whose function it is to consider afresh the questions at issue between the parties, whether of fact or law or both. Its business is to decide for itself, as a court of second instance, and its decision replaces the first instance decision for all purposes. ... From the appeal as thus defined, cassation is usually held to differ sharply. There is no devolutive effect; the role of a jurisdiction of cassation is said to be exclusively to examine the legality of the decision under attack—and 'attack' is here an appropriate word, which it is not in relation to appeal. No proofs are admissible on cassation—the facts must be taken as already found-and the court has only two options: it must either affirm or annul. In the latter event the parties are restored to the position in which they were before the defective decision was made; questions left outstanding must be resolved in another court, and that court must reach its own decision unfettered by any-thing that may have been said on cassation, even with regard to the correct interpretation of the law.[4]

Almost every feature of the code-oriented legal systems of Europe militates against the existence of an Anglo-Saxon appeal system. French judges (at every level of the hierarchy) have, in effect, the role and status of civil servants applying known rules and regulations to established facts; judges, part of a career-structured judiciary, are recruited directly into the lower levels of the judicial hierarchy, without having previously engaged in legal practice. Judicial creativity is largely precluded by adherence to the *Code*

---

[4] JA Jolowicz, *On Civil Procedure* (Cambridge, Cambridge University Press, 2000) pp 299–300.

Napoleon and (to quote Sir Carleton Allen) 'a judgment of a French court is, as we should expect of the Gallic genius, a meticulously-constructed piece of logic—a pared and polished judicial syllogism'.[5] Thus the *Code Napoleon* and the structure and role of the judiciary, allied with the highly decentralised character of the courts, all combine to discourage the development of anything resembling a doctrine of precedent.

Yet, are those processes of law so very alien to our own system? Jolowicz notes that the old English writ of error was based on something very similar to *cassation*, as defined above. Judges who purport to 'find' rules are a familiar feature of most legal systems. And, while no formal doctrine of *stare decisis* exists in France, we still find the French judge seeking *la jurisprudence* underlying a decision, including evaluation of a line of previous authorities. Although a judge in a lower court may not be strictly bound by a superior court's judgment, like any civil servant he or she will be loath to question decisions of senior judges who are not only more experienced, but are also his or her superiors in the judicial–bureaucratic hierarchy.

The prerequisites of a conventional appeal system are present. There exists an element of hierarchy, a watered–down notion of precedent, and reasoned decisions to form a basis for judicial review. The French may pay regard to the 'thereness' of codified law, but they too have been obliged to acknowledge the fallibility of trial judges, the rapid changes in modern social conditions, and the universal need for supervision and review within the judicial process. Appeal today, conceptually, is a plea to a court, higher in the hierarchy of courts, to reverse or uphold the decision of the lower court. The appellate method is by way of review, a flexible process of multiple, collegiate judicial ratiocination, to test the validity of the decision on both law and fact, under scrutiny.

THE RATIONALE OF ENGLISH CIVIL APPEALS

In his 1987 Hamlyn Lectures, Sir Jack Jacob, a Master of Civil Appeals, suggested six reasons to justify a facility for appeal from the outcome of a civil trial:

(1) to enable an aggrieved litigant to rectify a perceived judicial error;
(2) to advance the public and social interest in correcting judicial mistakes; unless corrected, such errors might undermine public confidence in the administration of justice;
(3) to achieve a fair and correct decision in the instant case;

[5] Sir Carleton Allen, *Law in the Making*, 7th edn (Oxford, Oxford University Press, 1964) p 180.

(4) to keep judges up to scratch by exposing their decisions to rigorous scrutiny;

(5) to enable senior and experienced judges, working collegially, to develop and refine legal doctrine;

(6) a court of appeal, through the operation of *stare decisis*, can prevent inferior courts from reaching inconsistent results; regularity of decisions promotes the ideal of equality before the law.[6]

Neil Andrews adds a seventh consideration: 'the appeal system provides a *cursus honorum* for judges; the prospect of promotion to superior courts drives the more ambitious judges to maintain the highest standards of adjudication.'[7]

This list resonates strongly with the distinction suggested by Blom–Cooper and Drewry, in their analysis of the appellate functions of the House of Lords, between 'review' and 'supervision'. The former is to do with rectifying error in the instant case; the latter is about maintaining systemic quality control in the administration of justice as a whole. Review is covered by points (1), (2), and (3); while the remaining points cover the 'supervision' function. Review is a particularly important function for a top–tier appeal court-and while in the United Kingdom that status formally lies with the House of Lords, it is important to remember that, in practice, the overwhelming majority of civil appeals in England and Wales go no further than the Court of Appeal.

It is arguable that the various justifications for permitting an appeal to a superior tribunal against the decisions of an inferior one must be set against the important principle of finality—the desirability of bringing litigation to an end as speedily as possible, and of drawing a line under a dispute once the parties have had their day in court. Andrews suggests that there are three potential dangers in allowing unrestrained access to appeal. First, an unsuccessful party may simply want to prolong the proceedings for as long as possible, perhaps out of vindictiveness towards the other party, or perhaps because they are simply bad losers. Secondly, there is the fact that appeals serve only to increase the cost of litigation. Thirdly, an unrestricted right of appeal might send out a message which undermines confidence in the soundness of decisions of civil courts: 'people might be led to believe that all civil courts are presumed to have committed error until the upper court has ratified each judgment.'[8]

These arguments, particularly the first two, are reflected in the thinking behind recent reforms of appellate procedure, following the Woolf and

---

[6] Sir Jack Jacob, *The Fabric of English Civil Justice* (London, Stevens, 1987) pp 211–12.
[7] Neil Andrews, *Principles of Civil Procedure* (London, Sweet and Maxwell, 1994) p 488.
[8] *Ibid*, p 489.

Bowman reviews-and in particular, the introduction of the requirement that litigants who wish to take their cases to the Court of Appeal must obtain permission to do so. A sieving process by the Court of Appeal is seen as a necessary basis for a sound appellate process.

APPEAL AND THE TRIAL PROCESS

So, whenever litigants in the twenty–first century find themselves on the losing side of a civil action-and become aspiring appellants-what do they, together with the prospective respondents, expect from the Court of Appeal? Assuming that permission to appeal is granted, does the litigant know what the hurdles are for upsetting the judgment of the trial court—for righting the presumed wrong or injustice of the decision?[9]

Until the recent reforms, appeals were conducted under Order 59, rule 3 of the Rules of the Supreme Court, dating back to the 1870s, when appeals were declared to be by way of a rehearing. But the term 'rehearing', as Jolowicz explains, 'cannot be taken at its face value.'[10] And its ambiguity is compounded by the fact that the word did not always have the same meaning. In cases where the appeal was from a Master of the Supreme Court to the Judge in Chambers under Order 58, rule 1—an interlocutory appeal—there was a 'rehearing', in the sense that the judge exercised any discretion afresh.[11] Otherwise, 'rehearing' in Order 59, rule 3 was considered to be the equivalent of a review by the Court of Appeal of the lower court's decision. It examined the judgment appealed against in the light of the evidence that had been presented to the trial judge, without the Court of Appeal hearing evidence in the court. The exercise was one of a retrospective examination of the case, and not deciding it afresh, untrammelled by the trial judge's conclusion. The limited contrast, pre-1999, between 'review' and 'rehearing' has unhappily survived in the language of rule 52.11(1) of the Civil Procedure Rules. The *Arab Insurance Group* case[12] in November 2002 seems, however, to have merged the two into the single concept of 'review', whatever that may now encompass in the function of the Court of Appeal. Rule 52.11 provides:

---

[9] *Assicurazioni Geurdi SpA v Arab Insurance Group (BSC)* [2002] EWCA Civ 1642, per Ward LJ, paras 194 and 195. The same approach to CPR r 52.11(1) was adopted by Auld LJ, in Meadow v General Medical Council, Attorney–General Intervening [2006] EWCA Civ 1390 at [125]-[128].

[10] Jolowicz, above n 4, pp 276-8.

[11] *Tanfern Ltd v Cameron–McDonald* [2000] 1 WLR 1311, para 31.

[12] Above n 9.

Hearing of Appeals

52.11 (1) Every appeal will be limited to a *review* of the decision of the lower court unless—

  (a) a practice direction makes different provision for a particular category of appeal; or

  (b) the court considers that in the circumstances of an individual appeal it would be in the interests of justice to hold a *re-hearing*.

  (2) Unless it orders otherwise, the appeal court will not receive—

  (a) oral evidence; or

  (b) evidence which was not before the lower court.

  (3) The appeal court will allow an appeal where the decision of the lower court was—

  (a) wrong; or

  (b) unjust because of a serious procedural or other irregularity in the proceedings in the lower court.

  (4) The appeal court may draw any inference of fact which it considers justified on the evidence.

  (5) At the hearing of the appeal a party may not rely on a matter not contained in his appeal notice unless the appeal court gives permission.

There was some force in the view that, when the Court of Appeal was conducting a review, it was adopting an approach different from the appeal by way of rehearing. But how different? 'Review' must be something less comprehensive than 'rehearing', but how much less? In the *Lloyds Insurance* appeal,[13] the Court proceeded, however, to hear a complicated appeal (lasting four court–working weeks) under rule 52.11(1)(b) without indicating any different approach to the appeal if it had been acting under rule 52.11(1)(a). Rule 52.11, on any view, needs revising so as to remove any doubt that all appeals to the Court of Appeal are 'reviews'. That is not, however, the end of the matter. What constitutes a 'review'? Is it even necessary to provide statutorily for anything but an 'appeal', in which case the Court of Appeal may adapt the forensic process most suitable to the nature of the particular case?

In essence, the 'review' approach involves the Court of Appeal considering the trial judge's judgment, testing it against the evidence available to the judge, and asking itself whether the decision was wrong (rule 52.11(3)(a)) or whether there was not a fair trial (rule 52.11(3)(b))—in effect, a replica of Article 6 of the ECHR. To what extent (if at all) does the Court of Appeal pay regard to the trial judge's assessment of the evidence? Two factors are claimed to place a restraint upon the appellate judges' view of the available evidence at trial. First, there is an instinctive awareness that 'judging the witness is more complex than merely judging the transcript'[14]—the

---

[13] *Jaffray v Society of Lloyds* [2002] EWCA Civ 1101.

[14] See Ward LJ in the *Arab Insurance Group* case, above n 9, at para 196.

former relying on intuition—or, as it is commonly said, the trial judge has the distinct advantage over the Court of Appeal in hearing and seeing the witness, and thus judging the witness's demeanour in the witness box. It is not so much 'more complex' as more confusing, since the spoken word is interpreted by the manner of its delivery. When the court of first instance is the judge of both fact and law (or even complicated factual events), a calm review, based on the cold formalism of a printed record and unencumbered by emotional reaction to human testimony at the personal level of oral hearing, is called for. A measure of detachment from the dust of forensic combat is the hallmark of the appellate court. It has only to contend with the voices, and perhaps the demeanour, of the advocates. Otherwise, it is distanced from the 'orality' of the trial process.

The second factor relates to the art of adjudication. The more complex the questions to be answered in the litigation, the more likely it is that different judges will come to different—all no doubt reasonable—conclusions. Hence, the harder it is to distinguish the right verdict from the wrong. This factor is inherent in the judicial process, as it proceeds along the continuum from trial to appeal. The very reason for a review by three judges—of eminent superiority in the judicial hierarchy—should accord, presumptively, a greater status than the single judge sitting alone, less able to test his own conceptions and prejudices-which, we are quick to observe, are not the same as bias.

But we think, respectfully, that the second factor is bound up in the first, which applies to witness actions. Where the appeal involves a case in public law, when the evidence is, other than exceptionally, in the form of written statements, there is less inclination to accord any priority to the first judicial input. Of course, an appellant in a case of judicial review under Part 54 of CPR (the old RSC Order 53) will always have the burden of seeking to upset the verdict of the judge in the Administrative Court. But, beyond that initial hurdle, is there any reason to prefer the reasoned judgment of the judge (no doubt a specialist in judicial review and hence entitled to special regard) to the review of three appellate judges? We think not.

The problem of 'review' arises where factual matters (primary facts and inferential facts) are the subject of mixed documentary material and oral testimony. It is at this point that deferential treatment is traditionally accorded to trial judges. But is it an advantage to have seen the witness give his or her evidence, a facility that is denied, other than exceptionally where fresh evidence is admitted, to the appellate judges?

The system of orality in the English common law tradition of legal process demands the hearing of the evidence which the witness gives. It does not include seeing the witness give that evidence, save for the fact that the ordinary means of giving evidence is by personal appearance in the courtroom, although the courts are now empowered to hear evidence by video-link. The recent decision of the House of Lords in *Polanski v Condé Nast Publications Ltd*[15] has, in effect, given the video recording of a witness's evidence the same legal status as the live witness in the courtroom.

There is, we perceive, a growing awareness among the higher judiciary that the demeanour of witnesses provides the trial court with nothing more than a distraction from the quality of the written or spoken word. The distinction can work both ways, advantageously to the accomplished witness and unfavourably to the nervous and inexpert witness. Thus, Steyn LJ said in *Compaq Computer Corporation and another v Dell Computer Corporation Ltd*:[16]

> Finally, I turn to a matter that troubles me very much. The judge commented unfavourably on the evidence of Mr Slagter, the managing director of Dell Computer Corporation Limited. The judge based his findings on the demeanour and tone of voice of Mr Slagter. Here I take the liberty of quoting what I regard as wise words of McKenna J on an extra–judicial occasion. He said this:
>
>> I question whether the respect given to our findings of fact based on the demeanour of witnesses is always deserved. I doubt my own ability ... to discern from a witness's demeanour or the tone of his voice whether he is telling the truth. He speaks hesitantly. Is that the mark of a cautious man whose statements are for that reason to be respected, or is he taking time to fabricate? Is an emphatic witness putting on an act to deceive me, or is he speaking from the fullness of his heart, knowing that he is right? Is he likely to be more truthful if he looks me straight in the eye, than if he casts his eyes on the ground, perhaps in shyness or natural timidity? For my part I rely on these considerations as little as I can help.

Steyn LJ observed:

> I am very much of the same mind. I readily accept, of course, that Harman J cannot possibly be criticised for approaching the matter in a way which is supported by legal convention. But I do wish to record that I am nevertheless not persuaded that his comments on Mr Slagter's evidence were justified. We have not heard full argument on that aspect, and I simply make clear that I must not be assumed to have endorsed the judge's views.

The 'legal convention' of paying full regard to the trial judge's sight (as well as sound) of the witness should by now have been dispelled by a more sober reflection of human capacity to accommodate the unusual (for most) experience of giving evidence orally. The overplay of the importance of the witness's demeanour had already been subjected to a devastating critique

---

[15] [2005] UKHL 10. And see ch 11.
[16] Unreported.

from Lord Bingham of Cornhill, in an article in 1985, drawing likewise on McKenna J's extra-judicial pronouncement. Lord Bingham's 'The Judge as Juror'[17] is an indicator of what the House of Lords (or the UK Supreme Court) may be saying in future about the value of witness demeanour. Contemporaneously, Lord Goff (when Robert Goff LJ) had uttered a similar view on the credibility of witnesses in a judgment that peculiarly has been under–reported. In *The Ocean Frost: Armagas Ltd v Mundogas SA*[18] he said:

> Speaking from my own experience, I have found it essential in cases of fraud, when considering the credibility of witnesses, always to test their veracity by reference to the objective facts proved independently of their testimony, in particular by reference to the documents in the case, and also to pay particular regard to their motives and to the overall probabilities. It is frequently very difficult to tell whether a witness is telling the truth or not; and where there is a conflict of evidence such as there was in the present case, reference to the objective facts and documents to the witnesses' motives, and to the overall probabilities, can be of very great assistance to a judge in ascertaining the truth. I have been driven to the conclusion that the judge did not pay sufficient regard to these matters in making his findings of fact in the present case.

We are conscious of another dimension to the view that attaches importance to the sight of the witness giving evidence. In its crudest form, it is commonly said that it is necessary to see 'the whites of the witness's eyes' in order to test accurately his or her credibility. We think this notion is wholly misplaced. It would mean that no blind person could be allowed to administer justice. If the blind were banned from the seat of justice, the Metropolitan Stipendary Magistrate, Sir John Fielding (the half-brother of the writer Henry Fielding) could not have sat at Bow Street Magistrates' Court with propriety. Only recently the former Lord Chancellor, Lord Irvine of Lairg, authorised the appointment of blind persons as lay magistrates. Our view is that the manner and style with which witnesses give their evidence in court should be treated as only one factor—and certainly not a vital factor-in the evaluation of evidence, and should not be accorded any great weight, as and when an appellate court reviews that evidence.

What then should properly constitute a 'review'? In a crop of recent cases the judiciary has pointed up the nature of appellate review when the issues are other than findings of primary fact. Where the appeal focuses on findings of primary fact, the courts still adhere to the approach of the appellate

---

[17] Thomas Bingham, 'The Judge as Juror: the Judicial Determination of Factual Issues' (1985) 38 *Current Legal Problems* 1

[18] The case is fully reported in the House of Lords and the Court of Appeal at [1986] AC 717; curiously the passage in the judgment of Robert Goff LJ is omitted, but can be found in the report of the Court of Appeal at [1985] 1 Lloyd's Rep 1, 57.

court depending upon the weight to be attached to the trial judge's findings. This is said to favour the primary adjudicator (the trial judge) over the secondary adjudicators (the appeal court judges) since 'the greater that advantage, the more reluctant the appellate court should be to interfere.' Clarke LJ elliptically added in the *Arab Insurance Group* case (at para 15): 'As I see it, that was the approach of the Court of Appeal [in the past] as a "rehearing" under the RSC and should be the approach of a review under the CPR.'

But where conclusions are drawn from primary facts, the appeal judges feel much less restrained from interference with the conclusions of the trial judge. And rightly so, since inference–drawing is a process that depends less on the primary facts (hard data) and more on an inferential assessment (soft data) of the established factual material. This distinction was best expressed by Mance LJ in *Todd v Adam*:[19]

> With regard to an appeal to this court (which would never have involved a complete rehearing in that sense), the language of 'review' may be said to fit most easily into the context of an appeal against the exercise of a discretion, or an appeal where the court of appeal is essentially concerned with the correctness of an exercise of evaluation or judgment-such as a decision by a lower court whether, weighing all relevant factors, a contract of service existed. However, the references in r 52 11 (3) and (4) to the power of an appellate court to allow an appeal where the decision below was 'wrong' and to 'draw any inference of fact which it considers justified on the evidence' indicate that there are other contexts in which the court of appeal must, as previously, make up its own mind as to the correctness or otherwise of a decision, even on matters of fact, by a lower court. Where the correctness of a finding of primary fact or of inference is in issue, it cannot be a matter of simple discretion how an appellate court approaches the matter. Once the appellant has shown a real prospect (justifying permission to appeal) that a finding or inference is wrong, the role of an appellate court is to determine whether or not this is so, giving full weight of course to the advantages enjoyed by any judge of first instance who has heard [but note, not 'seen'] oral evidence. In the present case, therefore, I consider that (a) it is for us if necessary to make up our own mind about the correctness or otherwise of any findings of primary fact or inferences from primary fact that the judge made or drew and the claimant's challenge, while (b) reminding ourselves that, so far as the appeal raises issues of judgment on unchallenged primary findings and inferences, this court ought not to interfere unless it is satisfied that the judge's conclusion lay outside the bounds within which reasonable disagreement is possible. In relation to (a) we must, as stated, bear in mind the important and well–recognised reluctance of this court to interfere with a trial judge on any finding of primary fact based on the credibility or reliability of oral evidence. In the present case, however, while there was oral evidence, its content was largely uncontentious.

---

[19] [2002] 2 All ER (Comm) 1, para 129.

Wherever inference-drawing is an evaluation, and hence more than an aggregate of primary facts, the appellate court will indulge in substituting its own view of the wrongness of the trial judge's decision all the more readily. It is at this point that reading the transcript can be geared more to evaluation than to testing the evidence as it unfolds in the trial process (we allude to this matter later). The most telling judicial observation comes, predictably we think, from Lord Hoffmann in *Biogen Inc v Medera plc*:[20]

> The need for appellate caution in reversing the judge's evaluation of the facts is based upon much more solid grounds than professional courtesy. It is because specific findings of fact, even by the most meticulous judge, are inherently an incomplete statement of the impression which was made upon him by the primary evidence. His expressed findings are always surrounded by a penumbra of imprecision as to emphasis, relative weight, minor qualification and nuance (as Renan said, *la vérité est dans une nuance*), of which time and language do not permit exact expression, but which may play an important part in the judge's overall evaluation.

The traditional caution of the appellate court towards interference with the trial judge's findings, evaluative or simply fact–finding, arises inherently from the nature of the appellate process. The party appealing has the formidable task of demonstrating that the decision of the lower court was wrong. The burden carries with it the implication that a trial judge's function, if not positive duty, is to produce the right decision, and his judicial experience and expertise entitle him to be accorded that initial recognition. As Lord Hoffmann points out, it is not just a question of professional courtesy, but an acknowledgement that litigation is a costly exercise and should be confined to a trial—hence the imposition of a need for permission to appeal—and that a civilised legal system entrusts the role of a trial court to competent (or better than competent), honest judges, with a honed intuition for handling complex material and employing evaluative techniques. Accountability alone determines that the correctness of the trial court's decision should be fully tested, without inhibition on the part of the appellate court.

A further—and we think compelling—reason for not placing additional restraints on the appellate courts beyond the fact of a successful appeal requiring a displacement of the burden of establishing wrongness, is the differential between the process of trial and appellate review. Put simplistically, the trial judge starts with a clean sheet, a *tabula rasa*. The Court of Appeal is presented with finite material with which to assess the correctness or otherwise of the decision. The approaches of the two judicial figures are both psychologically and forensically distinct and productive of discrete thought processes.

[20] [1997] RPC 1, at 45.

The trial judge is seen as setting out on a journey of discovery. His or her assessment of the evidence evolves as the case proceeds. He or she may judge the credibility or reliability of a witness instantly, or might defer forming a view until other witnesses have given their evidence. The process may be a shifting scene rather than a jigsaw puzzle. Throughout the days of the trial (which may last weeks or even months) the pendulum may swing back and forth. Even if the trend is all in one direction, the process is ongoing. Composition of the judgment, extempore or reserved, calls for reflection of the evidence heard. Even if the judge is wholly reliant upon a daily transcript, his or her assessment of the evidence will be coloured by the memory (even if of short duration) of the witness. It is a lonely journey. While the judge will normally receive assistance from the advocates, they will be delivering rival contentions. Any judge might reasonably wish to test the propositions put to him or her, through discussion with colleagues. But that advantage is denied. He or she must rely on his or her own judgment of the witnesses and the strength of partisanly delivered arguments. None of this is designed to quarrel with the forensic process. It is merely asserted to establish the peculiar features of trial by judge alone. The final product-the judgment-is the result of an overview of the trial process, in which the wood can be seen only after the trees have been negotiated and put in the correct order of things.

A review of a trial court's decision is a wholly different exercise from the trial process. The appellate judges read the transcripts of evidence as recorded and uninfluenced by the speaker of the written words. Subject to oral argument, the transcript can be seen in its entirety, unlike the trial judge's experience of hearing the evidence presented and out of any prescribed order. The wood and the trees are in their right places. Nowadays, the practice is for judges to read the case papers before coming into court. No such procedure can be adopted before the trial begins. In the Court of Appeal, views—even if they are only provisional—begin to form before and during the hearing. To have an open mind (the prerequisite of any judge's approach to jus-tice) is not to have an empty mind. A trial judge's open–mindedness is constrained by the fact that until he or she has heard all the evidence it will be empty. Even a provisional view gleaned from the pleadings will be bound, at best, to be tentative. The unfolding of oral testimony fills the emptiness.

The collegiality of the Court of Appeal, while preserving the independent judgment of each member of the Court (see chapter eight), provides a further distinct advantage over the trial judge. The interplay of views, both in the courtroom and in retirement, will enhance the process of deciding whether the judge got the right result in his judgment. The facility of measuring the judge's reasoned decision against the recorded evidence is a feature of review that assists and does not detract from sound decision-making. The production of draft judgments from each of the judges provides yet another opportunity to test the conclusions about the trial judge's decision.

Stripped of the supposed advantage accorded to the trial judge of having seen and heard the witnesses give their evidence, the two processes can be valued according to their intrinsic purposes and effects. We think that a trial conducted by a single judge giving a fully reasoned judgment meets the demands of a civilised system of justice. A review by three appeal judges likewise satisfies the dictates of an appellate process. The two processes are complementary, the higher court possessing the power of reversal over the lower.

3

Origins and Development of the Court of Appeal

The administration of the law is costly, dilatory and inefficient and that a competent Commission [the Royal Commission on the Judicature of 1869] having reported, the Government should in the next session [of Parliament], present a measure for its reform and reconstitution.[1]

THE CREATION OF the Court of Appeal dates from the Judicature Acts 1873–75. It was set up to hear appeals from the High Court and from the county courts. At common law the review of a case on the grounds that the trial court came to the wrong conclusion, whether in law or on the facts, was unknown. A complex system of challenging a decision by means of a writ of error was developed. If the official record disclosed no error on its face the decision stood.

THE POSITION BEFORE 1875

The appeal system as it stood before 1875 has been described as 'chaotic'. In 1869 the first report of the Judicature Commission was published.[2] This had been set up in 1867, under the chairmanship of Lord Cairns, to review and report on the existing structure of appeals and to consider the creation of a Supreme Court. It recommended precisely that. It is interesting to note that the phrase 'Supreme Court' then meant the High Court and the Court of Appeal together and did not include any reference to the House of Lords. The debate in 2003–04 about the creation of a Supreme Court referred only to the House of Lords in a new guise and stripped of its links to the upper chamber of the legislature. By contrast, in 1867 the Supreme Court was intended to be the (almost) final recourse for litigants in

---

[1] Vernon Harcourt QC, MP, speaking on 26 July 1872, *Hansard* (3rd series), 216.

[2] See particularly the second report, C 631 (HMSO, 1871). The political context is explained (with special reference to the appellate jurisdiction of the House of Lords) in Robert Stevens, *Law and Politics* (London, Weidenfeld and Nicolson, 1979) ch 2. See also Louis Blom-Cooper and Gavin Drewry, *Final Appeal* (Oxford, Clarendon Press, 1972) pp 25–29.

England and Wales, with only very limited further appeals to the House of Lords. As to the Court of Appeal, the recommendation was that a common appeal should lie from all divisions of the High Court. It was the immense structure of both the High Court and the Court of Appeal that would have constituted the Supreme Court, leaving the House of Lords to remain as it then was or, perhaps, as happened, to be reformed itself. It was a time of possible expansion for the Court of Appeal, but, ultimately, the right of appeal to the House of Lords was preserved with a more restricted role for the Court of Appeal than might have been the case. There was to be no restriction on appeals to the House of Lords. Thus the Court of Appeal became an intermediate appellate court and not a court of final appeal.

The legislative steps required to bring about this significant change were tortuous and controversial—at least for the small, elite group of lawyers and politicians who took an interest in these matters. The result of intense discussions that lasted five years was the Appellate Jurisdiction Act 1876.

At one stage, the Conservative administration of Disraeli in February 1874 would have brought about the entire abolition of the appellate jurisdiction of the House of Lords. The Court of Appeal (grandiosely referred to as the Imperial Court of Appeal) would have been the final recourse of litigants in England, Wales, and Ireland, and would also acquire jurisdiction over Scottish appeals. The Court of Appeal would also take on colonial and ecclesiastical appeals. The Court would be divided into three divisions, the first consisting of five and not three judges. It would hear all Irish and Scottish cases and would rehear any English case if either of the second and third divisions disagreed, that is if the judges were not unanimous or if they reversed a material part of the judgment appealed against on a question of law. The first division would determine what amounted to a 'question of law' or a 'material part'.

This Bill passed the House of Lords in its legislative capacity, but pressure then grew in the upper reaches of the legal profession (effectively the Bar only) to preserve some form of second appeal from the High Court and the lower courts. The Scottish judges, with whom government opponents agreed, did not like the idea of Scottish appeals going to a purely English court. Similar reservations were expressed by Irish interests. As the first division of the Court of Appeal was an elevated form of second appeal, in some cases the logic of abolishing the entire appellate jurisdiction of the House of Lords was somewhat undermined. The Bill passed all stages in the House of Lords and proceeded rapidly in the Commons. It had only to pass its report and third reading stage in the Commons when the government decided to abandon it for that session.

When new legislation was introduced in the following session it was initially almost identical to the proposal for an Imperial Court of Appeal as the final arbiter in all instances and would have abolished further appeals to the House of Lords. But this Bill ran into deep political difficulties and, eventually, a Bill was promoted to create the House of Lords in its judicial capacity as the final appeal court above the Court of Appeal. This Bill included the device of making Lords Justices of Appeal Privy Councillors even though they were paid less than the Law Lords. This cost nothing but flattered the judges in the Court of Appeal and went some way to ensuring a supply of judges of sufficient quality for the House of Lords from those sitting in the Court of Appeal.

An outline of the court structure before and after the passing of the Judicature Acts can be seen in Figure 1.

The distinguished historian RCK Ensor, author of a pioneering comparative study of European judicial systems published in the 1930s, professed himself bemused by the outcome of all this political manoeuvring. Why, he asked, was the Court of Appeal not abolished and its judges invited to serve as the first Law Lords? He added that 'litigation in England would

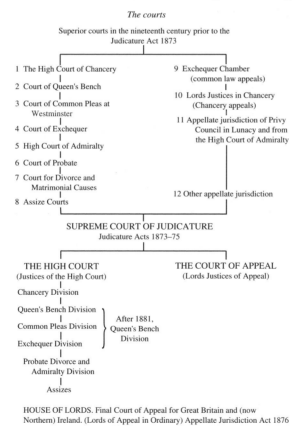

The courts

Superior courts in the nineteenth century prior to the
Judicature Act 1873

1 The High Court of Chancery
2 Court of Queen's Bench
3 Court of Common Pleas at Westminster
4 Court of Exchequer
5 High Court of Admiralty
6 Court of Probate
7 Court for Divorce and Matrimonial Causes
8 Assize Courts

9 Exchequer Chamber (common law appeals)
10 Lords Justices in Chancery (Chancery appeals)
11 Appellate jurisdiction of Privy Council in Lunacy and from the High Court of Admiralty
12 Other appellate jurisdiction

SUPREME COURT OF JUDICATURE
Judicature Acts 1873–75

THE HIGH COURT
(Justices of the High Court)

Chancery Division
Queen's Bench Division
Common Pleas Division
Exchequer Division
Probate Divorce and Admiralty Division
Assizes

After 1881, Queen's Bench Division

THE COURT OF APPEAL
(Lords Justices of Appeal)

HOUSE OF LORDS. Final Court of Appeal for Great Britain and (now Northern) Ireland. (Lords of Appeal in Ordinary) Appellate Jurisdiction Act 1876

Figure 1: Reorganisation of the superior courts of law in the nineteenth century. This diagram is adapted from fig. 1 of JR Spencer (ed), *Jackson's Machinery of Justice* (Cambridge, Cambridge University Press, 1989) p9.

certainly have been cheaper and more expeditious, had that course been adopted.'[3] He had a point, one that the later chapters of this book will seek to address.

A NEW HOME FOR THE NEW COURT

Upon its creation the Court of Appeal had five Lords Justices and two divisions. Prior to the passing of the Judicature Acts, the law courts in London were scattered across various locations, in premises that were notoriously inconvenient and ill suited to the purpose. In 1865 a Commission was established to find a site for a major new court building and to superintend its construction. Amid some controversy, a seven-and-a-half acre site on the north side of the Strand was purchased and an architect (GE Street) selected. The foundation stone of the handsome neo-gothic structure was laid in 1874, but the opening of the new Royal Courts of Justice did not happen until 1882.

This meant that, in its early days, the new Court of Appeal divided its sittings between Westminster Hall (for common law appeals from the Queen's Bench, Exchequer and Common Pleas Divisions of the newly established High Court) and Lincolns Inn (for Chancery and Probate, Divorce, and Admiralty appeals). The *Judicial Statistics* for 1880[4] shows that the Court sat for 135 days at the latter location and 194 days at the former. According to the *Judicial Statistics* for 1890,[5] the Court of Appeal, now relocated to the Strand, was sitting in two divisions: Appeal Court I (166 days of sittings on Queen's Bench business[6]); and Appeal Court II (184 days, hearing Chancery appeals).

By 1970 there were 14 Lords Justices. At the time of writing the Court has 37 Lords Justices sitting in up to 10 divisions. It occupies a wing of the Law Courts building in London which was modernised a few years ago to improve the public accommodation available in the shape of courtrooms and the private rooms for the Lords Justices.

RIGHTS OF APPEAL: FROM HANWORTH TO EVERSHED

A very significant factor for the work of the Court of Appeal in relation to further appeals was that no filter existed until 1934 to limit onward appeals to the House of Lords. It is very difficult to assess the effect of the

[3] RCK Ensor, *Courts and Judges in France, Germany and England* (London, Oxford University Press, 1933) p 15.

[4] C 3088, 1881.

[5] C 6443, 1891.

[6] In 1881, the former common law High Court Divisions of Common Pleas and Exchequer had been merged into the Queen's Bench Division.

Lords Justices' awareness in their decision-making that there would always be another round of litigation. Appeals to the Court of Appeal from the courts below required leave only if they were interlocutory in nature or if they came from the county court. The question of what is interlocutory and what is final used to occupy many pages of the law reports and in the standard commentary on practice, the *White Book*.

The creation of a court that could, without technicality, consider the legality of a decision of a lower court was entirely new. But the new court was very much a creature of the existing judicial system. The personnel of the court included, *ex officio*, the Lord Chancellor, any ex-Lord Chancellor, the Lords of Appeal in Ordinary, the Lord Chief Justice, the Master of the Rolls, the Vice-Chancellor of the Chancery Division, and the President of the Family Division. In practice, it is only the Master of the Rolls who sits in the Court of Appeal permanently. Further, the Judicature Act 1925 provided for judges and ex-judges of the Court of Appeal to sit in the High Court if requested to do so by the Lord Chancellor and with the consent of the Lord Chief Justice. This demonstrates how the Court of Appeal is not a separate court but is an integral part of the judicial system below the House of Lords.

The changes in 1934 reflected a general concern about the state of appellate litigation in the twentieth century. The government set up the Hanworth Committee to investigate the possibility of more expeditious dispatch of business in the Supreme Court.[7] Appeals from the county court did not generally go direct to the Court of Appeal. They had to pass through a High Court stage, the purpose of which was not immediately apparent. In the Administration of Justice (Appeals) Act 1934 the government achieved two striking changes through one very short and cogent statute. The High Court stage of appeals from the county courts was neatly abolished and a direct appeal introduced to the Court of Appeal. The question of whether leave would be required would be determined by rules of court and the monetary amount at stake. At the same time, appeals from the Court of Appeal to the House of Lords would proceed only with the leave of the Court of Appeal or of the House itself (we discuss the implications of the latter change in more detail in chapter five).

The procedure in the Court was reviewed in 1953 by the Evershed Committee on High Court Procedure.[8] The section in its report on appeals begins with a frank recognition that appeals are an important factor in the cost of litigation. At that time the rule that the loser paid the winner's costs was even more strictly applied than it is now, after the Woolf reforms. The very process of an appeal could increase the costs as fresh minds were brought to bear, new arguments were raised, and further issues arose for

---

[7] See the second interim report of the Committee: Cmd 4471, 1934.

[8] *Final report of the Committee on Supreme Court Practice and Procedure (Evershed Committee)*, Cmd 8878, pp 188ff.

consideration. With these factors in mind the Committee considered how the right of appeal might be preserved while reducing the costs involved. This led inevitably to a further question: should there be further limits on the right of appeal beyond those then in force?

In the first place the Committee considered whether the multiplicity of appeals could be reduced. It then went on to consider whether the procedure for appeals could be improved with a view to saving costs. As the law then stood, there was an absolute right of appeal against any final decision of the High Court. In the case of interlocutory orders, leave to appeal had, in general, to be obtained from the High Court or, failing that, from the Court of Appeal. When the possibility of an appeal to the House of Lords was set alongside this system, the Committee remarked that the cost to the ultimate loser might be very substantial and also unpredictable because nobody could predict the ultimate outcome. One suggestion was to deny an appeal from the High Court on a point of fact. That was then the position in appeals from the county court. This was summarily rejected as not being supported by any 'responsible' quarter. There was no analysis of the principles of appeals, and no discussion of the difference between appeals on fact and appeals on law. A proposal to limit appeals from the High Court to cases in which leave to appeal was granted was equally tersely rejected. (This is precisely the position that currently obtains since the Woolf reforms.) The Committee thought that it would be very difficult to formulate the grounds on which leave to appeal might be granted. This did not arise, the Committee said, in relation to interlocutory appeals. How the Committee could have ignored the substantial and impenetrable case-law on the difference between final and interlocutory appeals is not clear to us.

The problem of limiting appeals to those where leave was given seemed to the Committee to involve endless possible permutations of events and evidence, of inferences and primary facts, and of documents and oral testimony. That is true, but the Committee was clearly not as concerned about costs as it said it was. Had it been, it would have recommended a form of restriction on appeals that may have left a great deal to individual judges but would have recognised that there is no right to litigate endlessly. The further argument that it would be invidious for a judge who has disbelieved a witness to consider an application for leave to appeal on a point of fact is disingenuous. If the judge rejects the application it could be renewed in the Court of Appeal.

The Committee discussed at some length a proposal for a 'leapfrog' appeal from the lower courts direct to the House of Lords or, alternatively, for an appeal to the Court of Appeal only. The leapfrog appeal was enacted by the Administration of Justice Act 1969. As explained in chapter ten, it has not been much used. The broader idea that there should only be one appeal above a court of first instance received no support. Because the

Committee did not ask itself what appeals were for, it did not have to consider the principles behind such a radical reform.

After discussing some technical issues about appeals from Official Referees (now Technology and Construction court judges) and other specialist jurisdictions below the High Court, the Committee turned to the county courts. It recommended an absolute right of appeal on fact in most cases above a certain monetary figure. The difficulty presented by a lack of an accurate record of the evidence should, it said, be met by the eventual installation of reliable mechanical recording equipment, then in its infancy. This was no doubt a workable compromise but, again, it avoided any discussion of the central issue of what rights of appeal are for.

The report was a creature of its time. There was no academic input, the issue of the workings of the courts being reserved to practical people with experience of the legal system. Civil procedure was not at that time a topic in academic law schools. The Bar finals course included a rudimentary knowledge of civil procedure. The Law Society final examination did not include a paper in civil procedure—after all, counsel were the advocates. The solicitor had to prepare a case by eliciting the facts. Civil procedure was not thought to be capable of being taught to future solicitors. An ability to conduct litigation did not require a solicitor to know the details or even the principles of civil procedure. The few solicitors who ventured into the county courts were on their own. The demarcation line between the respective roles of counsel and solicitors was clearly understood and there was no intention of increasing rights of audience.

The few changes recommended by the Committee were adopted by changes to the Rules of the Supreme Court. The Bar had its way in opposing the cessation of the practice of counsel reading out loud the judgment given below, the various documents read by the lower court and passages of the evidence heard, and any cross-examination. There was an overwhelming case for changing the system. The Bar liked it for the very bad reason that it is easier to argue an appeal by this oral process, and the judges liked it because they did not have to prepare cases with any more than minimal advance reading. The expense of such indulgent practices fell either on private parties or on public funds where legal aid funded one or both of the parties.

A TRANSATLANTIC LESSON? SLOW MOVES TOWARDS MODERNISATION SINCE THE 1960S

In 1961 and 1962 there was a novel exchange between judges and, for the first time, academic lawyers in the United Kingdom and the United

States.[9] The UK participants found the limitations on oral argument and the emphasis placed on delivery of full written submissions pre-trial and pre-appeal in the United States unattractive. But the Court of Appeal was impressed with the practice of pre-reading. In a limited experiment the Court issued a practice direction stating that the members of the Court would read the pleadings, the order under appeal, the notice of appeal, and the judgment below, together with any cases cited in that judgment. Before the limited changes recommended by Evershed were adopted, the notice of appeal did not have to specify the grounds, thus leaving every point open to oral argument. The experiment was not taken any further, in that written summaries of points to be taken were not required and the practice of reading at length from relevant cases continued. It is well within the memory of the writers that counsel for each party commonly read to the court at dictation speed the main points they wished to make. The more enterprising counsel who provided a written summary were still expected to read out the summary slowly. As the use of photocopying equipment became common in the 1960s, written bundles of documents proliferated. Judges would often indicate that they had only dipped into the accompanying papers and would welcome an oral guided tour around the issues. The idea of an activist court which itself identified those issues and directed what arguments should be presented to it was far removed from the court over which Lord Denning presided from 1962 until 1982.

Until Lord Denning retired there was no serious pressure on the courts or the machinery of the administration of justice to modernise the workings of the appellate system. Management of the listing of cases, the compilation of papers for the Court, and liaison with solicitors preparing the appeals were in the hands of the clerks to the Lord Justices. These were employees of the Lord Chancellor's Department and may have been clerks to the judges before they left the Bar. They had no legal knowledge, but this did not matter because they performed no legal function. There were no lesser judges in the Court to handle issues that arose in the course of an appeal. Given the strong tradition of conducting appeals orally, there may have been no real need to worry about such issues. The Court would deal with all issues at the hearing. A minor concession to a more ordered system was to permit oral applications to be made to the Court each Monday morning. The Court would deal with any problems presented to it (such as the preparation of papers for the full appeal, security for costs, or issues of compliance with time limits) on a pragmatic basis.

This changed in 1981 when a Registrar was appointed to supervise the workings of the Court, to deal with applications arising in the course of

---

[9] See the interesting book that emerged from the visit: D Karlen, *Appellate Courts in the United States and in England* (New York, New York University Press, 1963), and an account of the visit by Lord Evershed MR in (1962) *The Times,* 12 April.

the appeal, and to ensure that delays in hearings were kept to a minimum. There was only one holder of this post, John Adams, a distinguished academic and also a practising lawyer who was eventually appointed as a circuit judge in 1997. Different arrangements were made for the management of the Court in 1998; these are discussed below in relation to the Bowman report.

INSIGHTS FROM WITHIN

There is no academic literature on the work of the Court of Appeal from the time of the 1934 Act until the Woolf reforms were enacted in the Civil Procedure Rules. Even then, most of the discussion was about procedure and not substance. However, some glimpses into judicial thinking are offered by four contributions in the form of lectures by Lords Justices and Lord Evershed MR. We begin with the latter's lecture in 1950 at University College London.[10]

Lord Evershed pointed out that the Court was a statutory creation of 1875. He spoke of the need for cautious modernisation as required by changing circumstances. At the time of his lecture he was engaged as chairman of the committee set up to review High Court procedure, referred to above. He was firmly committed to what, borrowing from Bagehot, he called 'growth bit by bit.' He pointed to the need to understand the procedural principles which governed, for example, appeals by writ of error to the Court of Exchequer Chamber, which was not an appeal at all in the sense of a rehearing. He gave a fascinating but necessarily brief account of the origin and methods of the reforms enacted in 1875. When he considered the role and function of the Court of Appeal in 1950 he paused to give some, again fascinating but arcane, references to the nature of the office of Master of the Rolls. He went on to the reforms of 1934 (above) and how, as a result of these, it had become necessary to appoint three more Lords Justices, making, at that time, nine in total. In addition, some judges of the High Court might be appointed by the Lord Chancellor to assist in keeping the Court up to date with its work. He did not say so, but we might reasonably infer that this would be a form of apprenticeship or testing for those who were thought to be suitable for later advancement.

The increase in the number of Lords Justices to nine had been intended to lead to those judges having one day (the exact number of such days was not specified) to think about and write reserved judgments. The expedient of cases suddenly settling was not available in appeals to the Court: it did not happen. Witnesses would not suddenly fall ill because there were no witnesses. But there was a disadvantage as Lord Evershed saw it. He

[10] *The Court of Appeal in England* (London, Athlone Press, 1950).

thought that the Court was unable to reserve as many judgments as perhaps it should. He linked this difficulty to the undoubted fact, which remains true today, that for the vast majority of litigants the Court of Appeal would be the final answer. He saw many problems in distinguishing between the *ratio* and *obiter* remarks after the event by reference to the written judgment. This was all the more so considering that the great majority of judgments were delivered *extempore* at the end of the hearing. He referred to the complexity of litigation on appeals from the county courts about and under the Rent Acts, which have now virtually disappeared from all courts. The judges had the role and the duty to supplement the legislation to make it coherent. He also thought that the Court of Appeal ought to develop a greater latitude concerning its rules of precedent (see below) by which, in general, the Court is bound by its previous decisions. He did not say how such a change might come about.

He then turned to the nature of a rehearing. He pointed out that, in the case of an appeal from the High Court, the appellant need not specify the grounds of appeal but that the rule was different in county court appeals. Here the notice of appeal had to set out the grounds of appeal and could not go beyond the points argued below. Lord Evershed had a vision of the county courts as places of immediate and binding decision-making on points of importance to the general public. He suggested (as was later recommended by his Committee) that in High Court appeals the grounds of appeal might be specified. But he thought that the case would probably have been argued fully in the High Court and no further specification of the grounds of appeal was necessary.

He concluded by considering the need for further reform. Here he raised a question of principle: why have appeals at all and, if there are to be appeals, where should they stop? He believed that the traditional role of the judge of first instance was to find the facts with as much expedition as possible, and the Court of Appeal could then, but only then, determine points of law arising on those facts. He did not explain why, if he was correct, judges at first instance need to be well versed in legal precedent.

As to the perpetual debate over the need for two or three appeals, he came to the pragmatic conclusion that because the House of Lords was the final court for England and Wales, Scotland, and Northern Ireland it should remain. There is an argument for that conclusion (today to be expressed in terms of the establishment of a Supreme Court) but it does not answer the question as to why there should be a third tier in purely English appeals which raise no issue of application throughout the United Kingdom.

In conclusion, Lord Evershed considered the 'leapfrog' system (introduced ten years later) and the question of introducing a system of written briefs and he disclosed, without any embarrassment, that the Court knew nothing of a case until it was opened by the appellant's counsel. That was the way the Court operated in 1950. It seemed self-evident that it should continue to do so, but Lord Evershed did concede that consideration should be given to the adoption of US and continental practices of written submissions, at least in heavy cases on appeal from the High Court. On the whole, he saw what he thought were great strengths in the existing system of no advance disclosure or reading, and an exposure of the case by dialogue between Bar and Bench. He then went on to discuss the benefits and disadvantages of single and separate judgments. He concluded with a forecast of further change to come but in an ordered manner.

In 1950 it was exceptionally rare for judges to speak in public, even in the form of a lecture at University College London. It is very unlikely that Lord Evershed would have answered questions in public following his lecture. His conversations about the reform of his Court would have taken place in private in the four Inns of Court. Apart from Professors Goodhart and Cross at Oxford, academic opinion would have counted for very little. That was the way the legal system operated in 1950. It could hardly be otherwise.

We now turn to the very limited but instructive public contributions of two Lords Justices to the even more limited literature on the internal workings of the Court. The items have to be seen in their historical context. Both were lectures given in 1950, significantly in the same year as the longer lecture given by Sir Raymond Evershed MR. The Court was then very much smaller than it is today (see above for brief details). It is reasonable to assume that the giving and publication of three lectures over a period of just a few months was planned or at least co-ordinated. The fact that the Evershed Committee[11] was considering possible changes to civil procedure might have led to the invitations to give the lectures and to their publication.

Asquith LJ, under cover of a bland title,[12] quite accurately pointed out that there was no treatise dealing comprehensively with the functions of the Court. He attributed this to the relative youth of the Court, its statutory origin in the 1870s, and the lack of a clear model for the development of the Court. In a rare declaration by a judge, he regretted the failure to develop any general theory of the appellate process after the Court was created. He had thought carefully about his daily activities and noticed that his eight years in the Queen's Bench Division had exposed him to crime (half of his work), personal injury cases (one quarter), and a range of other cases for the remainder. He was ill prepared for appellate work in other and more abstruse areas of the law. As examples, he gave tax, probate, shipping, divorce, Chancery, patent and trade mark, and, finally, housing in the form of the Rent Acts. It matters not that the context has changed significantly, that public law cases today occupy far more time than they

---

[11] See above.
[12] 'Some Aspects of the Work of the Court of Appeal' [1950] *Journal of the Society of Public Teachers of Law* 350.

did in 1950. The point that may still be made is that some of the work for some of the Lords Justices, and perhaps much for all of them, is not reflective of their previous work in practice or in the High Court. Whether this is significant for the quality of justice must await our later analysis of the manner in which the Court works. The work is described as 'grinding', 'back breaking' and 'exacting'. But there is also 'sharing, pooling, communication and consultation', which are absent, at least formally, in the High Court. However, concealed within this co-operative atmosphere is the need for each member of a three-man court (they were all men in 1950 and, indeed, until very much later) to keep up with the others. Although this is not stated in the text, there was virtually no preparation of cases by pre-reading, no skeleton arguments, no bundles of documents prepared in advance. Yet three quarters of judgments were given extemporarily. All of the work was done in open court between the Court and the Bar.

But Asquith LJ was not ignorant of developments in overseas jurisdictions. Should appeals be limited to points of law? (They were, in general, in appeals from the county court but not from the High Court.) He expressed no view, pointing out that the Evershed Committee was at work.[13] On written arguments he conceded that, at present, the Court tended to interrupt counsel frequently but he thought that this was a proven method of testing an argument or submission. He clearly liked the emphasis on oral advocacy. Perhaps that was because it was what he had come to know in practice. Perhaps he thought that this was the best manner in which the Court could give many judgments extemporarily. It is extraordinary to read that when an *extempore* judgment was given no shorthand writer attended to take a note of it-it was too early to expect recording equipment to be readily available. There was an almost private system of law reporting by which the legally qualified reporters (all members of the Bar, for obscure reasons) for the Incorporated Council of Law Reporting and the All England Law Reports would walk from court to court (there were then no more than three divisions at the most) and would take down in note form any *extempore* judgments given from day to day. The judge responsible for the judgment would be provided with a copy of the note and this would form the basis for the text that became the printed judgment. In effect the law reporters decided which cases would be reported and not the court. It may be that this is what Asquith LJ was hinting at when he protested at the absence of shorthand writers when *extempore* judgments were given. Their presence would restore to the judges the ability to at least pre-select those judgments that they would like to see reported while leaving the final choice of cases to the law reporters.

[13] See above.

In his lecture delivered to foreign jurists attending a special summer course in Cambridge,[14] Cohen LJ first spelt out the form of the jurisdiction of the Court for the benefit of those with little or no knowledge of the English legal system. He went on to explain that there were no written arguments lodged with the appeal papers and that, as stated by Asquith LJ, there was no general pre-reading of those papers; some judges thought that it would prejudice them in their attention to the oral arguments of counsel. He then graphically described the form of a hearing. The whole of the judgment below would be read out. So would much of the evidence heard and read below. As stated by Asquith LJ, most judgments were given extemporarily. To enable more judgments to be considered it would be necessary to give the members of the court an occasional day free from hearings. This could only be realised when the court had made more progress on its arrears than it had been able to do at that time.

He considered whether written arguments would assist the court. He was strongly opposed to this. Written arguments would have to be full and these would be expensive to produce. He did not seem to consider that the cost of a hearing prolonged by the absence of a written argument would also be substantial. The suggestion that abolishing hearings altogether would be inimical to achieving justice was one that had hardly been made and has not been advocated since then. The lecture was an elaborate justification of the status quo.

THE WOOLF REFORMS

We can now turn to the most significant change in the conduct of civil litigation in the twentieth century, the report of Lord Woolf entitled *Access to Justice*, published in July 1996.[15] The 'public management' impact of the Woolf proposals is considered in chapter four; the comments that follow seek to set them in a wider historical context.

Civil appeals were a small part of the vast enterprise for change led by one man. He identified the problems of civil litigation as being excessive cost, excessive delay, complexity, and a lack of equality between the powerful, wealthy litigant and the under-resourced individual or group. The courts played too small a part in the litigation: the parties dictated the speed of the case, and the rules of court were too often ignored and were not enforced by the court. Lord Woolf was successful in obtaining broad support for his reforms, the concrete result of which was the replacement of the diverse rules

---

[14] 'Jurisdiction, Practice and Procedure of the Court of Appeal' (1951) 11 *CLJ* 3.
[15] *Interim Report of Lord Woolf* (Lord Chancellor's Department, July 1995) and *Final Report* (Lord Chancellor's Department, September 1996).

of procedure in the county courts and High Courts by a single set of Civil Procedure Rules governing procedure in all courts. Further reform is contemplated. In 2005 the Department for Constitutional Affairs issued a consultation paper on a merger of the High Court and county court machinery, but not of the distinct judiciary.

The general principles that informed the Woolf review also governed his approach to appeals. A right of appeal was an essential feature of civil litigation for rectifying a mistake by a lower court. At the very least there should be a right to ask a higher court to consider whether an appeal against a lower decision should proceed any further. The dual purpose of an appellate system was noted. There is a private purpose in doing justice by correcting decisions in particular cases. There is also a public purpose in retaining public confidence in the administration of justice by making such corrections and in clarifying and developing the law. But such purposes must be free of the vices of much litigation: expense, delay, and complexity. The principles stated to be at the centre of the appellate part of the system of civil litigation were expedition, proportionality, saving expense, and assisting settlement.

Appeals had often been used as a delaying tactic but, in future, there was a danger that numerous appeals could undermine the system and use of case management by the courts, especially where a fixed timetable was to be introduced in the preparation of cases for trial. Case management might, of itself, generate more appeals, particularly if cases were disposed of summarily. A balance had to be struck between the need to ensure that litigation proceeds expeditiously and ensuring that the litigant has the opportunity to present an appeal where an injustice might otherwise be caused.

Case management would be the key to success and to achieving this necessary balance in the appellate courts themselves. As such, decisions below would often be discretionary: they would not normally be open to reversal by a higher court. The Bowman review was announced at the time that Woolf was preparing his final report, and he did not wish to pre-empt the detailed management review that had become necessary. Woolf did, however, set out the principles on which a right of appeal should operate.

Case management decisions might be divided into procedural decisions, such as fixing a date for a full hearing or for a pre-trial review, and substantive decisions, such as striking out a claim or granting an interlocutory injunction. Appeals from purely management decisions might be barred but this might also lead to much fruitless litigation about definitions of what is and what is not capable of being a procedural decision. In principle, and one senses with some regret, Woolf drew no distinction between procedural and management decisions. But he suggested that a requirement of leave to appeal be imposed for all interlocutory appeals and that further work should be done in defining which appeals should be classified as interlocutory and which should be substantive. In fact, a stronger requirement for leave (now known as permission) was later created for almost all appeals regardless of their classification: see the Access to Justice Act 1999.[16] The discussion of the machinery of permission to appeal was complex, but has been simplified to some extent since Woolf reported; this aspect of the work of the court is dealt with in more detail in chapter five.

As to the substance of the hearing of appeals, Woolf noted that the categories of appeal might be classified as a complete rehearing (which in effect would be a second hearing), a rehearing in the narrower sense of a review of the evidence on paper only without hearing witnesses afresh, and a review followed by a remittal if the appeal succeeds. There might be cases where a second hearing is appropriate, such as where one party took no part below for no fault on his part. But in most cases an appeal following the second method above would suit the needs of the parties and the broader requirement of justice. An appeal should not be an opportunity to re-litigate all issues arising between the parties. If a new trial is necessary, this should be passed to the lower court. This is, broadly, the manner in which almost all substantive appeals are heard today.

The time-honoured principle that an appellate court will not lightly interfere with findings of basic or primary fact was restated. This view has been criticised on the basis that in many cases the appellate court is in as good a position as the lower court to reach findings of fact.

Woolf went on to discuss the desirability of the court being able to encourage settlements, the need for a simplification of procedures, and the possibility of cases being referred to the Court of Appeal even where the parties themselves do not wish to appeal. Appeals in cases of judicial review and statutory appeals needed special attention and have been the subject of both a further report by Bowman and separate reform. Discussion of these and other related developments can be found in chapter five.

A VIEW FROM THE 1880S—PLUS ÇA CHANGE?

We conclude this chapter by looking back to 1886. In that year Bowen LJ, a strongly intellectual Victorian jurist, wrote an article entitled 'The Law Courts under the Judicature Acts'.[17] The origin of this piece is not clear. It reads as though the author were talking to intimate colleagues about the constant tensions between reform of the judicial process and the need to monitor reforms to avoid the cure becoming worse than the disease. The fascinating aspect of this article is its very modernity when placed alongside Evershed and Woolf.[18] The litany of complaints about delay, judges being

---

[16] 1999, c 22, and see also Part 52 of the Civil Procedure Rules.
[17] (1886) 5 *LQR* 1.

overburdened with many pressing cases, and the constant need to monitor the effect of reforms has a curiously contemporary flavour. After discussing some purely historical features of the changes brought about by the Judicature Acts, the author moved on to issues that remain under discussion today. How far should the pressure of work created by a reformed appellate jurisdiction be reduced by limiting or prohibiting entirely appeals where the pecuniary amount at stake falls below a given figure? Is it material that the legal significance of an appeal often bears no relation to the amount of money at stake? Further, is it equally material that the parties may well not measure the importance to them of the case in terms of the amounts involved? Should some or all appeals be subject to a requirement of leave? Is it an objection to a leave procedure that the Court is required to hear half a case to decide whether it should hear the whole of it? If this objection can be overcome, can leave properly be refused where a point seems to be arguable and, therefore, not liable to any doubt? If the leave process is placed in the hands of the judge whose decision it is desired to impugn, will the unsuccessful suitor ever be satisfied?

These are precisely the issues of principle underlying current debates on the nature and extent of the requirement for permission to appeal to the Court of Appeal. The language of Bowen LJ may be high Victorian English but the points of substance remain today. In many ways Bowen LJ discusses the perennial dilemmas of an appellate jurisdiction in terms of principle and not solely by reference to the resources available to the courts.

[18] Above nn 8 and 15.

4

New Public Management in the Court of Appeal: The Woolf and Bowman Reforms

... Bowman, like Woolf, is not intended to aid mere reform. They talk expressly and beguilingly of a change in culture. This too is deceptive. These reforms are not intended to build on or alter or adapt the Old World. The reports hardly argue the case for change. Indeed it is difficult to see how that could be done within the assumptions of the old ways. The language and the syntax and the grammar are all new. These reforms herald a New World. It owes little to the past ... One merely has to look at some of the recommendations in Bowman to see the magnitude of the shift from the traditional functions of the Court.[1]

It is clear that once even most of these changes are implemented the Court of Appeal as it has been since 1876 will cease to exist. Its pivotal role in the legal system will remain and may even be enhanced. But it will not be the same court and will not be doing the same things.[2]

T HE AUTHORS' RESEARCH into the operation of the Court of Appeal has been conducted against the background of a radical and continuing process of change in the machinery of justice. The Court of Appeal has been caught up in the numerous reforms that have followed the review of civil justice conducted by Lord Woolf in the late 1990s, complemented by the Bowman review of the Court of Appeal itself. These reforms had, in turn, been preceded by a decade or more of cumulatively significant incremental changes of various kinds. To say merely that the Court of Appeal has changed is to utter a commonplace. The questions addressed in this chapter are: Why has it changed? How has it changed? Do the many changes amount cumulatively to a complete transformation—a break with the past that has perhaps ushered in what the author of the epigraph to this chapter calls a 'New World' of civil appellate justice?

---

[1] Joseph M Jacob, 'The Bowman Review of the Court of Appeal' (1998) 61 *MLR* 390.
[2] *Ibid*, p 399.

We begin by setting the recent reforms of the machinery of justice in the wider context of public sector reform and modernisation of public services that have featured so strongly in the policy programmes of successive governments since the 1980s.

THATCHERISM AND THE NEW PUBLIC MANAGEMENT

Margaret Thatcher's term of office as Prime Minister from 1970 to 1990 marked the beginning of a revolution in the management and delivery of public services. In the United Kingdom, and in some other countries too, a newly fashionable 'New Right' political ideology, nourished by neo-liberal free market economic theories, condemned the inefficiency of traditional bureaucracies, while lauding the virtues of management, markets, and competition. Old-style public administration has been displaced, at least in part, by a 'new public management' (NPM),[3] which rejects traditional bureaucratic methods and structures in favour of market-based and business-like regimes of public service.[4] The radical nature and extent of the NPM phenomenon is well summarised by Owen Hughes:

> Since the mid-1980s there has been a transformation in the management of the public sectors of advanced countries. The rigid, hierarchical, bureaucratic form of public administration, which has predominated for most of the twentieth century, is changing to a flexible, market-based form of public management. This is not simply a matter of reform or a minor change in management style, but a change in the role of government in society and the relationship between government and citizenry.[5]

As Hughes observes, variations on the NPM theme can be found in the recent administrative histories of many developed countries.

---

[3] Other terms have been used as labels for the same phenomena: these include 'managerialism', 'market-based public administration', 'entrepreneurial government', and 'the contract(ing) state'.

[4] There is a very large literature on the nature and development of NPM. See, in particular, Owen Hughes, *Public Management and Administration*, 3rd edn (Basingstoke, Palgrave Macmillan, 2003); N Flynn *Public Sector Management*, 4th edn (Harlow, Financial Times/ Prentice Hall, 2002); BG Peters and DJ Savoie (eds), *Taking Stock: Assessing Public Sector Reforms* (Montreal, Canadian Centre for Management Development and the McGill-Queen's University Press, 1998); S Horton and D Farnham (eds), *Public Management in Britain* (Basingstoke, Palgrave Macmillan, 1999); D Oliver and G Drewry, *Public Service Reforms: Issues of Accountability and Public Law* (London, Pinter, 1996); C Pollitt, *Managerialism and the Public Services*, 2nd edn. (Oxford, Blackwell, 1993); S Zifcak, *New Managerialism: Administrative Reform in Whitehall and Canberra* (Buckingham, Open University Press, 1994); J Stewart and K Walsh, 'Change in the Management of Public Services' (1992) 70(4) *Public Administration* 499–518; C Hood, 'A Public Management for All Seasons' (1991) 69(1) *Public Administration* 3–20.

[5] Hughes, above n 4, p 1.

In Britain, many state-owned public service providers have been privatised, and functions and services have been extensively contracted out. One of the most significant NPM reforms of the Thatcher era was the 'Next Steps' programme, launched in February 1988, which transferred many of the executive functions of central government departments to semi-independent agencies, headed by chief executives employed on short-term contracts, many of them having been recruited from outside the civil service. By the turn of the millennium, more than three-quarters of all civil servants were working in Next Steps agencies or in departmental units organised along Next Steps lines. The Citizens' Charter, launched in 1991, then re-launched by the Blair Government in 1998 as 'Service First', added a further dimension to the NPM agenda, with its emphasis upon improved standards of service, transparency and citizen 'empowerment'. The election of a New Labour Government in 1997 did nothing to diminish the momentum of reform, and in 1999 the government published a major White Paper on *Modernising Government*. Cumulatively, all these reforms—and in particular the Next Steps initiative—have had an enormous impact on the machinery and the culture of public services in every sector and at every level.

To what extent has this revolution affected the courts—and, in particular, the Court of Appeal?

THATCHERISM CATCHES UP WITH THE JUDICIARY

Until the late 1980s the UK judiciary had co-existed in reasonable harmony with the executive. True, there had, from time to time, been grumbles about judicial salaries and calls for the recruitment of additional judges to reduce real or imagined overload of the courts. And it is also true that judicial review had been expanding since the early 1970s and that the judges had shown increasing signs of sympathy towards challenges to the exercise of executive power. But there was no real sense that the judiciary was trespassing to any significant degree upon governmental or parliamentary territory, and the Thatcher Government, like its predecessors, was generally deferential towards judicial independence, and initially seemed disinclined to expose the judicial process to the full rigour of the public management reforms that were being imposed on every other part of the public sector.

In a report on the administration of the courts, published in 1986,[6] the influential legal reform organisation, JUSTICE, ventured the observation that:

> The courts exist for the benefit of the public and provide, and should be seen to provide, a public service, as much as, say, the National Health Service. We would like to see a wider recognition of this fact. The customer in the law courts may

---

[6] JUSTICE, *The Administration of the Courts* (London, JUSTICE, 1986).

not always be right but it is he or she, and not the judges or lawyers, for whom the service is provided.

Twenty years on, this hardly looks like a radical statement. But in the mid-Thatcher era it was ahead of its time, and this way of thinking about legal services was not particularly evident in public policy.

One explanation for this lay in the office of Lord Chancellor, and in particular in the personal influence of Lord Hailsham, who held that office from the beginning of the Thatcher era until June 1987. The classic explanation of the Lord Chancellor's unique hybrid position as a Cabinet Minister and judge had been set out by a former holder of the office, Lord Birkenhead, in an essay published in 1922. If the Lord Chancellor's ministerial and judicial roles are 'totally severed', he claimed:

> there will disappear with them any controlling or suggestive force exterior to the Judges themselves, and it is difficult to believe that there is no necessity for the existence of such a personality, imbued on the one hand with legal ideas and habits of thought, and aware on the other of the problems which engage the attention of the executive government. In the absence of such a person the judiciary and the executive are likely enough to drift asunder to the point of a violent separation, followed by a still more violent and disastrous collision.[7]

Later, Lord Schuster, the Permanent Secretary of the Lord Chancellor's Department throughout the inter-war years (and probably the ghost-writer of Birkenhead's essay), wrote about the need for 'some link or buffer' between executive and judiciary; and his successor, Sir Albert Napier, later used the metaphor of a constitutional 'hinge' to describe the Lord Chancellor's position. Lord Hailsham, a Thatcher loyalist, but very much a legal traditionalist, strongly subscribed to this position and throughout his tenure of office fiercely defended judicial independence against any perceived threat—including innocuous moves to bring aspects of judicial administration (not substantive judicial decisions) within the purview of parliamentary select committees. However, even in the Hailsham era, some new public management themes, such as the Financial Management Initiative, had begun to impinge upon the Lord Chancellor's Department. In 1985 Hailsham himself instigated a major review of civil justice. But during his tenure of office, the judges themselves appeared to remain insulated from (or buffered against) such developments.

Soon after he left office things began to change. In June 1988 the report of the Civil Justice Review was published:[8] it recommended unification of the civil jurisdictions of county courts (local courts that handle all but the most serious civil litigation) and the High Court—although, for a variety of

---

[7] Lord Birkenhead, *Points of View*, vol 1 (London, Hodder and Stoughton, 1922) p 113.
[8] *Report of the Review Body on Civil Justice*, Cm 394 (1988).

reasons, this merger has never taken place. By this time a new incumbent of the Lord Chancellor's Office was in post—Lord Mackay of Clashfern. Mackay was a Scottish lawyer, and so not part of the English legal establishment in the way that Hailsham had been. Having been given a life peerage in 1979, he served as Lord Advocate, the senior Scottish Law Officer, in the early years of Mrs Thatcher's administration. But he was not a career politician (Hailsham, an MP before he went to the House of Lords, had once been a serious contender for the Conservative prime ministership)—and it is perhaps a certain lack of sensitive political antennae that goes some way to explaining why he quickly found himself in confrontation with the judiciary.

One of the present authors has told a fuller version of this story elsewhere[9] and we will not repeat the details here. Suffice it to say that, in 1989, following the earlier review of civil justice, Lord Chancellor Mackay published three consultation papers on legal services and the legal professions, one of which proposed a new system—including an advisory committee containing lay members—for licensing advocates to appear before the courts. The judiciary had always insisted that it was their absolute prerogative to determine who could argue cases before them and were furious at what they claimed to be an attack on judicial independence and the rule of law. In the House of Lords debate on the proposals they gave vent to their fury, in more than extravagant language:

> Lord Chief Justice, Lord Lane, attacked the new advisory committee procedure as a movement towards executive control over the judiciary, adding for good measure that: 'Oppression does not stand on the doorstep with a toothbrush moustache and a swastika armband ...'. Lord Donaldson, Master of the Rolls, said that, if necessary, he would tell the Government to, 'Get your tanks off my lawn'. Former Lord Chancellor, Lord Hailsham, said that he was 'shocked' by the prospective threat posed to judicial independence by the proposal that a member of the executive [ie the Lord Chancellor], advised by an advisory committee which is staffed secretarially by his own department and composed of a majority of persons unqualified in the law, would take charge of who was qualified to practice in the courts.[10]

Some of the details of the proposals were watered down and the row blew over, and the metaphor of the Lord Chancellor as a comforting 'buffer' or 'hinge' between the executive and the judiciary was now effectively consigned to the history books—although Tony Blair's first Lord Chancellor, Lord Irvine, tried to keep the tradition alive with a reference to his office being 'at a critical cusp in the separation of powers between Parliament, government and the judiciary.'[11]

---

[9] Oliver and Drewry, above n 1, pp 104–5.
[10] *Ibid*, p 105.
[11] HL Deb, 25 November 1997, col 943.

The episode described above—albeit based upon a considerable over-reaction on the part of the judges—underlines the rather obvious fact that modernising the machinery of justice requires tactful handling. But in the meantime, a senior member of the Court of Appeal, Sir Nicolas (later Lord) Browne-Wilkinson, had already addressed some of the issues in a public lecture delivered in 1987, and published in the following year. In his lecture he warned of threats to the continuing independence of the administration of justice that lay in the increasing application of strict value-for-money and financial management disciplines to the Lord Chancellor's Department:

> The requirements of judicial independence make the Lord Chancellor's Department wholly different from any other department of state. It is not for the executive alone to determine what should be the policy objectives of the courts. It is not for the executive alone to determine whether or not a particular judicial procedure provides 'value for money'. Justice is not capable of being measured out by an accountant's computer ... [U]nder our constitution it is for the judge to determine what is just, and what is not just, subject always to legislation passed by Parliament. As a result of such policy being applied to the Lord Chancellor's Department, that department is being required to formulate policy and to make determinations as to 'value for money' according to financial yardsticks and without, for the most part, even consulting the judges.[12]

NEW PUBLIC MANAGEMENT AND THE COURTS—THE RISING TIDE

All these judicial concerns, uttered in the late 1980s as the Thatcher years were about to come to an end, did nothing to hold back the tide of NPM that was already lapping the shores of the machinery of justice. Some of the reforms yet to come had been foreshadowed earlier in the decade.

To cite just one example, relating to the Court of Appeal, the Supreme Court Act 1981 had provided for the establishment of a new office of Registrar of Civil Appeals, with the judicial status of a Master of the Supreme Court. Up to this time, the Civil Division of the Court of Appeal (unlike the Criminal Division, and the High Court) had virtually no staff, apart from the judges' clerks. The establishment of the post of Registrar—implementing recommendations in the (unpublished) report of a working party on the Court of Appeal, chaired by Lord Scarman[13]—was intended to relieve the Lords Justices of the administrative burdens of dealing, in particular, with interlocutory business. In 1982 the office had 19 staff; by 2003 it

---

[12] Nicolas Browne-Wilkinson, 'The Independence of the Judiciary in the 1980s' [1988] *Public Law* 44, p 50.

[13] Report dated December 1978. See note to s 58 of the Supreme Court Act 1981 in *Current Law Statutes*, 1981, vol 2. The other relevant provisions of the 1991 Act are ss 88 and 89, and Sch 2.

had 70, including 10 lawyers, the office of Registrar having been abolished in the aftermath of the Bowman Report.[14] It was superseded by the senior managerial post of Head of the Civil Appeals Office (whose incumbent also has the judicial status of a Supreme Court Master), on the establishment of the Court Service Executive Agency—a product of the Next Steps programme. A major internal report, *Review of the Administrative Functions at the Royal Courts of Justice*, published in May 2006, recommended a number of further reforms relating to the administration of the courts that operate in the Royal Courts of Justice, including the Court of Appeal. These included the creation of a single post, with management responsibility for both divisions of the Court.[15]

Far from being recognised as 'wholly different' from other government departments, the Lord Chancellor's Department moved increasingly into the mainstream of public administration. The statutory requirement that the Permanent Secretary of the Department must have substantial legal qualifications and experience was repealed by the Supreme Court (Offices) Act 1997. Much of the Department's work and staffing has been concentrated in the large executive agency mentioned earlier—the Courts Service, which in 2005 was converted into a unified Courts Agency, which has absorbed the local committees that run the magistrates' courts (the bedrocks of the criminal justice system). There are courts charters, making commitments to improving standards of customer service, operating at all levels of the judicial system (and the Courts Service itself has won many 'chartermark' awards for service excellence). Since 1998, the Department negotiates Public Service Agreements with the Treasury, as the basis of securing three years' funding in return for achieving agreed targets. In January 2003 the Lord Chancellor's Department appointed its first Director General of Finance to oversee the Department's £3 billion annual budget.

It might appear odd that the modernisation of the administration of justice has been taking place under the auspices of a department whose ministerial head holds the antique and constitutionally rather strange office of Lord Chancellor, an office that has been in existence for some 1,400 years. We have already noted that the interesting position of the latter, at the interface between executive and judiciary, has been undergoing important evolutionary changes. And recently, the post of Lord Chancellor itself teetered on the brink of extinction. In June 2003, his Department became the Department for Constitutional Affairs (DCA), headed by a Secretary

---

[14] Access to Justice Act 1999, s 70.

[15] David Ryan and John Briden, *Review of the Administrative Functions at the Royal Courts of Justice*, May 2006 (unpublished), para 5.69. In July 2006 it was announced that the Civil Appeals Office and the Criminal Appeal Office would be united under a single administrative head. This entails the abolition of the posts of Head of the Civil Appeals Office and Master and Deputy Registrar of Criminal Appeals and the creation of a new post of Head of the Court of Appeal Office.

of State for Constitutional Affairs, who—contrary to the original intention of the Blair Government—retains the post and title of Lord Chancellor. The Secretary of State need no longer be a lawyer or sit in the House of Lords—although Lord Falconer, the holder of the office at the time of writing, is and does so.

These changes were given statutory effect by the Constitutional Reform Act 2005. The Lord Chancellor's judicial functions have been transferred to a President of the Courts of England and Wales. The same Act paved the way for the establishment of a new Supreme Court to take over the appellate functions of the House of Lords (see chapter ten), and an independent Judicial Appointments Commission, intended to curtail the extent of the Lord Chancellor's present powers of patronage over judicial appointments. The Constitutional Reform Bill proved controversial and ran into difficulties in the House of Lords, which delayed its enactment. The judges complained that they were not consulted about or even given advance notice of the proposals, and the Government agreed a 'concordat' to meet their objections by inserting additional provisions enshrining in law a duty on Ministers to uphold the independence of the judiciary. The initial judicial protests were led by the then Lord Woolf CJ, who was to become the new President of the Courts. As we will see in the following section, and as previously noted in chapter three, it is the same Lord Woolf who has played a key role in the recent modernisation of civil justice.

A new Directorate of Judicial Offices (DJO) has been established in the Royal Courts of Justice. This comprises a Judicial Office, to support the Lord Chief Justice (who has now taken over many of the 'head of judiciary' functions formerly exercised by the Lord Chancellor) and senior members of the judiciary in their new roles and responsibilities under the Constitutional Reform Act 2005. It is also responsible for upholding the concordat between the judiciary and the Lord Chancellor. In April 2005 a Judicial Communications Office was created as part of the DJO 'to enhance public confidence' in the judiciary (including magistrates and tribunal members). And, in April 2006, the Judicial Studies Board was brought within the management structure of the DJO, reporting to the Lord Chief Justice.[16]

THE WOOLF REPORTS ON CIVIL JUSTICE[17]

As already suggested, the momentum for civil justice reform—making the courts cost-effective and, at the same time, more accessible and user-friendly—built up slowly during the Conservative Thatcher–Hailsham

[16] See http://www.dca.gov.uk/constitution/reform/djo.htm
[17] See Charles Blake, 'Modernising Civil Justice in England and Wales' in M Fabri and P Langbroek (eds), *The Challenge of Change for Judicial Systems* (Amsterdam, IOS Press, 2000) pp 37–45.

era, and continued to gather pace with New Labour under Tony Blair and his first Lord Chancellor, Lord Irvine. The story told here, and in the sections that follow, begins some three years before the advent of the Blair Government, in 1994, when the Government of John Major commissioned a review of process of the civil courts in England and Wales, headed by Lord Woolf.[18] The object of the review was to find ways of:

— improving access to justice;
— reducing the complexity of rules of procedure, and modernising terminology;
— removing unnecessary inconsistencies in practice and procedure across the civil justice system.

Implicit in these terms of reference are some key elements that have driven NPM reform across the public sector—in particular, greater attention to the requirements of the citizen as customer, more cost-effective use of public resources (including expensive judicial manpower), and simplification of procedures and terminologies to make them more intelligible to non-lawyers and more user-friendly. The exercise was influenced by observation of reforms that had been taking place elsewhere, particularly in Australia and New Zealand.

The review produced an Interim Report in June 1995[19] and its Final Report in July 1996.[20] Details of the recommendations need not detain us here, but mention must be made of the core feature of the Woolf proposals—that judges should become proactive case managers. They would be required to manage proceedings, set timetables and deadlines for cases, and impose costs and other penalties (such as striking out claims) for non-compliance with judicial directions. No longer would the litigating parties be allowed to dictate the pace at which business is transacted. The case management role also includes encouraging the litigating parties to settle cases and to use mechanisms of alternative dispute resolution (ADR), such as mediation. The core principles recommended by Woolf were embodied in a new set of Civil Procedure Rules (CPR), issued in April 1999.

THE COURT OF APPEAL: FROM WOOLF TO BOWMAN

In October 1996, before the publication of Lord Woolf's Final Report, the Lord Chancellor (still Lord Mackay) commissioned a top accountant (formerly a senior partner of Price Waterhouse Coopers), Sir Jeffery Bowman,

---

[18] He was a Lord of Appeal (a judge of the House of Lords) at this time. He later (1996–2000) served as Master of the Rolls (head of the Court of Appeal), and has been Lord Chief Justice since 2000.

[19] http://www.dca.gov.uk/civil/interfr.htm.

[20] http://www.dca.gov.uk/civil/final/contents.htm.

to conduct a review of the Court of Appeal (Civil Division) in England and Wales. Lord Woolf did not include much direct reference to the Court of Appeal in his own report. However, he did emphasise the importance of applying the principles set out in that report to the appellate process.

Bowman's terms of reference were as follows:

To carry out a full review of the Civil Division of the Court of Appeal against the background of an increasing number of applications and appeals and consequent delays in the hearing of appeals. In particular the Review will examine:

a the rules, procedures and working methods of the Civil Division;
b the appropriateness of the scope of the Court's jurisdiction;
c the appropriate constitution of the Court for different categories of case; and
d the legal and administrative support to the court.[21]

Bowman noted the growing workload and consequent delays in the Court of Appeal. In 1996 the average time between the setting down and final disposal of 70 per cent of appeals was running at 14 months—which meant that 30 per cent of appeals were taking even longer than that, some indeed having been outstanding for over five years. And this calculation took no account of the interval between the judgment in the court below and the setting down of the appeal, nor of the time taken by any application for leave to appeal that might be required. Bowman quotes the then Master of the Rolls as saying that the delay in hearing some categories of appeal 'has reached a level which is inconsistent with the due administration of justice,' and the situation looked as though it was getting worse.

The review concluded that there were three options for improving matters:

— to increase the number of Lords Justices;
— to narrow the scope of the Court's jurisdiction; or
— to improve the way the Court worked so that it could deal with its caseload more quickly.

The first of these was regarded as a last resort, so the review focused on the second two options.

The Bowman Report was published on 6 November 1997.[22] It contained 146 conclusions and recommendations. The following is a slightly

---

[21] http://www.dca.gov.uk/civil/bowman/bowman1.htm.

[22] There is a substantial summary on the DCA website, http://www.dca.gov.uk/civil/bowman/bowman2.htm; see also a letter from Bowman to the Lord Chancellor, September 1997, http://www.dca.gov.uk/civil/bowman/bowman1.htm.

abridged version of Bowman's own summary, set out in a letter to the Lord Chancellor:

— the requirement for leave to appeal should be extended to nearly all cases coming to the Court of Appeal;
— leave to appeal against an interlocutory decision should be granted only if it is at an appropriate stage in the proceedings for an appeal to be heard;
— certain appeals which now reach the Court of Appeal should be heard at a lower level;
— it would still be possible for appeals which would normally to be heard in a lower court to reach the Court in certain circumstances. In particular, an appeal could be considered if it raises an important point of principle or practice, or one which for some other special reason should be considered by the Court;
— there is an increasing role for appropriate judicial case management;
— the Civil Appeals Office should be headed by a single administrative head, who must be accountable to the Chief Executive of the Court Service and have line management responsibility for every member of staff in the Civil Appeals Office;
— the judicial functions of the Registrar of Civil Appeals should be carried out by two designated legal officers. Anyone dissatisfied with the decision of a legal officer should be entitled to have that decision referred to a Lord Justice;
— if our recommendations are accepted, there will be no requirement for a judicial post of Registrar of Civil Appeals. When the present office holder leaves office, he should not be replaced;
— there is a need for more focused procedures. Cases should be better prepared at a much earlier stage in the process and realistic timetables should be set, which must be strictly observed;
— the Court should impose appropriate time limits on oral argument on appeals;
— the balance of judicial time should lean more towards reading and less towards sitting in court;
— there is a need to develop the use of information technology to support the other recommendations of this Review;
— information for litigants in person about the appeal process and what it can deliver must be available at an early stage. The information must be easily understandable and delivered through a range of methods;
— there should be an enhanced Administration Committee to assist the Master of the Rolls with his overall responsibility for the speed, efficiency, and economy with which the work of the Court is conducted;
— better information needs to be collected in order for the Court to monitor and evaluate its work satisfactorily.

IMPLEMENTING WOOLF AND BOWMAN: THE *TANFERN*
DIRECTION

The Bowman Report was accepted by the Government, with minor amendments, and—following further consultation—was implemented by a variety of legislative instruments[23] and by administrative action.

A helpful overview of the procedural implications of the post-Woolf–Bowman reforms can be found in a Court of Appeal decision in May 2000, *Tanfern Ltd v Cameron-MacDonald*.[24] The subject-matter of the case (a county court action for recovery of arrears of rent) was of no interest other than to the litigating parties, and the substantive legal issues involved appear to have been straightforward. What brought it to the Court of Appeal was a jurisdictional point arising out of the new provisions governing civil appeals in private law matters that had only just come into effect. Did an appeal lie from a district judge (sitting in effect as a circuit judge, hearing the case by the agreement of the parties, under the new multi-track procedure[25]) to a circuit judge of the county court—or to the Court of Appeal? The case presented a convenient peg on which their Lordships (Lord Woolf MR, Peter Gibson and Brooke LJJ) could hang a comprehensive practice direction relating to such novel matters as permission to appeal and the restriction of second appeals—and some more general issues to do with the nature of appellate proceedings (termed by the Court 'the appellate approach').

The following paragraphs summarise some of the main points of particular relevance to the present study. Brooke LJ delivered the judgment of the Court.

(1) Permission to Appeal

With a few exceptions—notably, in cases where the liberty of the subject is in issue[26]—permission to appeal is required. Permission may be granted either by the lower court at the hearing at which the decision to be appealed was made, or by the appeal court. If the latter (which of course includes the Court of Appeal itself) refuses permission without a hearing, a request may be made for consideration of that decision at an oral hearing. If the refusal

---

[23] In particular, by Part IV of the Access to Justice Act 1999, and the Access to Justice Act 1999 (Destination of Appeals) Order 2000, together with amendments to the CPR.

[24] [2000] 1 WLR 1311. See below pp 68 *ff*.

[25] The early allocation of cases to appropriate 'tracks' (small claims, fast-track or multi-track) is a central feature of the case management regime introduced by the CPR, in the interests of achieving greater efficiency and flexibility in the civil trial process.

[26] Thus an appeal against a committal order, a refusal of habeas corpus, or a secure accommodation order under s 25 of the Children Act 1989 lies as of right. There are other exceptions, mainly to do with certain categories of appeal in the lower courts.

of permission is confirmed at the oral hearing, that is the end of the matter. An order giving permission to appeal may limit the issues to be heard.

The Court noted the requirement in the new Rules that permission will only be given where the court considers that an appeal would have a real prospect of success or where there is some other compelling reason why the appeal should be heard. It reiterated an earlier *dictum* of Lord Woolf MR[27] that 'the use of the word "real" means that the prospect of success must be realistic rather than fanciful.'

Rule 52.14(1) of the CPR provides that, 'if the normal route of a first appeal would be to a circuit judge or to a High Court judge, either the lower court of the appeal court may order the appeal to be transferred to the Court of Appeal if they consider that it would raise an important point of principle or practice or there is some other compelling reason for the Court of Appeal to hear it.' Section 57(1) of the 1999 Act also gives power to the Master of the Rolls to direct that an appeal that would normally go to a circuit judge or to a High Court judge should be heard instead by the Court of Appeal.

We discuss the operation of the permission requirement, in the light of our research findings, in later chapters.

(2) Second Appeals

One of the questions at the heart of the present study—how many appeals do we need?—has been pre-empted at least in part by a statutory answer, to the effect that, in all but the most exceptional circumstances, one appeal must suffice. Thus section 55(1) of the Access to Justice Act 1999, based on recommendations in the Bowman Report, provides that:

> Where an appeal is made to a county court or the High Court in relation to any matter, and on hearing the appeal the court makes a decision in relation to that matter, no appeal may be made to the Court of Appeal from that decision unless the Court of Appeal considers that—(a) the appeal would raise an important point of principle or practice, or (b) there is some other compelling reason for the Court of Appeal to hear it.

This important change is designed—in the spirit of the Bowman recommendations—to reverse the steady increase in the number of cases reaching the Court of Appeal, and so to free up valuable and expensive judicial resources to give more and more effective attention to hearing first appeals. The effect is that, in the words of Brooke LJ:

> It will no longer be possible to pursue a second appeal to the Court of Appeal merely because the appeal is 'properly arguable' or 'because it has a real prospect of

---

[27] *Swain v Hillman* [2001] 1 All ER 91.

success' ... The decision of the first appeal court is now to be given primacy unless the Court of Appeal itself considers that the appeal would raise an important point of principle or practice, or that there is some other compelling reason for it to hear this second appeal.

He went on to note the significance of this change from the point of view of those tenacious litigants who, under the old procedure, might have been tempted to pursue their grievances up every rung of a long appellate ladder:

> All courts are familiar with the litigant, often an unrepresented litigant, who will never take 'no' for an answer, however unpromising his/her cause. Under the new appeals regime, however, such litigants must appreciate that the general rule will be that the decision of the appeal court on the first appeal will be the final decision. If they wish to pursue the matter further, and to incur the often quite heavy costs involved in paying the court fee and preparing the appeal papers, the Court of Appeal may dismiss their application quite shortly, saying that the appeal raises no important point of principle or practice, and that there is no other compelling reason for the court to hear the appeal.

This section of the judgment ends by noting the consequent importance of providing clear documentation of the previous history and present status of each application, so that the staff and lawyers in the Civil Appeals Office can ascertain whether the Court has jurisdiction.

(3) The 'Appellate Approach'

CPR rule 52.11 provides that, 'as a general rule [with minor exceptions noted later in the judgment], every appeal will be limited to a review of the decision of the lower court ... The appeal court will only allow an appeal where the decision of the lower court was wrong, or where it was unjust because of a serious procedural irregularity in the proceedings in the lower court.' The Court noted that this marked a significant change in relation to interlocutory appeals from district judges or masters, which formerly involved a full rehearing and scope for the appellate judge to exercise his or her discretion *de novo* in substitution for the decision of the court below. We have already discussed the concepts of 'review' and 'rehearing' in chapter two.

The Court went on to explain the two grounds on which an appellate court, conducting such a review, may interfere with the decision of the court *a quo*. So far as the 'wrongness' of a decision below is concerned, it quoted from a House of Lords judgment by Lord Fraser of Tullybelton, who had pondered on the use by different judges of such terms as 'blatant error', 'plainly wrong' or (simply) 'wrong', before concluding that:

> All these various expressions were used in order to emphasise the point that the appellate court should only interfere when it considers that the judge of first instance has not merely preferred an imperfect solution which is different from an alternative imperfect solution which the Court of Appeal might or would have adopted, but has exceeded the generous ambit within which a reasonable disagreement is possible.[28]

As for the 'procedural or other irregularity' ground for interference, the Court noted that the irregularity must be 'serious', and be one that 'caused the decision of the lower court to be an unjust decision.'

JUDGES AS CASE MANAGERS?

Some of the Bowman recommendations were narrowly technical in character and do not require detailed discussion in the present chapter. In the following discussion we will focus on just one crucial aspect—one which permeates the Woolf and Bowman Reports, and which is particularly relevant to a discussion of NPM's impact on the judicial process: the significance of the moves, in the Court of Appeal and elsewhere, to introduce judicial case management.

The Lord Chancellor's Department subsequently commissioned a research review to evaluate the impact of the reforms in the Court of Appeal (Civil Division), and the report based on that review, by Joyce Plotnikoff and Richard Woolfson, published in November 2002,[29] forms a valuable background to this chapter and, in particular, to the sections that follow.

Elsewhere, one of the present authors, Charles Blake, has questioned whether management is compatible with a judicial function. He believes that on balance it is—although there may be potential dangers:

> If the judge becomes involved very closely in a case during its preliminary stages, will that judge get to see too many of the internal papers showing the strength and weakness of the case which, arguably, should be adjudicated upon later on evidence placed before the court at the trial? This assumes that judges should only ever do what they have always done. It is most important that decisions about the conduct of cases should be taken by judges and not merely by court administrators. There is room for the use of administrators in marshalling cases and putting them in a suitable state to be placed before judges. Judges

---

[28] *G v G* [1985] 2 All ER 225, 229; [1985] 1 WLR 647, 652.
[29] There is an executive summary on the DCA website, at http://www.dca.gov.uk/research/2003/5-03es.htm. The full report can be obtained from the DCA.

must be wary of making irrevocable decisions even on procedural matters before sufficient information is placed before them. But it is the very experience of a judge as a former practitioner (the absence of a career judiciary in England may have this advantage) that should enable a correct judgment to be made on procedural matters yet one which will not compromise the impartiality of the trial process.[30]

However, he goes on to acknowledge the importance of avoiding the obvious risk that an obsession with moving cases forward may lead judges to compromise on the quality of their decisions (he cites some instances in the area of social security adjudication as a reminder of the dangers of excessive haste in pursuit of performance indicators).

But are the budgetary constraints imposed by government necessarily consistent with the need to maintain the independence of the judiciary in dispensing justice between litigating parties? Blake notes that Woolf addressed this issue by appointing a senior appellate judge as head of civil justice to supervise the reforms, and the creation of a Civil Justice Council to assist in this role.[31] (The Council takes a particular interest in the use of ADR; see chapter 5.)

Reservations about the continuing tendency to combine judicial and administrative functions in pursuit of constitutional modernisation were recently expressed by Moses LJ in his Margaret Howard Lecture, 'The Mask and the Judge', delivered in Oxford in May 2006. He observed:

> Judges have no training in administration; the Judicial Appointments Commission does not ask whether alongside the qualities of decisiveness, fairmindedness and such other qualities as they seek to see demonstrated look for management skills. But the higher a judge ascends the judicial ladder the greater the need for skill and subtlety of the mandarin. And the dangers of so obvious a necessity lie not so much in the possibility that ... some judges reaching the top may be good at judging and bad at administration but rather in blurring the very boundary which the new constitutional changes sought to clarify and preserve. The danger lies in the elision of administration and the process of judging.[32]

Many of his remarks related to the effects of the Constitutional Reform Act 2005 and the new responsibilities transferred to the Lord Chief Justice and other senior members of the judiciary, which have led to the creation of the Directorate of Judicial Offices (see above). We ourselves venture to doubt whether there is in fact such an inherent incompatibility between judging

---

[30] Blake, above n 17, p 43.

[31] The council's website is: http://www.adr.civiljusticecouncil.gov.uk/Home.go;jsessionid= baad6NwqOJ3oAu.

[32] An edited extract of the lecture appeared in (2006) *The Times*, 23 May. The full text can be accessed at timesonline.co.uk/law.

and administration (and in our own interviews with members of the Court we found no echoes of Moses LJ's views). It is certainly the case that some judges have more enthusiasm and/or aptitude for administration than others, but that is a different issue.

Returning to our own, more specific concerns with the impact of the Woolf–Bowman reforms, the sixty-four thousand dollar question remains. Has the implementation of the Woolf report, whose principles have been carried over into the appellate process by the Bowman review, brought about as fundamental a culture shift in the judicial role as the drivers of change might have hoped? The verdict appears to be a 'yes'—but a somewhat qualified 'yes'. For one thing, it should not be imagined that judges have in the past had no responsibility at all for 'managing' court business and the flow of litigation (including management of their own time). Judges have, for instance, always had the power to rule against 'vexatious' litigation. Moreover, it is an axiomatic corollary of judicial independence that only (senior) judges—and not administrators—can ultimately give instructions to other judges. Judicial independence is an important constitutional principle. But that principle operates in tandem with sub-constitutional professional concerns that have accompanied NPM reforms throughout the public sector—concerns about, for example, the extent to which the managerial criteria for prioritising the allocation of scarce resources in the National Health Service should be allowed to override the medical judgements of hospital consultants.

The 2004 Public Service Agreement (see above) of the DCA includes the following commitment:

To achieve earlier and more proportionate resolution of legal problems and disputes by:

— increasing advice and assistance to help people resolve their disputes earlier and more effectively;
— increasing the opportunities for people involved in court cases to settle their disputes out of court; and
— reducing delays in resolving those disputes that need to be decided by the courts.[33]

While these principles resonate strongly with the objectives and proposals set out in the Woolf and Bowman reports, including judicial case management, they are couched in broad managerial terms that leave unspecified the part to be played by the judges. This and other Public Service Agreements vest responsibility for delivery in the Minister—in this case the Secretary of State for Constitutional Affairs, who is of course advised by his civil servants, who administer and manage the system on his behalf.

---

[33] http://www.dca.gov.uk/dept/sr2004.htm.

In practice, even after Woolf and Bowman, many aspects of case management have always been and remain—and properly so—essentially an administrative/bureaucratic function. The Civil Appeals Office—part of the Courts Service, which is an executive agency of the DCA—has a permanent staff of about 70 administrators and lawyers, about 25 of whom are employed in one of three 'Case Management Groups', each headed by a senior lawyer.[34]

Many of the post-Bowman developments (eg the requirement of permission to appeal, which has generated a huge number of time-consuming applications, and the shift towards more judicial 'reading time' outside the courtroom) have undoubtedly impacted upon judicial work-patterns—albeit to initially mixed judicial feelings, as interviews carried out by Plotnikoff and Woolfson make clear. Our own interview data suggest that the Lords Justices seem generally, in many respects, to have welcomed their role as case managers, although not to the extent that the traditional judicial culture has been significantly displaced by managerialism.

One important feature of the new case management regime is the working relationship between Supervising Lords Justices (SLJs), who were first introduced in November 1997 to oversee particular types of appeal, and the lawyers in the Civil Appeal Office. The Plotnikoff and Wolfson review paid close attention to the role of the SLJs, and found little evidence of managerial enthusiasm on the part of these key actors, nor indeed much apparent effort on the part of others to define and manage their role:

> SLJs generally saw their role as reacting to problems when they arise. There was little judicial appetite to get involved in strategic planning, communication with lower courts or forging closer links with the administration. The full vision of the role set out in the Bowman report was therefore not being realised ... Despite an intention that SLJs should be drawn from the ranks of experienced Lords Justices, many had taken on the role months or even weeks after joining the Court of Appeal. This was a factor in how the role was perceived. One judge saw it mainly as a way of enriching the career structure for Lords Justices by providing a first rung on the ladder to becoming a presider [presiding Lord Justice] ... SLJs received no preparation other than a short briefing from their predecessor, where one was available, and a discussion with an office lawyer. No-one had oversight of the way different SLJs approached the role and there was no formal exchange of ideas about the role between SLJs.[35]

They concluded that 'persuading SLJs to adopt a more managerial approach may take time. The transition could be assisted by introducing an element of coordination and the development of guidance on carrying out the role.'

---

[34] *The Court of Appeal, Civil Division: Review of the Legal Year 2002–2003*, p 27.
[35] Plotnikoff and Woolfson, above n 29, para 9.6.

However, these conclusions were based on data from the early days, when the reforms were still bedding down. Our own findings suggest that, in this and other areas, things have moved on. Our general conclusion is this: even though the direct impact of judicial case management may not in practice amount to quite as much as the attention given to it might have led one to expect, the overall impact of the Woolf–Bowman reforms has been substantial (and evidently beneficial in terms of significantly reduced backlogs and a quicker throughput of cases).[36] The Court of Appeal has become a much more 'modern' and streamlined institution—the extensive use of information and communications technology, as recommended by Bowman, is just one very visible manifestation of this.[37] The Master of the Rolls and his senior judicial colleagues use more 'managerial' language in public contexts—for example in the Annual Reports of the Court of Appeal—than their predecessors, and they evidently do take very seriously the managerial aspects of their role, in relation to performance indicators and so on, and fighting for necessary resources.

One interesting observation, illustrative of potential tensions between judicial and managerial priorities is to be found in a comment by the Vice-President of the Court of Appeal, Brooke LJ, referring to the Treasury's expectation that the Court will to try to cover its costs from the income generated by appeals. He is concerned about the substantial amount of expensive judge-time that is wasted in disposing of hopeless applications for permission to appeal, and goes on to note that no one seems to have calculated the full economic cost of a Lord Justice's time.[38] And the radical step—one which would certainly need to accompany any full-blooded attempt to 'managerialise' the judiciary—of introducing formal performance indicators for the judges themselves appears to lie a very long way in the future.

In summary, the recent reforms do seem to have succeeded in raising the awareness of judges of the managerial context in which they operate; but turning them into managers is not what this has been about. The more substantial changes have been in the bureaucratic and technical infrastructure—turning *administrators* into managers, as has happened across the rest of the public sector.

Nevertheless, if we were looking for a particularly vivid piece of *symbolism* to mark the importation of NPM principles into the administration of the courts we surely need to look no further than the Woolf–Bowman

---

[36] Statistics and commentary that appear to bear this out can be found in the annual reports of the Court of Appeal entitled *The Court of Appeal, Civil Division: Review of the Legal Year* available on the DCA website. And see ch 6.

[37] For a commentary on continuing developments in this area, see Brooke LJ, 'Behind the Times? IT in the Court of Appeal' [2004] *NLJ*, 5 March, pp 331–32.

[38] *The Court of Appeal, Civil Division: Review of the Legal Year 2002–2003*, p 8.

move—albeit probably more rhetorical than real—to harness the judges themselves to the proactive management of cases. Judges of an earlier generation would have had apoplexy at the very idea: many of those of the present generation seem quite willing to entertain the idea, and can see real advantages in it, even if some of them have embraced it more enthusiastically than others. And it is of course worth remembering that Lord Woolf, the main driver of change—and the changes have largely been 'judge-driven'—is himself a senior and respected judge rather than a management guru.

5

A Right of Appeal?

If no appeal were possible ... This would not be a desirable country to live in ...[1]

IN THIS CHAPTER we consider critically the changes brought about by the Woolf and Bowman reforms to the existing procedure in the Court of Appeal. Under the former procedure, a litigant generally had an absolute right to appeal against a lower and final decision. In the case of an 'interlocutory' decision—broadly a decision taken in the course of litigation and not finally dispositive of the rights of the parties—leave to appeal was required. Moreover, the jurisdiction of the Court of Appeal could normally only be engaged after the interlocutory decision had first been appealed to the next level in the lower courts. So, a decision of a district judge had first to be taken to a circuit judge, and a corresponding decision of a High Court master had first to be taken to a High Court judge. Such an appeal would take the form of a full rehearing. Appeals to the Court of Appeal were limited rehearings.

In chapters three and four we have set out the principal recommendations of both the Woolf review of civil litigation and the Bowman review of the management and jurisdiction of the Court of Appeal. The fundamental principles of the Woolf reforms were to be applied to the Court of Appeal. These were: access to and delivery of justice, expedition in the handling of cases, and moderation of costs, which would be proportionate to the nature of the litigation in any one case. An unfettered right of appeal had outlived its utility. So had a distinction in the right of appeal based on whether a lower judgment had been final or interlocutory in nature. The only right a litigant has is to ask a higher court to look at the lower decision and see if ought to be considered afresh. This is the 'permission' stage of appeals. Only in a very limited number of cases does a litigant possess a right of appeal without the need for antecedent permission to appeal.

THE NEW PROCEDURE IN OUTLINE

Sections 54 to 59 of the Access to Justice Act 1999 and Part 52 of the Civil Procedure Rules came into force on 2 May 2000. There is now one

---

[1] Bowen LJ in R v Justices of the County of London [1893] 2 QB 492.

universal system of appeals, but not all appeals lie to the Court of Appeal. The general principle is that an appeal lies to a judge in the next court in the hierarchy of civil courts. In general, there can only be one appeal. A second appeal will lie in strictly limited circumstances.

It would be otiose to repeat what is found in standard procedural guides to the jurisdiction of the Court of Appeal. We wish to analyse the reasoning of the Court of Appeal in a few key cases concerning the procedure after Woolf and Bowman. In *Tanfern Limited v Cameron Macdonald (Practice Note)*[2] Brooke LJ had identified the appeal as one in which the Court could usefully explain the effect of the Woolf and Bowman reforms. The case concerned an action for unpaid rent on commercial premises. It turned on the proper interpretation of the pre-Bowman and Woolf procedure rules.

The claim was for about £20,000 rent and about £7,000 in interest on the unpaid debt. It began in the High Court. It was transferred to the county court, where it was heard by a district judge who gave judgment for the defendants. The claimants tried to appeal by lodging the necessary documents for a hearing before the circuit judge. However, the court staff had been directed to refer the parties to the Court of Appeal because the case had proceeded under the multi-track—broadly as a claim for over £15,000 with some legal complexity. In brief, they thought that the district judge had acted as if he were a circuit judge and any appeal would then lie to the Court of Appeal. The staff in the Court of Appeal took the view that the correct location of the appeal was before the circuit judge and not the Court of Appeal. The Court eventually decided that the appeal lay to the local circuit judge.

Brooke LJ (for the Court) set out the nature of the changes that had come into force on 1 May 2000. The judgment was given on 12 May 2000. It is not clear from the transcript whether the hearing had been before or after 1 May 2000. In a detailed exposition of a complex set of rules, the Court set out which appeals now went to which court, what the conditions were for giving permission to appeal in second appeals from lower courts, and the criteria the Court would apply in deciding whether or not to give permission to appeal. Such a didactic function may be thought unnecessary. Are the rules of court not accessible to all practitioners? Why should the Court have to modify its usual role of deciding issues of law to providing guidance to litigants and their advisers? The answer may be that the legal profession was not yet familiar with the import and impact of the new rules. A further reason is probably the difficulty court staff had in both the lower and higher courts as to how they should deal with a purported appeal in which they were uncertain about the true destination of that appeal. It is true that this decision is an accretion to the text of the procedure rules and increases the amount of reading a practitioner will have to master. But this

---

[2] [2000] 1 WLR 1311. See above, pp58 ff.

may have been the most effective way in which the new procedures could be implemented.

THE REQUIREMENT FOR PERMISSION TO APPEAL

This is the major innovation for almost all appeals. The Court desires that all litigants first seek permission from the lower court, although this does not always occur.[3] There is no sanction for not so applying. There may be cases where legal representation changes after a decision by a lower court or where legal advice changes, both of which may render it impossible in the time obtaining to apply for permission to the lower court.

Initial application to the lower court at the time of the judgment is, however, strongly advised. In *Re T (A Child)*[4] the Court approved the following reasons for taking this course:

(1) The judge below is fully seized of the issues in the case and the application will take a minimum of time. The judge may already have formed a view about the merits of such an application.
(2) No additional costs are involved.
(3) No harm is done if the application fails. The application can be made again to the Court of Appeal.
(4) No harm is done if the application succeeds but the litigant decides not to pursue the appeal.
(5) If the application succeeds and the litigant decides to proceed to a full appeal, the costly and time-consuming process of obtaining permission in the Court of Appeal is avoided.

The only difficulty with this guidance is that the judgment in the lower court will sometimes be reserved and only given at a later date. The parties may receive such a judgment by post, and there will be no opportunity to apply for permission to appeal at the time the judgment is given. It would be possible for the judge below to consider a notional application for permission to appeal whenever a written, reserved judgment is given. This is not the current practice.

DEALING WITH AN APPLICATION FOR PERMISSION TO APPEAL

As we have seen, the Court may decide an application on paper alone or may refer the application for oral hearing without any initial consideration

---

[3] See ch 6.
[4] [2002] EWCA Civ 1736, paras [12]–[13].

on paper. This course is often taken where it is likely that a refusal on paper will lead to the litigant renewing application orally.

A refusal on paper leads to the opportunity of an oral hearing at which the application may be renewed. This means that in one way or another a disappointed litigant may have at least a brief hearing of an application for permission to appeal. In *Jolly v Jay*[5] the Court clarified at some length the position where a litigant attempts to use the application procedure to challenge a decision itself given on appeal by a lower court. The Court of Appeal has no jurisdiction to hear such an appeal and, therefore, none to hear a preliminary application for permission to appeal from such a decision. It indicated that it would take administrative steps to prevent such 'appeals' going any further.

The essential reason for a near-universal permission requirement is that unmeritorious appeals are identified and brought to an early conclusion. Costs are saved. If permission is granted the Court has an early opportunity to make case management directions.

How has the Court applied the test of an appeal having a 'real prospect of success' or there being 'some other compelling reason why the appeal should be heard'—the words used in CPR rule 53.3(6)? The test is the same as that used when considering summary judgment.[6] This phrase is not capable of enlargement. It means that the prospects of success must be real rather than fanciful. Clearly what one judge sees as a real prospect of success will not necessarily so appear to another.

In *Swain v Hillman*[7] Lord Woolf MR discussed the requirement for success in an application for summary judgment under CPR rule 24.2. His reasoning was that his reforms had been introduced partly to ensure that claims or defences that had no real prospect of success ought not to be pursued. Likewise with an appeal: if the appeal has no real prospect of success it should not be pursued.

The same may be true of the other ground for granting permission: 'or there is some other compelling reason why the appeal should be heard'.[8] The word 'or' is disjunctive: see *Morris v Bank of India*.[9] At first sight, the phrase is puzzling. If a litigant has failed to persuade the Court that an appeal has any real prospect of success, what justification can there be for permitting that appeal to go further at great cost to him or her and to the other party? And why should the other party be put to the expense and trouble of defending a hopeless cause? The origin of this ground for granting permission to appeal lies in paragraphs 37–38 of the Bowman

---

[5] [2002] EWCA Civ 277, para [19].
[6] See CPR r 24.2.
[7] [2001] 1 All ER 91.
[8] See CPR r 52.3(6).
[9] [2004] EWCA Civ 1286, [9]–[10].

report. It was pointed out that the public interest might require that the law in a given area be clarified. But if this is so, would the litigant seeking permission not have a real prospect of success, at least where the expected or promised clarification operates in favour of the appellant? Perhaps. But this ground of granting permission operates as a valuable reserve power where an appeal may not satisfy the merits test but there is good reason in the public interest for the appeal to proceed. There may be the rare occasion when the litigant faces insurmountable authority at Court of Appeal level, yet the Court may wish to grant permission and immediately dismiss the appeal to enable the litigant to petition the House of Lords for permission to appeal. (It is not clear why, in such a hypothetical case, the lower court would not permit a leapfrog appeal to the House of Lords.)

SECOND APPEALS

Section 55(1) of the Access to Justice Act 1999 provides that where an appeal is made to a county court or the High Court and a decision is made by that court on that appeal no further appeal may be made to the Court of Appeal unless:

(a) the Court of Appeal considers that the appeal raises an important point of principle or practice, or
(b) there is some other compelling reason for the Court of Appeal to hear it.

This provision is largely repeated in CPR rule 52.13.

At first sight, it may seem strange that the Court of Appeal as the pivot of the judicial system should have exceptional measures in place to limit second appeals from the host of lower courts merely because the jurisdiction of some of those courts has been extended to hearing some kinds of appeals. It may be thought that such inferior appellate courts are in greater need of guidance than superior appellate courts. The need for any limitation on second appeals arises because the lower courts exist as both courts of trial and courts of appeal. So, a circuit judge in a county court will hear trials. So will a district judge. He or she will also act as an appellate judge from decisions of a district judge whether those decisions are about case management or are taken as a trial judge. The court system is inching towards the merger of the High Courts and the county courts, which is logically the proper course, as all civil courts apply the Civil Procedure Rules. But this will take some years to complete. Meanwhile, some of the lower courts are both trial courts and courts of appeal. Bowman saw as a particular problem those litigants who had brought successive appeals, all of which had failed.

The Court of Appeal in *Tanfern Ltd v Cameron-Macdonald*[10] commented on this provision. While not using the above language, it pointed out that the quality of Lords Justices of Appeal was a scarce and valuable resource. It was necessary to impose a tough requirement for permission to appeal to ensure that the Court did not become overburdened by matters that had no place coming before it.

The result of this is that the Court is no longer properly called 'the Court of Appeal'. It is but one of a number of courts which exercise an appellate jurisdiction. Consider how the Court has striven to maintain the level of the hurdles that have to be surmounted before a full appeal may be heard. In *Aoun v Bahri*[11] it had to consider an issue about the grant of security for costs—that is, where one party is unlikely to be able to meet any order for costs made against him or her and is required to deposit (usually) cash, failing which the action is stayed. Such an order was made in commercial litigation being pursued in the High Court. Mr Aoun appealed against that order. The defendants were prepared to defend the appeal on its merits but were concerned that yet more expense would be incurred in doing so. They wanted an order for security for costs of the appeal, payment of the sum decided upon below as the amount of security to be provided, and a stay of the appeal until the claimant met his obligations to provide such security. Mr Aoun had been found to be an unreliable and untruthful witness when asked questions about the amount and location of his assets. The judge below had no doubt that Mr Aoun should have to provide security for costs. Given that the issue in such applications is one of discretion and that on the facts as disclosed in the judgment it was a very proper order, it is hard to see why and how permission to appeal was ever granted. Brooke LJ and Wall J were careful not to make any criticism of Mance LJ, who granted permission to appeal.

The question before the Court was whether the order granting permission to appeal should be set aside or suspended for so long as Mr Aoun did not comply with the order for security made below. CPR rule 52.9 permits the Court to deal with appeals in a broad manner by setting aside the grant of permission, varying it, or imposing conditions. CPR rule 52.9(2) makes it clear that an order granting permission is not to be set aside, etc, unless there is a compelling reason to do so. This shows the significance that the Court attaches to one of its orders obtained only after proof of a 'real prospect of success'. Mr Aoun had not applied to stay the order made below directing him to give security. The defendants said that a grant of permission to appeal is all very well but if Mr Aoun were allowed to pursue his appeal and did not have to comply with the order for security made below,

[10] [2000] 1 WLR 1311, see above n 2.
[11] [2002] EWCA Civ 1141.

he would in effect have had the benefit of a stay on the order for security without having applied for it.

The Court was not so persuaded. The effect of the order below was to stay Mr Aoun's action if he did not produce the security as and when ordered. He also had to pay the security ordered in respect of the appeal itself. The action was now stayed because of his default. But he was entitled to pursue an appeal against that order, and he should not lightly be deprived of the benefit of the grant of permission to appeal. The Court then revealed that Mance LJ had not seen fit to impose conditions on the grant of permission to appeal despite being strongly pressed to do so. The Court was not prepared to admit what was, in effect, a challenge to the grant of permission to appeal.

There is a paradox here. The grant of permission to appeal against a matter that involves exercise of discretion is itself a matter of discretion or, at least, of the making of a fine judgment. The judge below may have been wrong to grant security in the first place. Perhaps not all Lords Justices would agree that permission to appeal such an order should have been granted. But once it was granted it should not easily be set aside or subjected to conditions. The unasked question is whether, and if so under what conditions, the other party to litigation should be invited (or at least permitted) to take part in the process of granting permission to appeal. In *Jolly v Jay*[12] the Court said that respondents to an appeal should file submissions only if they are addressed to the point that the appeal would not meet the relevant threshold test or (and this may come to much the same point) there is a material defect in the papers placed before the Court. Advocates should be heard only sparingly at the permission stage. Permission is essentially a 'without notice' procedure.

RESTRICTIONS ON APPEALS ABOUT CASE MANAGEMENT

Paragraphs 4.4 and 4.5 of the Practice Direction limit such appeals. The Court must take into account the significance of the appeal, the likely costs, the delay or other disruption an appeal will cause, and whether the issue could and should be dealt with at the trial. Case management was seen by Bowman as the key to success in expediting trials and appeals. Interlocutory appeals could cause delay for little advantage. A balance must be struck in deciding which appeals should be allowed to proceed before a trial has taken place. Further, a case management decision within a judge's discretion is not to be lightly overturned: see *Royal & Sun Alliance v T & N Limited*.[13]

[12] [2002] EWCA Civ 277.
[13] [2002] EWCA Civ 1964.

APPEALS FROM SPECIALIST TRIBUNALS

Tribunals are increasingly seen as an adjunct to the courts in specialist areas of jurisdiction. Yet the link between the courts and tribunals remains. The courts retain the right and obligation to resolve significant legal issues, however specialised those issues may be. In *Cooke v Secretary of State for Social Security*[14] the Court considered the circumstances in which a second appeal should lie when permission to appeal is sought from the very specialised and experienced Social Security Commissioners. After an initial decision there will have been a hearing before a specialist tribunal with a further appeal (with permission) to a highly expert and specialised body. Appeals from the Commissioners should be approached with a degree of caution. A similar degree of reticence has been shown in the case of appeals from other specialist bodies, particularly with those from the Asylum and Immigration Tribunal.

The Court has adequate powers to limit the grant of permission to appeal to selected areas of dispute between the parties. It can also make costs orders relevant to the grant of permission. In one case,[15] the Court granted permission to appeal on condition that even if successful the appellant should not be entitled to the costs of the appeal. The appellant was a large corporation with an admitted strong commercial interest in the outcome of the appeal, whereas the respondents were a number of individuals.

REFORM OF PERMISSION TO APPEAL

In 2005 the Department for Constitutional Affairs issued a consultation paper on this topic.[16] The Court had identified a large number of applications for permission which were totally devoid of merit or, more simply, hopeless. It thought that such cases were wasteful of the resources of both litigants and the Court, might maintain an applicant's unrealistic expectations of the outcome, and created uncertainty for the respondent because finality in the case was postponed. Moreover the resources employed to deal with such applications would be better used in dealing with meritorious applications.

Hopeless applications fell into two main categories. There were those in which the application was refused on paper and renewed to an oral hearing, and those which were fast-tracked to an oral hearing because experience showed that there was a likelihood that the applicants would renew any paper refusal of permission by seeking an oral hearing. The paper did not

---

[14] [2001] EWCA Civ 734.
[15] *Lloyd Jones v T Mobile (UK) Ltd* [2003] EWCA Civ 1162.
[16] CP20/05: available on DCA website under 'Consultation Papers'.

say so but it is clear to us that these applications were almost invariably brought in person.

In order to establish whether the proposal to restrict access to an oral hearing would lead to injustice by denying a meritorious application an opportunity to proceed to a full hearing, a research exercise was undertaken by Professor Dame Hazel Genn of University College London.[17] All non-family applications for leave to appeal for one term in 2004 were examined by one Lord Justice, who was asked to say whether in his or her opinion the application was totally devoid of merit. That Lord Justice would not be asked to deal with the application when it came to its turn for consideration. The Lord Justice hearing the oral application was also asked to say whether, at that stage, the application was totally devoid of merit.

The exercise led to 497 assessments. Of those, 372 were made following a paper assessment and 125 after oral hearings. There were 112 cases which proceeded from a paper assessment to an oral hearing for permission to appeal. In one third of those cases, the judge at both the written and oral stages considered the cases to be without merit. In another third of cases, both judges agreed that the cases were not wholly without merit. In 15 per cent of cases there was a discrepancy that might have operated against the applicant: that is, on paper the case appeared to have no merit but this was not apparent after an oral hearing.

If there were no right to renew an application refused on paper an injustice might be caused to an applicant for permission to appeal. There were only 17 such cases. None was designated to be wholly without merit after an oral hearing. Tracing those cases to a full appeal hearing and setting them in the context of the total number of cases analysed, it was found that there were only three cases in which an injustice would have been visited upon an applicant. On this basis the proposal was for the Court to be able to order that a rejected written application for permission should not be renewed at an oral hearing.

The justification for such a change was said to be that some inconsistency in decision-making is an inevitable part of the common law, that the principles of the CPR concerning proportionality and cost-effectiveness might lead to an occasional injustice, and, finally, the number of cases where there would be any such disadvantage was small, both absolutely and as a proportion of the decisions made. These possible losses had to be weighed against the releasing of judicial time and resources and sparing parties the cost of attending an oral hearing.

The recommended change was brought into effect by way of a new paragraph (4A) in CPR rule 52.3, which came into force on 2 October 2006. Other than in family law proceedings, the single Lord Justice considering

---

[17] Available on the Court of Appeal's website at http://www.hmcourts-service.gov.uk/cms/files/PTAFinalReportMarch20051.pdf.

an application for PTA now has the discretion to decide that an application is 'totally without merit' and that the would-be appellant should not have the right to renew the application at an oral hearing.

The DCA consultation did not make it clear that the majority of such cases are likely to be those of litigants in person, whose applications have been fast-tracked to an oral hearing. The research did not establish in how many cases an oral hearing was ordered because the papers were unclear as to the prospects of success. Nor do we know in how many cases a litigant in person had to be contacted by the Court for elucidation of the grounds of appeal.

A further unknown element is whether the ability of a single Lord Justice to reject an application and to order no oral renewal might lead to a defensive exercise of this power because of the drastic effect of the rejection of the application. It is, however, impossible to say that a power to prevent oral renewal, to be exercised only in a clear case of no merits, has no place in the array of powers that the Court possesses.

ALTERNATIVE DISPUTE RESOLUTION: MEDIATION, COSTS, AND LOWER COURTS

The courts must deal with cases justly.[18] This includes 'encouraging the parties to use an alternative dispute resolution procedure, if [the court] considers that appropriate, and facilitating the use of such a procedure.'[19] The costs rules in the CPR require the Court, when assessing costs, to consider the conduct of the parties both before and during proceedings, which specifically includes the efforts made before and during the proceedings to try to resolve the dispute.[20]

The Court of Appeal has recently considered the circumstances in which alternative dispute resolution (ADR) might be used in litigation. In *Halsey v Milton Keynes General NHS Trust*[21] the Court set out general guidance as to when any court should impose costs sanctions on a litigant who refuses to take part in ADR. The context was an action for medical negligence in which the claim was dismissed at the trial. The defendants would normally be entitled to a costs order, but the claimant said that as the defendants, after a number of invitations, had refused to participate in mediation, they should be deprived of their costs. The Court was opposed to compelling parties to enter into mediation. Mediation was not yet proven as a universal alternative to litigation. The courts should encourage mediation, even robustly, but should

---

[18]   CPR r 1.1(2).

[19]   CPR r 1.4(2)(e).

[20]   CPR r 44.5. For a general guide and commentary on the place of ADR in the courts see David Gladwell (administrative head of the Court and a Master), 'ADR and the Courts' [2004] *Civil Court News* 27.

[21]   [2004] EWCA Civ 576.

not force mediation on unwilling parties. It was for the lawyers for the litigants to consider mediation. After a full survey of the advantages of mediation, the Court pointed out that if parties declined to mediate they would have to be able to justify that decision when the judge came to consider the appropriate costs order. But this approach would stop short of compelling the parties to undertake mediation or some other form of ADR.

In *Halsey* the claimant was the wife of an elderly man who died in hospital because, she said, of medical negligence. The claim was strenuously defended. The defendants refused to mediate, asserting that the expense of mediation would be greater than preparing for and attending a trial in what they considered to be a very weak claim. The action went to trial. The claimant lost. The trial judge had to consider the position as to the costs of the action. The claimant funded the action by a conditional fee arrangement. The judge decided, and the Court of Appeal upheld him, that the defendants should be given their costs. The defendants had not acted unreasonably. They genuinely believed, on grounds vindicated at the trial, that they had a strong defence. The attempts to persuade the defendants to agree to mediation were tactical. Although the value of mediation was undoubted, it should not be invoked in a case where the defendants honestly and reasonably believe that they have a good defence and wish to have the issues adjudicated by the courts.

In the later case of *Burchell v Bullard*[22] the Court of Appeal summarised the effect of *Halsey* as requiring the lower courts considering liability for costs when mediation is requested by one party and refused by the other to take account of the nature of the dispute, the merits of the case, the costs of ADR, and whether ADR has a reasonable chance of success. On the facts the costs order made by the Court of Appeal reflected the conduct of the parties and the relative success of both in parts of the claim and counterclaim. The defendant had refused the claimant's request for mediation. The Court of Appeal declined to mark such conduct by refusing the defendant his costs. He had acted on the advice of his surveyor at a time when the *Halsey* principles were not yet well known (it appears that the decision below was made at about the same time as that in *Halsey*).

Mediation in the Court of Appeal

The principles in the two above cases have yet to be applied in an appeal to the Court. But the Court has not merely waited for appeals to arise in which these principles might be tested; a scheme for mediation has been in operation since 2003.[23] Its administration has been contracted out to

[22] [2005] EWCA Civ 538.
[23] See *Court of Appeal, Civil Division: Review of the Year 2003–2004 and Court of Appeal, Civil Division: Review of the Year 2004–2005*, available on the Court's website at www.hmcourts-service.gov.uk/cms/files/mr_review_legal_year_2004_5.pdf.

CEDR Solve.[24] After a research study for the DCA by Professor Dame Hazel Genn[25] the Court decided to require the Lord Justice considering a PTA application to assess whether the appeal is suitable for mediation. If so, the Court writes to both parties urging them to 'seriously consider mediation' and to notify the Court within 14 days whether they agree to such a course. The parties are free to make their own arrangements but they may choose to use the CEDR scheme. They then pay a fee of £850 and select the mediator from a list of three provided by CEDR. The fee covers nine hours of the mediator's time, which includes reading and preparation time. In 2003/04 (in fact, a 15-month period) 63 cases were referred to CEDR by the Court. The success rate was 66 per cent, which includes six cases settled before mediation took place. Fourteen cases did not proceed and 15 did not settle. In 2004/05 (a 12-month period) there were 21 referrals to mediation. Writing in the *Review of the Year 2004–2005*, Rix LJ said that the reason for the drop in the number of cases was not clear. He thought that the decision in *Halsey* might have had a temporary cooling effect in so far as it held that ADR should be encouraged but not mandated. If mediation was undertaken without success the parties knew that they were committed to a judicial answer to their dispute.

A draft report by CEDR for 2004/05 makes the same point as Rix LJ regarding the beneficial effect of even a failed mediation. Settlement of cases is not the only measure of the success of mediation. The report went on to say that 'in appeal cases where mediation leads to revised outcomes between trial and appeal ... [it] may have a role in checking that an appeal is worth the Court's time.' On this view, mediation is an adjunct to, and perhaps a form of, case management. Overall the report concluded that mediation was underused in the Court.

Family cases were not part of the CEDR scheme. The reasons are not clear, but it may be that CEDR is used rather to call on mediators who are active in the commercial world. The Court offers a service in collaboration with the UK College of Mediators. In 2004/05 nine cases were submitted for mediation. Four were settled by mediation, two by other means and three were continuing.

AFTER PERMISSION TO APPEAL HAS BEEN GRANTED: REVIEW OR REHEARING?

CPR rule 52.11(1) sets out the general rule: appeal means review unless the Practice Direction makes special provision for this or there are individual circumstances that make a rehearing necessary in the interests of justice.

---

[24] See the CEDR (Centre for Effective Dispute Resolution) website: http//www.cedr.co.uk.
[25] See www.dca.gov.uk/research.

CPR Practice Direction 52, paragraph 9 does so in relation to an appeal against the decision of a minister or similar public body and there was no hearing below or, if there was, no hearing was held before the decision in question was reached. This is a rarely applicable provision because such appeals are scarce indeed and are likely to have first been heard in the Administrative Court.

The wording of the rule does not clarify the distinction between review and appeal. This only emerges from a reading of the case-law together with the further provisions of CPR rule 52.11(3). An appeal can be allowed only if the decision of the lower court is wrong, or unjust because of a serious procedural or other irregularity. To see whether there is such a ground for allowing the appeal the Court has first to determine whether it should hold a rehearing or merely a review. The case-law represents a collective decision by the Court to leave such a decision to the panel hearing the instant case yet to set out some broad principles by which such discretion ought to be exercised. Before turning to a discussion of the jurisprudence we must make it clear that 'rehearing' cannot be read literally. It does not mean that the Court will hear all of the oral witnesses (if there were any) again. The evidence taken below will normally have been in the form of written witness statements. Then there will be findings made by the lower court, partly of facts and partly of inferences to be drawn from such facts, then there will be a ruling on matters of law. A review of such a decision will take that decision as the starting point. There will be a difference between decisions involving findings of primary fact reached after an evaluation of oral evidence or cases of the exercise of a discretion and those cases where there has been an evaluation of written material.

The key decisions of the Court of Appeal on the proper application of CPR rule 52.11(1) are *Audergon v La Baguette Ltd*,[26] *Assicurazioni Generali SpA v Arab Insurance Group*[27] and *EI Du Pont Nemours & Co v ST Du Pont*.[28] It is very difficult to encapsulate the effect of these decisions in terms of the gloss or clarification they place upon the wording of CPR rule 52(11). The Court was very careful in each of these cases to emphasise that the decision whether to hold a review or a rehearing is for the panel of the Court of Appeal. Everything depends on the circumstances of the case under appeal. Three examples of how the issue of the form of review or of rehearing is to be made by the Court of Appeal emerge from a trilogy of cases heard in 2003. In *Hackney London Borough Council v Driscoll (No 1)*[29] the Court of Appeal allowed a second appeal and directed that the case should be remitted to a different circuit judge for rehearing. The case

---

[26] [2002] EWCA Civ 10.
[27] [2003] 1 WLR 577.
[28] [2003] EWCA Civ 1638.
[29] [2003] EWCA Civ 614.

concerned an application by a public sector landlord for possession of a rented property. The appeal was complicated because the issue remitted for rehearing was whether an order for possession that had been made in the county court should be set aside by the county court itself. The Court of Appeal appears to have thought that the new circuit judge would both hear the tenant's application to set aside the possession order and, if the order was set aside, would earlier have given case management directions so that if the application were successful, a full new hearing could immediately follow. In terms of CPR rule 52 this was complicated. The remittal by the Court of Appeal was of an appeal against an original decision of a circuit judge. Was that a first appeal to be followed, on a setting aside of the possession order, by a new first instance hearing, or, if the second circuit judge refused to set the order aside, was that a decision at first instance or on appeal? There are two issues to notice here. First, there was a complex human tale behind the making of the original order for possession. Secondly, the order of the Court of Appeal did not accurately reflect that court's intention. It was quite unclear whether the decision to refuse to set aside the possession order was appealable to the Court of Appeal as a first appeal or to the High Court as a second appeal. An essentially simple and verifiable intention in CPR rule 52 and in section 55 of the Access to Justice Act 1999 turned into a matter of great complexity and uncertainty.

In *Fowler de Pledge (a firm) v Smith*[30] Brooke LJ pointed out how important it is for appeal courts, at all levels, to show on the face of an order for a rehearing whether that rehearing would be at appellate level (so any subsequent appeal would be a second appeal) or whether the order is for rehearing at first instance. He further said that such cases could travel back and forth from the High Court to the Court of Appeal. The necessity for clarity was probably addressed as much to the lawyers in the Court of Appeal, to the Court Associates (effectively the clerks sitting below the judges) and to the advocates for the parties as to fellow Lords Justices.

The issue of the form of a rehearing arose again in *Southern & District Finance plc v Turner*.[31] The claimants made a secured loan to the defendant. She fell into arrears. The county court made a suspended possession order to enable the claimants to enforce their security by selling the property. The defendant then sought to reopen everything on the grounds that that the original loan agreement had not been properly executed under consumer protection legislation and that the bargain was unenforceable as an extortionate credit agreement. The district judge ordered the possession order to stand but allowed the defendant to pursue her counterclaim on a strictly limited basis. At a later date a circuit judge dismissed an appeal against the

---

[30] [2003] EWCA Civ 703.
[31] [2003] EWCA Civ 1574.

order of the district judge. The question was then to which court an appeal against the dismissal of that appeal should be made. The Court of Appeal pointed out that this was another occasion on which the court below had not paid sufficient attention to the form of its order and this had led to confusion as to which court had jurisdiction to hear any consequent appeal It is not necessary for us to recount the outcome of the substantive appeal as the facts of the case would make that a lengthy and tedious task.

The one point that needs to be made in consequence of this complexity does not appear in the various relevant judgments of the Court of Appeal, nor is it found in CPR rule 52. If the outmoded distinctions between the High Court and the county courts had been, if not abolished, at least made less restrictively divisive, much of the above difficulty would disappear. (We have alluded to this point elsewhere.[32])

THE OUTCOME OF AN APPEAL

We have seen that an appeal will be allowed if the decision below was wrong, or unjust because of a serious procedural error or other irregularity in the proceedings in the lower court.[33] It is also important to note that the overriding principles of the CPR[34] apply equally to appeals as they do to decisions at first instance. In *Tanfern*[35] the Court said that the word 'wrong' applied to the substance of the decision below. If the appeal is against the exercise of a discretion below it is very well established that to succeed on this ground it must be shown that the lower court has reached a view with which the Court of Appeal disagrees but is one which goes beyond the generous degree of choice within which a reasonable disagreement is possible.

CPR rule 52 applies not only to the exercise of power by the Court of Appeal but also to appeals to lower courts in the court system which exercise an appellate jurisdiction, for example to a circuit judge from the decision of a district judge. Further, the exercise of an appellate jurisdiction will range from private law disputes to public law issues decided on an application for judicial review from decisions of tribunals in complex areas of, for example, social security, immigration and asylum. The right of appeal to the body from which an appeal is brought to the Court of Appeal may lie in fact, law or both. An error of law will include, depending on the context, the proper construction of a statute or of secondary legislation and the equivalent construction of a private law document such as a will or

---

[32] See ch 3.

[33] See CPR r 52.11(3).

[34] See Part 1 of the CPR: the need to save expense, to deal with the case in a way that is proportionate to the sums and issues involved, and to ensure that it takes up no more than an appropriate share of the Court's resources.

[35] See above n 2.

a contract. But another far more malleable area of jurisdiction is included in the scope of an error of law. A lower court may have reached a finding of fact which is not supported on the evidence. It is not common for oral evidence to be tape-recorded in either the county court or the High Court. The very court that is said by an appellant to have made a finding that is not supported by the evidence will also have been the only authoritative source of a record of the evidence.[36]

The deference to which a decision of a lower court is habitually entitled is normally founded on that court having had the advantage of seeing and hearing the witnesses. But the weight of the authority in this area derives from Victorian cases in which great weight was placed on the character and demeanour of the witnesses long before the invention of photocopying, word processing and tape recording. Further, far more evidence is now prepared in written form, with oral evidence being relegated to an examination with the witness of the meaning and significance of documentary evidence. In our view this long line of authority needs re-examination.

---

[36] For a more detailed consideration of this topic and of much else we have included in this chapter see Roger Venne, David Di Mambro, Phillipe Sands, Louis Di Mambro and Ian Joseph, *Manual of Civil Appeals*, 2nd edn (London, Butterworths, 2004), ch 2.

6

The Court of Appeal at Work— Some Facts and Figures

While it is not always profitable to analogise 'fact' to 'fiction', La Fontaine's fable of the crow, the cheese, and the fox demonstrates that there is a substantial difference between holding a piece of cheese in the beak and putting it in the stomach.[1]

THIS CHAPTER SEEKS to provide a profile of the work of the Court of Appeal. The first part presents a broad overview of the volume, outcome, and throughput of appeals and applications, drawing upon material published in recent annual volumes of *Judicial Statistics*[2] and in the Court of Appeal's own annual *Reviews of the Legal Year*. The second part of the chapter, based on some of our research data, focuses in particular on some detailed aspects of the operation of the permission to appeal (PTA) procedure during a 12-month period following the introduction of the new Civil Procedure Rules (CPR). Finally, we look at the handling and progress of applications from the litigant's perspective.

THE OFFICIAL STATISTICS

For the most part, the following tables are self-explanatory. Table 1 shows the number of appeals filed annually (the total has hovered around the 1,000 mark), and what became of them. We were struck by the high proportion of cases that are dismissed by consent. Why do parties, having cleared the high hurdle of obtaining PTA, then throw in the towel? At least part of the explanation seems to lie in the fact that an acknowledgement that there is a real chance of the appeal's succeeding provides a sharp injection of reality for the respondent, who then comes up with an offer sufficiently tempting to save at least the further legal costs and uncertainty. Looking at the cases which were actually decided by the Court, we find that the success rate—the percentage of appeals allowed—is about 42 per cent.

Table 2 shows the origins of appeals that are set down for a hearing in the Court of Appeal, distinguishing between final and interlocutory cases.

---

[1] Frankfurter J in *Alleghany Corp v Breswick and Co*, 353 US 151, 170 (1957).
[2] Published by the Directorate of Judicial Offices for England and Wales: http://judiciary.gov.uk.

Table 1: Final appeals set down and disposed of, showing results

	Set down/ filed	Allowed	Dismissed	Dismissed by consent	Struck out for failure to provide documents	Other	Total
1999	876	279	434	300	21	93	1,127
2000	1,101	282	442	237	14	90	1,065
2001	1,071	338	445	244	2	91	1,020
2002	981	344	432	2064	4	102	1,088
2003	1,127	334	401	209	3	128	1,075
2004	966	295	413	229	2	120	1,059

Source: *Judicial Statistics 1999–2004*, Table 1.9.

Not surprisingly, the largest single source of business is the county court, which handles the great bulk of first-instance civil litigation. A significant proportion of appeals are administrative law cases from the Administrative Court (formerly the Crown Office List), although the proportion diminished slightly during the period covered by the table. Another significant sub-category came from the Immigration Appeal Tribunal (now the Asylum and Immigration Tribunal), and the number in this sub-category increased during the same period.

Table 3 provides the equivalent data in respect of applications—most of which are applications for PTA,[3] as confirmed by the figures in Table 4, which shows the annual number of applications for PTA filed, disposed of, and outstanding at the end of each year. Table 5 shows the method of disposal of PTAs, as described more fully elsewhere. It will be seen that the Court decides more than 40 per cent of these applications solely on the papers, without recourse to an oral hearing.

Table 6 shows the steady reduction in the backlog of appeals outstanding at the end of each legal year, following the post-Bowman reforms and the introduction of the CPR.

PERMISSION TO APPEAL: THE PROCEDURE IN PRACTICE

Having set the scene with information gleaned from the official statistics, we turn now to a more detailed account of the work of the Court in its

---

[3] See J Plotnikoff and R Woolfson, *Evaluation of the Impact of the Reforms in the Court of Appeal (Civil Division)*, for the Lord Chancellor's Department, November 2002. Their report (in Figure 1) shows that, in 1999, 74.8% of applications were for PTA and, in 2001, 76.9%.

Table 2: Appeals set down for year ending september (2001/02 to 2004/05)

	2001/ 02	% of Total	2002/ 03	% of Total	2003/ 04	% of Total	2004/ 05	% of Total
Queen's Bench Final	150	11.7%	166	13.0%	120	10.9%	123	10.4%
Queen's Bench Interlocutory	64	5.0%	35	2.7%	11	1.0%	27	2.3%
Queen's Bench Administrative Court (formerly Crown Office)	176	13.7%	152	11.9%	130	11.8%	107	9.0%
Queen's Bench Commercial Final	70	5.4%	81	6.3%	86	7.8%	62	5.2%
Queen's Bench Commercial Interlocutory	27	2.1%	15	1.2%	12	1.1%	8	0.7%
Chancery Final	172	13.4%	188	14.7%	159	14.4%	165	13.9%
Chancery Interlocutory	58	4.5%	31	2.4%	13	1.2%	10	0.8%
High Court Family Final and Interlocutory	33	2.6%	34	2.7%	25	2.3%	32	2.7%
County Court Final	260	20.2%	284	22.3%	242	22.0%	281	23.7%
County Court Interlocutory	39	3.0%	20	1.6%	2	0.2%	7	0.6%
County Court Family Final and Interlocutory	70	5.4%	59	4.6%	54	4.9%	82	6.9%
Employment Appeal Tribunal	66	5.1%	75	5.9%	78	7.1%	50	4.2%
Social Security Commissioners	17	1.3%	20	1.6%	11	1.0%	23	1.9%
Immigration Appeal Tribunal	66	5.1%	104	8.2%	132	12.0%	172	14.5%
Asylum/ Immigration Tribunal	0	0.0%	0	0.0%	0	0.0%	26	2.2%
Other	19	1.5%	12	0.9%	26	2.4%	12	1.0%
All Appeals	1,287		1,276		1,101		1,187	

Source: *The Court of Appeal, Civil Division: Review of the Legal Year 2004–2005*, Table 1 (www.civilappeals.gov.uk).

Table 3: Applications set down for year ending september (2001/02 to 2004/05)

	2001/02	% of Total	2002/03	% of Total	2003/04	% of Total	2004/05	% of Total
Queen's Bench Final	289	9.1%	334	10.5%	335	10.7%	342	10.1%
Queen's Bench Interlocutory	157	4.9%	80	2.5%	32	1.0%	58	1.7%
Queen's Bench Administrative Court (formerly Crown Office)	426	13.4%	524	16.5%	416	13.2%	357	10.6%
Queen's Bench Commercial Final	119	3.7%	110	3.5%	107	3.4%	118	3.5%
Queen's Bench Commercial Interlocutory	64	2.0%	24	0.8%	14	0.4%	13	0.4%
Chancery Final	348	11.0%	402	12.6%	398	12.7%	401	11.9%
Chancery Interlocutory	143	4.5%	61	1.9%	28	0.9%	26	0.8%
High Court Family Final and Interlocutory	118	3.7%	121	3.8%	156	5.0%	199	5.9%
County Court Final	638	20.1%	650	20.4%	643	20.5%	675	20.0%
County Court Interlocutory	106	3.3%	46	1.4%	15	0.5%	13	0.4%
County Court Family Final and Interlocutory	294	9.3%	256	8.0%	302	9.6%	315	9.3%
Employment Appeal Tribunal	207	6.5%	246	7.7%	213	6.8%	198	5.9%
Social Security Commissioners	18	0.6%	23	0.7%	25	0.8%	34	1.0%
Immigration Appeal Tribunal	215	6.8%	289	9.1%	427	13.6%	410	12.1%
Asylum/Immigration Tribunal	0	0.0%	0	0.0%	0	0.0%	195	5.8%
Other	34	1.1%	16	0.5%	32	1.0%	29	0.9%
All Appeals	3,176		3,182		3,143		3,383	

Source: *The Court of Appeal, Civil Division: Review of the Legal Year 2004–2005*, Table 2 (www.civilappeals.gov.uk).

Table 4: Applications for permission to appeal (2000/01 to 2004/05)

Year (ending 30 September)	Filed	Disposed	Outstanding
2000/01	2,330	2,437	817
2001/02	2,398	2,433	708
2002/03	2,499	2,448	672
2003/04	2,430	2,402	724
2004/05	2,541	2,415	853

Source: *The Court of Appeal, Civil Division: Review of the Legal Year 2004–2005*, Graph 1 (www.civilappeals.gov.uk).

Table 5: Method of disposal of permission to appeal applications (1999/2000 to 2004/05)

Year (ending 30 September)	Only Paper (refused)	Only Paper (allowed)	Paper then Oral (refused)	Paper then Oral (allowed)	Only Oral (refused)	Only Oral (allowed)
1999/2000	17%	23%	6%	7%	38%	9%
2000/01	13%	28%	14%	7%	30%	8%
2001/02	11%	28%	13%	7%	33%	8%
2002/03	14%	30%	13%	7%	29%	7%
2003/04	16%	25%	13%	6%	33%	7%

Source: *The Court of Appeal, Civil Division: Review of the Legal Year* (for years 1999/2000 to 2004/05)

Table 6: Throughput of appeals (1997/98 to 2004/05)

Year (ending 30 September)	Filed	Disposed	Outstanding	Dismissed with consent
1997/98	1,647	1,917	1,319	440
1998/99	1,436	1,684	1,071	420
1999/2000	1,324	1,501	894	336
2000/01	1,316	1,382	829	282
2001/02	1,287	1,415	703	259
2002/03	1,274	1,296	680	227
2003/04	1,101	1,227	563	257
2004/05	1,115	1,182	630	191

Source: *The Court of Appeal, Civil Division: Review of the Legal Year* (for years 2001/02 to to 2004/05)

handling of PTAs, and the subsequent progression of successful applications (those that are not settled) to full appeal, using some of our own research data.

The Progression of Permission to Appeal Applications

All applications for PTA lodged with the Civil Appeals Office are recorded on a case-tracking computer system (RECAP). In the first instance, details such as the title of the case, the names of the parties, whether or not the parties have legal representation, and the name of the referring court are entered into the system. The following account is based on research into the progress of 800 PTA applications over a 12-month period, from the moment they were inputted by the front desk staff, until the moment that a final determination was reached. It should be borne in mind that the final outcome is not always determined by way of a judgment by or order from the Court. Sometimes the parties themselves chose to settle out of court: as noted above, many appeals are dismissed by consent after PTA has been granted. Sometimes applicants for PTA changed their minds and withdrew. Sometimes applications for PTA were lodged as a tactical move in litigation: the other party might then be more willing to negotiate in order to avoid the cost and delay of further litigation. Sometimes applicants failed to comply with a procedural direction and their application was dismissed without a hearing.

The year chosen for our analysis was divided into four blocks, each of which contained 200 applications. Group 1 includes the first 200 applications lodged from the beginning of June 2000; the last group, group 4, contains the first 200 cases lodged from the beginning of May 2001. Our analysis of these 800 applications was augmented by extensive observations of proceedings in the Court and by unattributable interviews with judges and other court personnel. For ease of reference, we have, in most contexts, aggregated the results for each group.

The Courts Below

This section should be read in conjunction with Tables 2 and 3 above. PTA applications can be brought to the Court of Appeal from lower courts, including various tribunals, throughout England and Wales. Elsewhere[4] we have analysed the law and practice surrounding the PTA process, with reference to the applicable rules of court and the case-law of the Court

---

[4] In ch 5.

Table 7: PTA applications: from which court did the application come? (May 2000 to May 2001)

County Court	304
High Court, QBD	144
High Court, PRFD	40
High Court, Admin	72
High Court, DC	8
High Court, ChD	73
High Court, Commercial	15
Immigration Appeal Tribunal (IAT)	43
Employment Appeal Tribunal (EAT)	43
High Court, CO	42
Social Security Commissioners	9

of Appeal. We first gathered data about the numbers and types of cases being appealed from the various courts below. Are some kinds of case (for instance, commercial cases) more likely to generate applications for permission? We only considered applications made to the Court of Appeal for PTA.

In terms of absolute numbers, as already noted, county courts generate the largest number of applications. However, this is in fact a minute proportion of the more than one million cases heard each year by county courts across the whole of England and Wales. Moreover, county courts have jurisdiction in a very wide range of civil matters, so any further breakdown (eg by subject-matter) yields very small numbers in each sub-category.

Tribunals also constitute a large source of applications. Between them, the (former) Immigration Appeal Tribunal (IAT) and the Employment Appeal Tribunal (EAT) sent more cases to the Court of Appeal than did the Chancery Division of the High Court. However, when one considers the high social impact and political salience of issues of immigration and asylum and employment, perhaps this is not surprising. Cases that raise public law issues are fairly well represented.

The range of the subject areas of PTAs was diverse. Within the commercial and Chancery subject categories, issues of civil procedure, contractual disputes, and costs were the most prominent. The area of costs emerges as a large sub-group. This is not altogether surprising. Indeed, Lord Phillips MR in a published interview went so far as to say that, from the Court's perspective, 'the problem area is undoubtedly costs.'[5] Personal injury claims are also well represented. Issues that arose during the period covered by our

[5] S Hawthorne, *Counsel*, April 2002, p 8.

analysis included the levels of compensation being awarded, the appropriate test for psychiatric harm to be used by the court, causation, and the duty of care owed by hospitals and others. There was also a cluster of family law matters, ranging from contact between fathers and their children to issues of residence, ancillary relief, and adoption orders.

The county court applications were understandably the most diverse. Landlord and tenant applications, neighbour disputes (often relating to the positioning of land boundaries), contract issues, and various torts were all well represented.

THE HUMAN RIGHTS ACT 1998

A significant factor in the content and timing of our research project was the coming into effect of the Human Rights Act 1998 (HRA) in October 2000. To what extent would this legislation—and the Articles of the European Convention on Human Rights, scheduled to it—impact upon the courts in general, and the Court of Appeal in particular? Across the range of subjects, and throughout our sample period of one year, by far the most common ECHR Article cited in the context of PTA applications was Article 6(1): the right to a fair and impartial hearing in the determination of civil rights and obligations. Article 8, the right to private and family life, was also widely cited.

In our sample we found 118 applications in which HRA issues were raised. There was a noticeable increase in the number of cases as our sample year progressed, probably explained by the fact that the Act had only just come on to the statute book at the point where our research began, meaning that initially there would not have been sufficient time for the applications to be processed. Our findings confirm that there was not the 'flood' of human rights applications predicted (and in some cases feared) by some commentators. From the beginning of January 2001 to the end of that year, the figure was 387, or 16 per cent of the total number of PTA applications lodged during 2001. In many of these cases the human rights element was more or less tangential to the application—even perhaps tacked on to a PTA application, almost as an afterthought—and the overall impact of the HRA on the pattern and outcome of applications appears to have been slight.

The last subject group of interest was the group where applications had been brought for judicial review, where there were 100 applications in the period June 2000 to May 2001. Numerically this represents a very significant sub-set of the applications in our sample, although judicial review is a procedural rather than a substantive category, embracing a wide variety of subject-matter (including human rights issues).

WHERE WAS PTA APPLIED FOR?

The rules relating to seeking PTA are complex but, in sum, state that in order to appeal a lower court decision, the party seeking permission must first ask the judge at the lower court hearing.[6] Failure to do this or making such an application which fails necessitates approaching the court that will sit as the appeal court. Where an application for PTA is first heard, that application is considered a first-tier appeal. Where an application is being brought for the resulting order to be itself appealed, the application is considered to be a second-tier appeal. The possible fora are either the High Court or the Court of Appeal (see below).

This has important ramifications for applications being brought to the Court of Appeal, as the rules state that applications from a county court or from some tribunals will be second appeals. The test formulated under section 54(1) of the Access to Justice Act 1999 and affirmed by the Court of Appeal in *Tanfern Ltd v Cameron-Macdonald*[7] is stricter for second-tier appeals than for first-tier appeals.

We may note in passing that the *Tanfern* decision exemplifies how procedural errors made by the courts albeit in good faith can lead to uncertainty and delay in the handling of appeals by the Court of Appeal. By agreement of the parties, a decision was made by a district judge and not a circuit judge in a commercial dispute between a landlord and his tenant, a restaurant operator. A question arose as to whether an appeal from that decision lay to the Court of Appeal or to the local circuit judge. A special two-judge court was convened to determine this arcane question. The Court decided that the appeal lay initially to the circuit judge and not to the Court of Appeal. The Court then went on to consider which appeals were first-tier and which second-tier. The judgment is detailed, directed towards practitioners and replete with practical advice as to how appeals from a lower court should be prepared if the appeal to the Court of Appeal is to be treated as a second and not a first appeal. It is interesting that the British lack of familiarity with codes of procedure led the Court to spell out in over 50 paragraphs how the above statutory provision and Part 52 of the CPR should be interpreted and applied. Part 52 was intended to state the current practice in appeals in some detail but the judges clearly thought that such practice should be set out in the familiar form of a common law judgment.

With reference to our sample of PTA applications we asked two questions: first, in how many cases was PTA refused by the lower court; and secondly, in how many cases was the application a first or second appeal?

---

[6] See ch 5.
[7] [2000] 1 WLR 1311. See above, pp 58 *ff*.

In a surprisingly large number of cases, the Civil Appeals Office recorded that the parties had apparently not sought PTA from the court below. The computer records these cases as 'nk' (not known). One assumes that, if an applicant had asked for permission below, he or she would record the fact in the application paperwork. If this is an accurate picture of how PTA requests are being handled by the lower courts, it could mean that a large number of applicants are not asking the lower court for PTA but, rather, are seeking permission from the Court of Appeal at a later date. One explanation could be that litigants need time to digest a lower court's order before they decide what further action to take. At this point, they cannot approach the lower court judge again, but must apply directly to the Court of Appeal. Applications to a lower court are best made when judgment is given. But many such judgments are delivered in written form and sent to the parties rather than being delivered orally in open court. The opportunity to seek PTA therefore passes.[8] However, in the absence of data showing why no application for PTA was made below, it is difficult for us to draw any conclusions about the utility of this two-stage approach.

The relevant figures, based on our sample groups, are as follows:

Table 8: PTA applications in the court below (June 2000 to May 2001)

PTA refused by lower court	433
Numbers marked 'nk'	367
First-tier appeal	651
Second-tier appeal	149

There is a further matter of jurisdiction to be borne in mind in this context. The CPR are very specific about where each application should be lodged. This means that for second appeals the High Court might be the court designated to hear a PTA application. Where a High Court judge refuses permission to appeal to himself from a decision of a county court judge, a further application for PTA cannot be made to the Court of Appeal. The matter is over. Where a party in such circumstances does apply to the Court of Appeal, the civil appeals Master or Deputy Master has to return the application to the party seeking permission, as being 'Not our Jurisdiction' (NOJ). This excludes the application from being determined by the Court of Appeal. It appears that the chances of a case entering the Court of Appeal system before being considered to be outside the court's jurisdiction are relatively small, and this is confirmed by our statistics, which show that just 22 applications were designated as NOJ.

---

[8] See also CPR r 52.6.

REPRESENTED AND UNREPRESENTED APPLICANTS

Most of those initiating PTA applications are legally represented, but a substantial minority (litigants in person—abbreviated hereafter to LIPs) are not. We found that LIPs accounted for 187 (36 per cent) of the 800 applications in our sample. However, it should be noted that unrepresented parties have the opportunity to seek assistance from the Citizens Advice Bureau located in the Royal Courts of Justice[9] and that there is provision for lawyers to represent LIPs on a non-fee-paying, or *pro bono* basis.

A recurrent problem that faces the Court of Appeal in responding to applications from LIPs is the inability of a majority of such applicants to draft the relevant paperwork (in particular, the skeleton arguments) in proper form, to prepare the requisite bundle of documents, and to present their applications competently. This led the Civil Appeals Office to recruit a corps of judicial assistants to assist the Lords Justices in assessing the history of the case, the issues raised, points of law, and the merits of an application brought by unrepresented applicants. This scheme was instigated in 1996, in the run-up to the Bowman review of the Court, largely on the initiative of Otton LJ.[10] The judicial assistants prepare a bench memorandum for an application for the Lord Justice, serving much the same function as a skeleton argument prepared by a legal representative.

During our study period, this procedure was questioned by one LIP who sought access to the bench memorandum. In *Attorney General v Covey*,[11] Lord Woolf CJ made it clear that this document is designed not as a formal part of the documentary bundles, but rather as a private document to assist the Lord Justice to be fully cognisant of the issues relevant to the application. It is not revealed to the parties. The position of LIPs, and the continuing debate about ways of reforming the procedures for dealing with applications from unrepresented parties, are discussed more fully in chapter nine.

However, one point that did emerge from our sample was that many LIP applicants do not in fact have a bench memorandum prepared for their appeals. The Civil Appeals Office (CAO) computer database recorded just 117 out of 287 LIP applications (40.8 per cent) as giving rise to bench memoranda during the sampling period. However, the Civil Appeals Office's own figure is much higher—63.2 per cent in 2001—so it is possible that our sample may be unrepresentative in this context. One possible explanation for this is that there may not be enough judicial assistants to cover the growing number of such applications. And it is possible that some cases are called for hearing before the judicial assistant has had a chance to prepare the memorandum.

---

[9] See Plotnikoff and Woolfson, above n 3, p 69.
[10] See *ibid*, p 123. The *Reviews of the Legal Year*, produced annually by the Court of Appeal, include a section on the judicial assistants scheme.
[11] [2001] EWCA Civ 254, (2001) *The Times*, 2 March.

TIME TAKEN FOR APPLICATIONS TO BE PROCESSED

Delay, and the costs and mounting backlogs associated with delay, has been an issue for a long time in the Court of Appeal. Streamlining procedures in the interests of greater efficiency and speed in the disposal of business was an important part of the rationale of the Woolf–Bowman reforms, discussed elsewhere, particularly in chapters four and five. Prior to the introduction of the CPR it was not uncommon for the final resolution of an appeal to take two years. The Civil Appeals Office has worked, with some success, to shorten waiting times substantially. Lord Phillips MR reported in his *Review of the Legal Year* for 2001 that in his Practice Note of 4 July 2001 he was 'able to announce a further reduction in the longest date [for the disposal of full appeals] to 10 months.' Table 6 above indicates that the backlog of appeals still outstanding at the end of each legal year has steadily declined since the late 1990s.

We used our own sample data to ascertain how long it took for the Court to dispose of PTA applications and full appeals. The figures for the four data-sets combined were as follows.

Table 9: Time taken for disposal of pta applications and full appeals (June 2000 to May 2001) (N = 800)

Time taken	Number of cases
<3 months	422
3–6 months	271
6–9 months	70
9–12 months	31
12–15 months	6
>15 months	0

Only six of the 800 cases (0.75 per cent) took more than a year from initiation to conclusion, while 422 (52.75 per cent) took less than three months. Our research data suggest various reasons why a few applications take such a long time to reach a conclusion. In those cases, 55 of which (6.9 per cent) appeared in our sample, where an application is considered on the papers, and then adjourned for a hearing before a full court (AFC), the application necessarily has to enter the listing for full appeals, as this list is where three-judge court time is allocated. This will of itself result in delay. Moreover, the papers will need to be given to the judges sitting in the full constitution, and they will need time to study them.

Delay can also occur where a litigant, whether appearing in person or represented by lawyers, is for some reason threatened with having their application dismissed. Each Wednesday morning, a hearing list is drawn up where all cases listed as being threatened with dismissal are examined by the Court, with the applicant being invited to show 'due cause why they should not be dismissed.' Often, there are between 10 and 20 such cases listed. In our sample, 125 applications (15.6 per cent) appeared in a dismissal list. There are various reasons why an application can be threatened with dismissal. They include a failure to complete the PTA application form correctly; a failure to present the required papers with an application; and a failure to obtain a copy of the decision of the court below. One task of the Civil Appeals Office is to ensure that applications are correct in every particular. A failure by a minority of applicants to comply with the relevant requirements inevitably results in delay.

Only 30 (3.8 per cent) of the applications in our sample were actually dismissed in this way. If we add to this the figures for those applications that were adjourned, and those where the parties had to correct a defect in the paperwork, it becomes apparent that these two reasons alone are enough to explain why a significant minority of applications are delayed for six months or more. In addition, a few cases are held back by the office; indeed, a few are 'stood out'. The two main reasons for this are as follows. First, occasionally, a case will be brought before the court containing facts that raise very similar issues to other applications that are awaiting a hearing. Where this occurs, the civil appeals Master will select one case to be determined as a test case, whilst the other applications await the outcome. A positive aspect of this process is that costs are saved by the parties whose applications are put on hold, as the outcome of the test case may well determine the relevant issues, in which case there is no need for them to continue.

Secondly, a case will occasionally progress to the House of Lords for a ruling designed to be authoritative for other applications. Although the figures are small, the cases in these two groups more than account for the numbers represented in the groups where applications have waited more than nine months, or even more than 15 months, to be determined by the court. Fourteen cases in our data-set were 'stood out'.

One further reason why an application might be delayed is that one or more of the parties might wish to consider Alternative Dispute Resolution. (ADR). The Woolf reforms have actively encouraged ADR in all of its forms: arbitration, adjudication, and mediation. The Court of Appeal has developed a system whereby litigants can ask for ADR to be considered. Where this occurs, the other party is sent a letter asking for comments and responses to the idea. Although the uptake for ADR was very small (a larger number of litigants do consider ADR at the full appeal stage), the time taken for the parties to contemplate this course of action can result in delay, as the application will be stayed during the process. In our data-sets, we found 32 cases in which ADR had been in some way mentioned and/or explored.[12]

---

[12] For a comprehensive overview of ADR see David Gladwell, 'Alternative Dispute Resolution and the Courts' [2004] *Civil Court News* 27.

DETERMINATION ON THE PAPERS, AND ORAL HEARINGS

Where an application has progressed through the case management stages, and has been finally processed by one of the case management groups, it will be sent to a Lord Justice for a determination on the papers. Whilst some applications brought by litigants in person may go directly to an oral hearing, the majority of applications—488 out of the 800 applications in our sample (61.0 per cent)—receive a 'paper' determination (compare Table 5 above).

Where the application is granted, it proceeds directly to be processed for a full appeal hearing by a full court. However, few of these paper applications are granted—just (13.9 per cent) of our sample. Indeed, of the group of 200 applications in the June 2000 sub-sample, not one such application was allowed, perhaps because the CPR were still in their infancy, and the transition from the previous practice of deciding applications orally was not yet complete.

Where an application is refused on a paper determination, the CPR provide that the applicant can request to have the application determined at an oral hearing. The renewal process involves the application being processed by the listing office, to go before a Lord Justice. However, a substantial minority of applicants whose 'paper' applications are unsuccessful do not apply for an oral hearing. In our sample, 272 paper applications were refused, and 148 of these applicants (54.4 per cent) sought an oral hearing. Moreover, some applications (21 in our sample) are dismissed by consent (DBC) and do not actually proceed to an oral hearing. In some cases the parties manage to reach a settlement. Occasionally, ADR has been successful. Sometimes the applicant, perhaps after listening to legal advice, may have had second thoughts about the wisdom of proceeding in the face of a paper dismissal. A legal aid certificate may have been withdrawn following the rejection of the paper application.

A DBC request has to be made to the Civil Appeals Office, to be granted by a Master or Deputy Master. Both parties have to consent to the dismissal. The timing of DBC applications is a matter for the parties, and these applications do appear to occur at various stages. There were 93 DBCs in our sample.

Some applications, although originally submitted for a determination on the papers, progress directly to an oral hearing. Sometimes this is because the judge decides that the application requires both sides to be heard—for example in complex commercial cases. It may also arise where there is an issue that affects many other applications waiting to be heard—the 'test case' scenario.

Sometimes, the case is expedited or adjourned to a full oral hearing, often before two or even three judges, instead of the usual single judge. This situation sometimes occurs in family cases, where the issue is very pressing—for example, adoption or cases where there is the possibility of harm to a child. In our sample, 360 applications went directly to an oral hearing (this includes the few applications where a paper determination was ordered but not completed for the kinds of reason noted above).

Altogether, 182 of the 800 applications in our sample (22.8 per cent) were granted PTA, either on the papers or following an oral hearing. The overall success rate for applications heard orally was 71 out of 402 (17.7 per cent). This figure includes cases that were initially 'paper' applications but were eventually determined after oral hearing; of the 239 applications decided only on the basis of an oral hearing, 32 (13.4 per cent) were successful. A small number (28) of applications were refused permission on paper, but subsequently granted permission at an oral hearing.

During the period covered by our sample, there were signs of a slight increase in the success rate of applications. This was probably due, at least in part, to the growing familiarity of lawyers with the new CPR and with the criteria applied by the Court in considering the merits of a permission application. However, a 12-month period is much too short to form the basis of any firm conclusion about such trends.

JUDICIAL TIME TAKEN TO HEAR PTA APPLICATIONS

Various factors can affect the time taken for the determination of a PTA application, and the time spent considering such applications is (as several judges confirmed in interview) a very significant part of their workload. The resource implications of this are considerable, particularly in the case of time-wastingly hopeless applications submitted (mostly) by LIPs—many of whom, having been rejected on the papers, have gone on to insist on taking another bite of the cherry at oral hearing. This is why (at the time of writing) the Department for Constitutional Affairs is taking steps to curtail the availability of such oral hearings (see chapter five).

However, quantifying the amount of judicial time expended is difficult if not impossible because the time taken by the Lords Justices, in the privacy of their own offices, to consider 'paper' applications is not recorded—probably not even by them. Moreover, no record is kept of the time that judges spend reading the paperwork prior to an oral hearing. (Most cases that are dealt with only on the papers by a Lord Justice and then progress to an oral hearing will have the same judge to determine the application. This cuts down on judicial time, but still means that the Lord Justice has had to give his or her time to the application twice.)

The only figures available (gleaned from the Court Associates' notebooks) relate purely to the time taken at the oral hearing. It is worth noting that the time recorded includes both the time spent in case presentation and judicial questioning, and the time the Lord Justice spent handing down the decision.

What is revealed is that only a relatively small number of applications were determined within 20 minutes—the time given in the CPR for this purpose Most were determined within one hour, but a number took longer than this—some took a whole day or more.

Some cases are very complex, for example large commercial applications. All applications, regardless of their subject-matter, are subject to the rules governing PTA applications. This means that the legal representative or the LIP must try to present very large volumes of information in a very short time. The use of the skeleton argument was designed to help the Lord Justice to identify the issues in argument. However, many counsel and LIPs rehearse the skeleton, or read it out. It might be more beneficial if the party making the application were able to condense the issues to three of four points that are central to the application, but many applicants do not do this.

Certainly, 20 minutes does not leave much time for questions to be raised and arguments to be made on matters that may arise within the hearing. The vehicle used by the Lords Justices of adjourning complex cases to a full hearing is useful in this context, in that it saves long arguments occurring at an oral hearing that then have to be reheard by a full court.

It may also be said that one function of a paper determination is to elicit those cases where many or complex questions will need to be asked of the applicant by the judge. By having an understanding of the issues prior to meeting the party, the Lord Justice is better placed to conduct the oral hearing as one where the issues can be canvassed without a full recital of the case being necessary.

The aggregate figures for our four sample groups are shown below:

Table 10: Time taken at oral hearing (June 2000 to May 2001) (N = 800)

Time taken	Number of cases
Less than 20 minutes	58
20 minutes to 1 hour	232
1–2 hours	80
2–3 hours	25
3–4 hours	3
4–5 hours	10
More than 1 day	14

From these figures, one can see that only 133 cases in the sample (16.6 per cent) took more than an hour. One can of course argue that that is 133 cases too many.

In addition, some PTA applications are so complex that the hearing is listed to be before more than one judge. This is relevant as the rules provide that a single judge may determine the PTA application, either on the papers or at an oral hearing. One exception to this is the situation where an applicant's application to have their case re-listed following the making of a *Grepe v Loam* order (preventing a litigant from making further applications in a particular set of existing proceedings without first obtaining the court's permission)[13] is refused by a Master or Deputy Master. Where the applicant wishes to appeal that decision before a Lord Justice at an oral hearing, under the rules as affirmed by the Master of the Rolls, two judges can finally determine the application on the papers.

In our sample, most cases (509) were determined by a single Lord Justice, on the papers and/or at an oral hearing. However, 99 cases went to a two-judge court and 37 to a three-judge court.

Outcome of Appeal Application

We examined the cases in our sample that progressed to a full appeal to see the final success rate. The figures must be treated with some caution because an appeal may be partly successful. For example, an appellant may succeed under some heads but not others. A financial judgment may be for less than the appellant sought. The respondent to the appeal may have cross appealed with some success.

Of 185 cases in our original sample where PTA was granted, the appellant succeeded in 62 full appeals. We were particularly interested to see how LIPs fared if they did obtain PTA and proceeded to a full appeal. It is even more difficult for an LIP to appear and succeed in a full appeal than to obtain PTA. LIPs succeeded in only 14 cases.

PERMISSION TO APPEAL GRANTED BY THE COURT BELOW

Even though we have drawn attention to the apparent failure by many appellants to seek PTA from the court below, we examined our figures to see whether conclusions could be drawn about comparative success rates where PTA had been granted by the lower court.

PTA given below	166
Full appeal allowed	49

One advantage of obtaining leave from the lower court is the avoidance of delay and complexity in obtaining PTA from the Court of Appeal. Our figures are as follows:

Table 11: Length of time before appeal is heard

Length of Time before Appeal Heard	Where PTA Given by Court of Appeal	Where PTA Given Below
<6 months	94	59
6–12 months	61	79
> 12 months	5	24

---

[13] *Grepe v Loam* [1887] Ch 168. The order has subsequently been revised as a Civil Restraint Order. See also *Ebert v Venvil* [2000] Ch 484.

However, account must be taken of the judicial time taken in a full appeal where PTA has been given by the court below. We found that the time taken by such cases is longer. There may be several reasons for this. Where the Court of Appeal has given PTA the papers will have been seen and put into good order. From the court below there may be no more than a short judgment, and the preparation of bundles may have been complicated. The PTA process will also have led to closer case management before a full hearing. The PTA process is often an opportunity in itself for effective case management.

The final success rate of appeals is very similar wherever PTA is given.

PTA given by CoA	33.84%
PTA given below	32.32%

Does it matter, then, whether PTA is given below or by the Court of Appeal itself? Would litigants who do not currently do so be better advised to seek leave below before approaching the Court? We think that the need to apply to the court below should be better enforced than it is now. The lower court may be better placed to decide whether PTA should be granted than the Court of Appeal. The facts will have been found recently. The lower court will be well placed to distinguish between a trial that has turned solely on factual issues and one in which a real point of law of some difficulty and importance is raised.

On the other hand, the number of PTA applications lodged each year in the Court of Appeal is substantial. There is also the question of whether the Court of Appeal should predominantly decide which cases it wishes to hear, as is the case with the House of Lords. And this may depend in part upon the extent to which the Court of Appeal exercises a 'review' rather than a 'supervisory' function—see chapter two.

THE JOURNEY OF AN APPLICATION: AN APPLICANT'S EYE VIEW OF THE COURT OF APPEAL

The remainder of this chapter seeks to outline the process by which an application for PTA is prepared for a determination by the court, as seen from the litigant's standpoint.

An application must be lodged at the Civil Appeals Office Registry. This can be done by post but is most frequently achieved by visiting the office in person. The relevant forms can be found on the Court Service website. A copy of the order made by the court below is essential. This is not the written judgment, rather it is the formal order drawn up by the court to reflect the content of the judgment. In either case a copy of the order that was made by the court below is essential. For LIPs, the form has to be produced at the registry desk. Solicitors can give an undertaking that they will produce the order with their bundles. The registry needs to see the order to determine whether or not the court has jurisdiction to hear the appeal.

This is a result of statutory regulation (section 54(4) of the Access to Justice Act 1998) and of CPR Part 52, which came into operation in May 2000. Under the legislation and the rules, there are strict criteria as to which cases may be heard in which court. The Court of Appeal hears only those appeals that are second-tier appeals (under s 54(4)) and those that have been allocated to the 'multi track', and only those seeking a final determination of the order. Other appeals lie to the High Court and the county court.

The staff who process the initial application will be able to determine from the order which court the appeal lies to. This can be a difficult judgement as the capacity in which a lower court gives its decision is not always readily apparent from the formal order embodying that decision. In addition, some litigants do not agree with the allocation of tracking that the lower court made. Where there is a query, the case file has to be examined by a Deputy Master of the Court of Appeal, who will investigate the matter and determine, with the help of the court below, which court has jurisdiction to hear the appeal.

On the first visit, LIPs will be given an appeals pack which contains an Appellant's Notice. This document is essential, as it contains all the information that the Civil Appeals Office needs in order to process the application. It requires the prospective appellant to set out the grounds for appeal, details of the order or parts of the order appealed, and details of whether or not permission to appeal was granted by the court below. The notice also contains a checklist of the necessary supporting documents.

In order to assist this group of litigants, the pack contains advice as to how to complete the notice accurately. It is recognised that many LIPs may find the process of completing the necessary form complex and difficult. In this case, there is assistance to be found: as noted earlier, within the court precinct there is a Citizens Advice Bureau where staff will be able to assist with the process.

When the form is completed, the applicant has to return with all forms to the Civil Appeals Office, where the appropriate details from the papers are formally entered into the office computer. At this point a number is allocated to the application, which will apply to the case at all stages of the action. The papers are put into a file that is checked by the office staff and sent to a case manager to be processed for a hearing. At this stage, the issue of obtaining permission to appeal is all-important. The staff have to determine whether or not the court below did make an order—that is, whether an application was made below for permission to appeal, and if so what order the court made on that application.

As noted above, our figures reveal that in a substantial number of cases, no such order was made, or, if it was, it was not obtained by the litigant. The court office needs to know whether it is processing an application for leave to appeal or whether permission has been obtained below, in which case it is processing a full appeal. At present there is no centralised computer system for county court, High Court, and Tribunal appeals. As the office cannot immediately see what happened below it must rely on a review of the documents filed.

All supporting documents have to be handed in at the registry desk. These are called the 'bundles'. They are stamped and sent to the case manager's offices to be processed with the notice. A receipt is given to the applicant or their legal advisor. In the case of a full appeal, three sets of bundles have to be lodged, so that all the appropriate persons have a full copy of all the papers, including the Lords Justices, who will have to read all of the papers in good time for the hearing.

Whilst the application papers are at this initial stage, it is the job of the office staff to ensure that all relevant details are completed. Litigants will often have queries, mostly concerning the correct way to prepare and to lodge the forms. It is the Registry staff who will answer these. It is important to note that the Civil Appeals Office does not give legal advice.

When the papers have been assessed as being complete they are sent to the relevant section of the Civil Appeals Office. The Office is separated into three sections—Groups A, B and C. This is because cases fall into many different subject areas. Each group has its own set of staff headed by a case manager. In addition, a Department for Constitutional Affairs lawyer is allocated to each group, who specialises in the legal issues handled by that group. Each group also has allocated to it a supervising Lord Justice who is an expert in the particular fields of law covered by the group. Group A deals with commercial cases, tax cases, patents, Admiralty cases, probate, negligence, all the cases from the Chancery Division of the High Court, trusts and land law, and professional negligence. Group B takes all the cases from the county courts where final orders have been made, family cases, county court interlocutory cases, and bankruptcy and insolvency cases. Group C handles public law cases, those where immigration and asylum matters are at issue, and applications seeking a judicial review.

The difference between the groups originates from the subject-matter of the cases handled. A commercial case will often contain many complex issues and multiple parties to the action. By comparison, a matter from a county court will in the main originate between private parties.

Due to the differences in the subject areas, the workload of the sections varies. Group A lawyers have to communicate with their supervising Lord Justice on a regular basis. This is due to the complexity of many cases. Where a commercial case is being prepared for a hearing, there will often be many parties—usually large companies. All the parties will need to be apprised of the progress of the papers. The role of the supervising Lord Justice is to give directions where needed to ensure that all ancillary matters are attended to in advance of the main hearing. Often, a directions hearing is needed. In addition, solicitors or litigants themselves may want to write to the supervising Lord Justice or speak directly to the office lawyer. Where this occurs, the other parties will need to be informed. It is a feature of Group A cases that not many litigants appear in person. This is thought to be due to the fact that most disputes arise from a commercial scenario, where companies will often have in-house legal teams, or will elect to use legal advisers who are specialists in the commercial field of law.

Parties to an action managed by Group A often decide to settle their dispute during the preparatory stage of their legal action. The commercial realities may necessitate agreement before heavy legal costs are incurred, or there may be other commercial reasons for reaching an agreement. In some cases, the parties may wish to resort to mediation. If so, their case is stayed while the mediator is at work.

Group B processes smaller cases. In this respect, their need to refer to a supervising Lord Justice reflects different problems. The issue of tracking is most acute. The rules relating to the tracking of a case are laid down in the CPR. An application may have been lodged incorrectly and should be before the High Court. Cases in the fast track do not belong in the Court of Appeal as a first-tier appeal. The correct track will have to be identified at an early stage.

One other feature of Group B that does not occur so much in Group A is that of linking cases. Where a case is heard in a county court, the court and parties will often be unaware that other cases with very similar issues are also being lodged for hearing in other parts of the United Kingdom. Where this occurs, the CPR state that the cases may be joined or that one appeal may be treated as a test case and other actions stayed in the meantime.

Litigants in person, are heavily represented in the workload of Group B.[14] As a result, Group B uses the services of the judicial assistants on a regular basis. As noted earlier, these judicial assistants write bench memoranda to assist the Lords Justices in understanding the arguments presented by the litigant, especially at the permission stage.

Group C also handles many cases where there is an issue of linking. This helps to reduce the risk of different judgments being given in the same area. The court office uses its sophisticated computer system to identify areas of commonality between appeals. Human rights issues are also frequently cited in applications to Group C.

The usual respondent in cases processed by Group C is the government. This group handles all cases where a judicial review is being sought of a governmental or local authority decision. The group also handles judicial reviews (from the High Court) where there is no statutory appeal to a second-tier tribunal or to a court such as the Mental Health Review Tribunal.

---

[14] See ch 9, on litigants in person.

In this group, as in Group B, many litigants act in person. Many will be bringing an action against a local authority, or seeking to appeal a tribunal decision. This again means that a large number of applications will need a judicial assistant to prepare a bench memorandum. It also means that a number of people will need the case manager to assist them in satisfying the procedural validity requirements of their applications.

In our sample, the majority of cases were processed by the appeals office in under three months (see above), but it is relevant to make a comparison between the three sections. Group B has many more cases yet is able to process them in less time, because Group A cases are more complex and protracted. Group C will process many cases, but where there is a need for government input, the case will proceed more slowly. It is therefore unrealistic for litigants bringing applications in Groups A and C to expect an early resolution of their appeals.

This issue also affects the aspect of actual court time. The CPR lay down that a PTA hearing—that is, the oral stage of the case—should last no more than 20 minutes. However, for some Group A cases, this time constraint is unrealistic. Such is the complexity and bulk of the issues involved that counsel or the LIP will often need hours, if not days, to present their case. One such case in our sample lasted three days, involved three QCs, a full complement of junior counsel, the requisite solicitors, and several senior members of the parties involved. The Lord Justice who heard the PTA application noted that the case 'stretched the notion of the PTA mechanism to its limit.' Our sample reveals that many PTA hearings take far more time than some full appeals. This disproportionate use of judicial resources has major implications, which are discussed elsewhere in this book.

7

The Judges

Few judgments were reserved and all work was disposed of with despatch ... His reasons for judgment were comprehensible, felicitously expressed and eminently quotable. His reasons for judgment did not resemble the 'position papers' then churned out by the Court of Appeal on matters their Honours [judges of the New South Wales Court of Appeal] deem to be of current social interest—which has no resemblence to matters which are actually before the Court ... Nor did his Honour favour the judicial technique of writing totally verbless sentences. He has what for Sir Robert Megarry is the greatest judicial attribute ... [No one] left court feeling any sense of grievance.[1]

LEADING THE COURT: MASTERS OF THE ROLLS

IF THE COURT of Appeal is the pivot of the civil justice system, as Bowen LJ once described it,[2] the Master of the Rolls has traditionally been its distinctive pilot.[3] As President of the Court since 1881,[4] the Master of the Rolls has been uniquely placed to display the qualities of incisiveness and intellectual flair in the articulation of legal principles that lie at the heart of civil justice. At the pinnacle of the court hierarchy, the Master of the Rolls has, moreover, been in command of the Court's practice and procedure that both determine the efficiency and effectiveness with which the Court does its business and present to the public the image of the appellate system.

---

[1] A portrait of Sir Laurence Street, Chief Justice of New South Wales, 1975–90, in Roddy Meagher and Simon Fieldhouse, *Portraits on Yellow Paper* (Rockhampton, Australia, Central Queensland University Press, 2004) p 92.

[2] *R v London County Justices* [1894] 1 QB 543.

[3] The title of the office derives from the fact that the office–holder was originally a clerk responsible for keeping the 'Rolls', or records, of the Court of Chancery. The post eventually evolved into a judicial one, but the MR retained his clerical functions in the modern era by serving as the nominal head of the Public Record Office (PRO), until the Public Records Act 1958 transferred responsibility for the PRO (now subsumed in The National Archives) to the Lord Chancellor. Until the Supreme Court Act 2005 the MR was the third most senior judge in England, the Lord Chancellor traditionally being the head of the English judiciary, followed by the Lord Chief Justice (LCJ). With the removal of the Lord Chancellor as the head of the judiciary, the MR can be said to rank after the LCJ and the senior Law Lord who will take the title of President of the Supreme Court.

[4] The holders of the office are listed in Annex A at the end of this chapter.

The first incumbent, Sir George Jessel (1875–83),[5] amply exhibited the highest qualities of judgeship, combined with personal attributes of a prodigious memory and an astonishing mastery of any subject-matter under judicial scrutiny. He was acknowledged to be a tower among the tiny coterie of five Lords Justices.

For nearly a century thereafter, successive Masters of the Rolls steered the ship of the civil appellate system with variable distinction and uniformly sparse public recognition, and often professionally unsung. Apart from a gradual increment in the number of Lords Justices and a few changes in the management and operation of the court, until the Second World War, the public image of Masters of the Rolls remained curiously inconspicuous outside the legal fraternity. By the time Lord Denning took office in 1962 the situation was ripe for a dramatic change in the functioning of the Court, prompted by governmental activity after 1945, and, as a corollary, an emerging public awareness of this high judicial office. Lord Devlin wrote in 1983[6] that Lord Denning's decision to step down from the House of Lords to accept the post of MR was 'coupled with the determination to seize the power of the office,' a power that resided strictly with the Lord Chief Justice, at the time Lord Parker of Waddington. Lord Parker was a distinguished Chief Justice who was the first Lord Chief Justice to have had no political association and who had acquired considerable expertise in the burgeoning field of administrative law as Treasury Counsel (the government's advocate in the courts) and as a member of the Franks Committee on Administrative Tribunals in the mid-1950s.

Within the two decades of Lord Denning's tenure of office (1962–82) the Master of the Rolls (or MR, as he is invariably referred to) had become an international as well as a public figure. Following the publication of the report into the notorious Profumo affair,[7] an inquiry which was conducted in private by a single judge acting as prosecutor, judge, and jury, Lord Denning captured the public imagination in a manner not witnessed in English legal history since Lord Mansfield at the end of the eighteenth century. The publicity was sedulously fostered. Newspaper headlines singularly declared 'Lord Denning decides ...' in cases decided in the Court of Appeal. None, least of all himself, would have regarded Lord Denning as the self-effacing servant and instrument of the law, which by tradition characterised the position of the English judge. The posture in Court Three of the Royal Courts of Justice (the Master of the Rolls' invariable courtroom) was manifest daily by a sprinkling, and sometimes a substantial gathering.

---

[5] The Master of the Rolls was made the presiding judge by the Judicature Act 1881.
[6] Foreword to JL Jowell and PWB McAuslan (eds), *Lord Denning the Judge and the Law* (London, Sweet & Maxwell, 1984) pp vi–vii.
[7] *The Security Service and Mr Profumo*, Cmnd 2152 (1963).

of the public in his court. The Master of the Rolls was, to all intents and purposes, the Court of Appeal, and the latter (then sitting daily in three divisions) was the Master of the Rolls.

The capacity for so conspicuous a judicial publicist was greatly assisted by previous holders of the office who favoured judicial anonymity, or at least public obscurity. Lord Denning's immediate predecessor, Lord Evershed (1949–62) left no enduring mark in English law; his judgments, in a period of contentious governmental activity largely unchecked by what was then a conservative-minded judiciary, were often prolix and lacked clarity. He is memorable for having once disqualified himself from sitting in an appeal because he knew one of the parties to the case, his anaesthetist. Lord Evershed commented, with unintended humour: 'I have slid into unconsciousness under his care.'[8] His name survives only as the chairman of a committee on Supreme Court practice and procedure in 1953[9] which had made some suggestions for changes in the functioning of the Court of Appeal; their implementation was either not forthcoming or (apart from the introduction of a facility for 'leapfrogging' appeals, noted in chapter ten) had to await the post-Denning era.

Lord Evershed's predecessor, Lord Greene (1937–49), was, in sharp contrast, a distinguished jurist. With a natural lucidity of thought, he brought to his judgments a felicity and elegance of expression and occasionally a whimsical wit. His name will forever be associated ineluctably with the landmark decision in *Associated Provincial Picture Houses Ltd v Wednesbury Corporation*[10]—'*Wednesbury* unreasonable' must daily cross the lips, or at least the minds, of advocates and judges in almost every case of judicial review. His entry in the *Dictionary of National Biography* concluded that '[his] technical virtuosity in making coherent sense of legally troublesome wartime fiscal legislation was universally admired.' His tenure of office—12 years—proved exhausting.

Exhaustion was not a characteristic of Lord Denning, who lasted 20 years and would have stayed longer had it not been for a forced retirement at the age of 83 (having spent 38 years on the bench, 33 of them as an appellate judge) for an ill-considered racist remark in one of his many autobiographies. Of his successors, only Lord Donaldson got into double figures (1982–92); the three most recent holders of the office, preceding the appointment of Sir Anthony Clarke in 2005, served only four or five years. It is likely that the pattern of holding office will never emulate the longevity of the Denning era.

---

[8] (1958) *The Times*, 13 March; he also disqualified himself from hearing an appeal on the ground that he was an *ex officio* member of the Church Commissioners for England, who were parties to that appeal; see Shimon Shetreet, *Judges on Trial* (Amsterdam, North-Holland Publishing Company, 1996) p 310.

[9] See ch 3.

[10] [1948] 1 KB 223.

What, then, characterised the Denning court which has so significantly disappeared since 1982? The most notable perquisite of the office from Lord Denning's point of view was the power it gave him to hand-pick the cases that came into his court. At a time when the Court of Appeal sat in only three or four divisions it is hard to recall any high profile case that was not deliberately steered into Court Three. Sir Michael Kerr, in his auto-biography, *As Far as I Can Remember*,[11] said that Lord Denning selected the appeals he wanted to hear. For the rest, he left the administration to his clerk and the clerks of the other participants. Further, the composition of the court was determined by the Master of the Rolls. Even if his judicial colleagues could not be described as book-ends, their scope for delivering a distinctive assenting or dissenting judgment was severely limited. Since Lord Denning invariably (literally) delivered the first judgment, the two Lords Justices were constrained, because of the Master of the Rolls' authority as the lead appellate judge. (Even a reserved judgment, which would have been seen in advance by the other two appeal judges, was liable to change in the course of its delivery. Reserved judgments are now handed down and not read out—this has been the case at least since the 1980s.)

Life in the Master of the Rolls' court was always a source of unpredict-ability, relieved by his geniality and personal warmth as the presider. Lord Denning was, if nothing else, a past master of court-craft. No litigant in per-son and no advocate was ever treated other than with the utmost courtesy and judicial attentiveness, all conducted in that distinctive, but suspiciously affected, Hampshire burr. It is little wonder that the Court of Appeal was so strongly personified by Lord Denning. We are, of course, referring to the Civil Division of the Court: he never ventured into the Criminal Division, following its establishment in 1968.

If that dominance, with its procedural trappings, was not swept away in a tide of reaction, it has in effect gone for ever, in a typically English way of quiet, unheralded change. That change must be credited to Lord Donaldson, who came to the position of Master of the Rollswith a reputation for judi-cial orderliness and an administrative predisposition. As Donaldson LJ, he had earlier been embroiled in legal, political and media controversy as the one and only president of the National Industrial Relations Court (NIRC) during Edward Heath's prime ministership, from 1970–74. At the NIRC Donaldson often decided against the trade unions, culminating in a tussle with the Amalgamated Union of Engineering Workers[12] in which he ordered sequestration of £75,000 of funds for contempt of court. Some 181 Labour MPs signed a Commons motion for his removal. The NIRC saga gave credence to the popular view of judicial hostility towards left-

---

[11] Oxford, Hart Publishing, 2006.
[12] Unreported.

wing politics generally. However, the truth is that the trade unions mostly lost their cases because that is what the legislation inevitably intended. If controversy over Lord Donaldson persisted—as it did while Labour was in power (1974–79)—he was deliberately and shamefully passed over for deserved promotion. The time he spent judicially adrift was, however, well spent in preparation for the role of Master of the Rolls. After the NIRC was abolished, Donaldson LJ, as he had by then become, was given the task of cleaning up the mess left by the Lord Chief Justice, Lord Widgery, in the prerogative order work of the Divisional Court. This was the period of the nascent application for judicial review. The huge backlog of cases was cleared and the emergence of a vibrant public law was put on a sure footing.

Donaldson's way of conducting speedy hearings without jeopardising the justice of the case was to become a feature of his period as Master of the Rolls. As a passionate sailor he was adept at calming the waters of the Court of Appeal, after the waves generated by Lord Denning, without fuss and bother. His style was quite the opposite of his predecessor. Supported now by a Registrar, he effectively sorted out the mess behind the scenes, streamlined procedures, and encouraged all and sundry to get a move on so that justice was not delayed. His espousal of the technique of the skeleton argument by counsel was an innovation which did much to distil the point of an appeal and save much time in oral argument. This practice has happily persisted, although skeleton arguments tend nowadays not to be all that skeletal. The move from Denning to Donaldson was noticeable in the courtroom, with unfussy determination to decide appeals with expedition and efficiency. Unlike his predecessor, he retired earlier than expected, the foundations of a modernised Court of Appeal being well laid.

Each of the three incumbents since 1992, Lord Bingham of Cornhill (1992–96), Lord Woolf (1996–2000), and Lord Phillips of Worth Matravers (2000–05), became Lord Chief Justice, a feature of the judicial hierarchy that looks to be uniformly repeated. The most recent Master of the Rolls— appointed while the present book was being completed—is Sir Anthony Clarke (2005–). The shuffling of the judicial pack reflects the very different practice of the appellate judiciary in the twenty-first century.

THE COURT TODAY

Today the pilot is—if Lord Woolf, a firm believer in ridding legal language of non-English archaisms, will forgive the resort to a Latinism—*primus inter pares* of himself and 37 Lords Justices, three of them in fact Lady Justices. The judicial strength of the Court of Appeal is, however, not simply reflected in its statutory composition, if only it is numerically in striking contrast to the Denning era. The actual strength of the Court is significantly supplemented by the President of the Family Division and the Chancellor of the Chancery Division (until the Constitutional Reform Act 2005 the Vice-Chancellor, reflecting the previous link with the Lord Chancellor as head of the judiciary). Both of the heads of the two divisions of the High Court preside in the Civil Division of the Court of Appeal for a number of weeks in the year, sharing the pilotage of the court. The Lord Chief Justice too has infrequently sat, on occasion with the Master of the Rolls as his seconder. Further, whether because of pressure of business on the Court or the wish to give High Court judges some experience in the Court of Appeal and, perhaps, to test their ability, a number of High Court judges have sat in the Court of Appeal. Occasionally they have given the lead judgment. Now, given that the Lord Chief Justice is the head of the judiciary and as such is detached from any governmental link, the new practices noted above will continue apace. Since the last three Masters of the Rolls moved on to the Chief Justiceship the holistic aspect of the Court of Appeal—civil and criminal—has emerged. As noted in chapter four, there is now to be a rationalisation of the respective administrative offices of the two divisions.

There are other hands at the wheel. Retired Lords Justices return from time to time as part-time members of the Court. Even a retired Law Lord has been known to sit as a supernumerary member. None of this reliance on judicial labour is entirely new, but it has been accentuated over recent years. It all adds up to a greater spread of judicial work, which tends to present a picture of enhanced collegiality.

While the Civil Division of the Court of Appeal can look to outside assistance, it often exports its own talent. In terms of the actual available strength at any one time, a number of the Lords Justices of Appeal—between five and seven—are seconded to preside in the Criminal Division of the Court of Appeal. Others are not infrequently allotted to the Queen's Bench Divisional Court and, more recently, to the Administrative Court. A member of the Court may not infrequently be engaged in conducting public inquiries, and others may be performing other public duties away from the Courts of Law.

Over the years the Court's resources were stretched to the point where it became incapable of providing a tolerable service to the litigant seeking review on appeal. Thus in his annual report for 1993/94, Sir Thomas Bingham (now Lord Bingham) concluded his Master of the Rolls report with the warning that unless substantial progress could be made in the ways that he indicated, 'the outlook is bleak'. In the following decade the struggle has continued, with some success in the period following the requirement, in almost all cases, of permission to appeal against the verdict of a court of first instance. A major source of absorbing excessive judicial work-hours is the litigant in person on application for permission to appeal. The Court is currently developing a sieving system, which weeds out those cases which are 'totally without merit'. In chapter nine we float the idea of restricting all applications for permission to appeal to aspiring applicants who are legally represented. In several European countries parties are required to conduct their litigation through the agency of a qualified legal representative.

WHO GOES UPSTAIRS?

Although the practice of promoting inferior court judges to the High Court has witnessed a noticeable upsurge in recent years, the personnel of the Court of Appeal has, since 1946, been drawn exclusively from among the serving judges of the High Court. A vacancy in the Court of Appeal may be filled, however, directly from the Bar, but such advancement has been infrequent, and there has not been such an appointment since Lord Somervell (a former Law Officer in a Conservative government, appointed by the post-war Labour administration) in 1946, and very few in earlier times. After the claims of the Law Officers to the most senior judicial offices had been put to rest—effectively at the time of the appointment of Lord Parker of Waddington as Lord Chief Justice in 1958 (against the assumed claims of the then Attorney-General, Sir Reginald Manningham-Buller, later Viscount Dilhorne, Lord Chancellor, and subsequently a Lord of Appeal in Ordinary)—every Lord Justice of Appeal over the last half-century has been promoted from the High Court.

There can be little doubt that the refusal to appoint practising lawyers direct to the Court of Appeal has meant that there has been some obvious loss of talent to the highest judiciary. Paradoxically, there have been one or two instances of appointments directly from the Bar to the House of Lords: Lord Reid in 1948 (from being Lord Advocate during the war), and Lord Radcliffe in 1949. Lord Wilberforce (unusually promoted in 1964 directly from the Chancery Division of the High Court) and Lord Simon of Glaisdale (promoted from President of the Family Division) similarly demonstrated judicial aptitude and correspondingly evidenced outstanding juristic qualities.

It has been the traditional view that a Lord Justice of Appeal must, of necessity, have undertaken judicial work as a trial judge. The theory is that the functions of an appellate judge can be performed only after a kind of apprenticeship as a judge of first instance. There have been members of the Bar who would willingly have taken judicial appointment as an appellate judge, but were unwilling—often for domestic or social reasons—to start at the lower rung of the judicial ladder. In modern times there have been two instances of High Court judges who would have been expected to reach the Court of Appeal resigning prematurely. Sir Henry Fisher resigned from the

Queen's Bench Division in August 1970 after only two and a half years on the Bench. Part of his reason for giving up, in favour of a City appointment and later as head of an Oxford College, was a sense of boredom and the lack of any intellectual stimulus to an outstanding lawyer in trial work. In 2005 Sir Hugh Laddie, an intellectual property judge, publicly declared that the boring nature of his work in the Chancery Division had led him to resign and take up a consultancy post in a firm of London solicitors. The Court of Appeal might profitably have accommodated both these talents, and many others who were aware of the possibility of spending the remainder of their professional careers as High Court judges, but sensibly would have avoided the opprobrium of successive Lord Chancellors.

The traditional view is that there is no promotion of judges in the English system. The historian Professor RCK Ensor wrote in 1933 in his comparative study, *Courts and Judges*, that a judge, at whatever level, 'does not look for promotion but takes his job ... as something final: an apex, not a ladder.'[13]

While that is no longer true of the stipendiary magistrate (now district judge), circuit judge, or county court or circuit court judge moving to higher things up the judicial ladder, it was still posited as the true position for High Court judges in 1967 by Lord Scarman (then Scarman J). He asserted that a judge does not hope for promotion: 'He does not come to the Bench looking for further promotion, judicial office is of itself the apex of a legal career.'

Even if one takes no account of the disparity in the levels of remuneration (which became the case only in recent years), we cannot think that those who take judicial appointments abdicate all hope of attaining the appellate rank within the judicial hierarchy. Indeed, many a High Court judge has preferred to remain a puisne judge, trying cases in the Crown Courts up and down the country rather than being stuck in the centralised system of the Royal Courts of Justice and never again having direct contact with litigants and witnesses. The late Caulfield J (famous for his 'fragrant' remark about the wife of Jeffrey Archer) was known to avoid ever sitting in London, never mind becoming a permanent judge in the Court of Appeal. Another notable judge, Lynskey J (the Chairman of the tribunal in 1948 inquiring into the bribery of a junior Minister of the Crown), was, at his own request, a notable omission from the Court of Appeal. And doubtless there have been others.

We think that the traditional view defies reality. We think that it is human nature for any High Court judge to contemplate the prospect of promotion and, if favourably disposed towards appellate work, to expect that it might happen. If indeed there has been an in-built attitude among

---

[13] RCK Ensor, *Courts and Judges in France, Germany and England* (London, Oxford University Press, 1933) p 5.

Lord Chancellors to observe this traditional view, we think that the Judicial Appointments Commission should make it clear that, for the future, promotion is potentially available to all High Court judges as well as to members of the legal profession—barristers, solicitors, and academic lawyers. Under the new arrangements, no High Court judge need put his name forward for promotion to the Court of Appeal.

If there is no publicly available evidence of an individual High Court judge's desire to seek promotion to the Court of Appeal, there is some declared desire among Lords Justices of Appeal to sit in the final court of appeal. In his autobiography, Sir Michael Kerr testifies that in 1985 'there remained one thing which could still be achieved in my work and career: the House of Lords ... it was something about which I thought nearly every day, and not only I.'[14]

ANNEX A: MASTERS OF THE ROLLS, 1873–2006[15]

Sir George Jessel (30 August 1873–21 March 1883) (died in office)
William Baliol Brett, Lord Esher (3 April 1883–19 October 1897)
Sir Nathaniel Lindley (19 October 1897–9 May 1900)
Richard Everard Webster, Lord Alverston (9 May 1900–24 October 1900)
Sir Archibald Levin Smith (24 October 1900–24 October 1901)
Sir Richard Henn Collins (24 October 1901–6 March 1907)
Herbert Cozens-Hardy, Lord Cozens-Hardy (6 March 1907–3 May 1918)
Sir Charles Swinfen Eady (3 May 1918–3 November 1919)
William Pickford, 1st Lord Sterndale (3 November 1919–16 August 1923) (died in office)
Ernest Murray Pollock, Viscount Hanworth (11 October 1923–7 October 1935)
Robert Alderson Wright, Lord Wright (7 October 1935–26 April 1937)
Wilfrid Arthur Greene, Lord Greene (26 April 1937–1 June 1949)
Raymond Evershed, Lord Evershed (1 June 1949–19 April 1962)
Alfred Thomson Denning, Lord Denning (19 April 1962–30 July 1982)
John Francis Donaldson, Lord Donaldson of Lymington (30 July 1982–1 October 1992)
Thomas Henry Bingham, Lord Bingham of Cornhill (1 October 1992–4 June 1996)
Harry Kenneth Woolf, Lord Woolf (4 June 1996–6 June 2000)
Nicholas Addison Phillips, Lord Phillips of Worth Matravers (6 June 2000–3 October 2005)
Sir Anthony Peter Clarke (3 October 2005–)

---

[14] Above n 11, p 320.
[15] Adapted from a www.nowtryus.net article, 'Master of the Rolls'.

ANNEX B: THE JUDGES OF THE COURT OF APPEAL
(CIVIL DIVISION)[16]

Master of the Rolls: Sir Anthony Clarke

Born 13 May 1943; called to the Bar (Middle Temple) 1965; QC 1979; a Recorder 1985–92; High Court judge (Queen's Bench Division) 1993–98; Admiralty Judge 1993–98; Lord Justice of Appeal 1998–2005; Master of the Rolls 2005–.

Other Heads of Division who sit in the Court of Appeal

Lord Chief Justice: Lord Phillips of Worth Matravers

Born 21 January 1938; called to the Bar (Middle Temple) 1962; Junior Counsel to Ministry of Defence and to Treasury in Admiralty matters 1973–78; QC 1978; a Recorder 1982–87; High Court judge (Queen's Bench Division) 1987–95; Lord Justice of Appeal 1995–98; Lord of Appeal in Ordinary 1999–2000; conducted BSE Inquiry 1998–2000; Master of the Rolls and Head of Civil Justice 2000–05: head of judiciary, April 2006–.

President of the Queen's Bench Division: Lord Justice Judge (Sir Igor Judge)

Born 19 May 1941; called to the Bar (Middle Temple) 1963; a Recorder 1976–88; QC 1979; High Court judge (Queen's Bench Division) 1988–96; Presiding Judge, Midland and Oxford Circuit 1993–96; Lord Justice of Appeal 1996–; Senior Presiding Judge for England and Wales 1998–2003; Deputy Chief Justice 2003–06: President of Queen's Bench Division, April 2000–.

President of the Family Division: Sir Mark Potter

Born 27 August 1937; called to the Bar (Gray's Inn) 1961; QC 1980; a Recorder 1986–88; High Court judge (Queen's Bench Division) 1988–96; Presiding Judge, Northern Circuit 1991–94; Lord Justice of Appeal 1996–2005; Chairman, Legal Services Advisory Panel 2000–05; Treasurer, Gray's Inn 2004; President of the Family Division and Head of Family Justice 2005–.

Chancellor of the Chancery Division: Sir Andrew Morritt CVO

Born 5 February 1938; called to the Bar (Lincoln's Inn) 1962; Junior Counsel to Secretary of State for Trade in Chancery Matters 1970–77;

---

[16] Adapted from www.hmcourts-service.gov.uk/cms/civilappeals.htm, visited May 2006.

Junior Counsel to Attorney-General in Charity Matters 1972–77; QC 1977; Attorney-General to the Prince of Wales 1978–88; High Court judge (Chancery Division) 1988–94; Vice-Chancellor of County Palatine of Lancaster 1991–94; Lord Justice of Appeal 1994–2000; President, Council of the Inns of Court and the Bar 1997–2000; Vice-Chancellor 2000–5; Chancellor 2005–.

Vice-President of the Court of Appeal (Civil Division): Lord Justice Brooke (Sir Henry Brooke), retired July 2006

Born 19 July 1936; called to the Bar (Inner Temple) 1963; Junior Counsel to the Crown, Common Law 1978–81; QC 1981; a Recorder 1983–88; High Court judge (Queen's Bench Division) 1988–96; Chairman, Law Commission 1993–95; Lord Justice of Appeal 1996–; Judge in charge of modernisation 2001–04; Vice-President, Court of Appeal, Civil Division 2003–06.

Vice-President of the Court of Appeal (Criminal Division): Lord Justice Rose (Sir Christopher Rose), retired 2006

Born 10 February 1937; called to the Bar (Middle Temple) 1960; QC 1974; a Recorder 1978–85; High Court Judge (Queen's Bench Division) 1985–92; Presiding Judge, Northern Circuit 1987–90; Lord Justice of Appeal 1992– ; Vice-President, Court of Appeal (Criminal Division) 1997–2006; Chairman, Criminal Justice Consultative Council 1994–2000; Treasurer, Middle Temple, 2002.

Vice-President of the Court of Appeal (Civil Division): Lord Justice Latham (Sir David Latham), from July 2006

Born 18 September 1942; called to the Bar (Middle Temple) 1964; Recorder 1983–92; QC 1985; High Court judge (Queen's Bench Division) 1992–2000; Presiding Judge, Midland and Oxford Circuit 1995–99; Lord Justice of Appeal 2000–; Vice-President, Court of Appeal, Criminal Division 2006–.

Other Lords and Ladies Justices of Appeal (in order of seniority)

Lord Justice Auld (Sir Robin Auld)

Born 19 July 1937; called to the Bar (Gray's Inn) 1959; QC 1975; a Recorder 1977–87; High Court judge (Queen's Bench Division) 1987–95;

Presiding Judge, Western Circuit 1991–94; Lord Justice of Appeal 1995–; Senior Presiding Judge for England and Wales 1995–98; conducted Criminal Courts Review Inquiry 1999–2001.

Lord Justice Pill (Sir Malcolm Pill)

Born 11 March 1938; called to the Bar (Gray's Inn) 1962; a Recorder 1976–87; QC 1978; High Court judge (Queen's Bench Division) 1988–95; Presiding Judge, Wales and Chester Circuit 1989–93; Lord Justice of Appeal 1995–.

Lord Justice Ward (Sir Alan Ward)

Born 15 February 1938; called to the Bar (Gray's Inn) 1964; QC 1984; a Recorder 1985–88; High Court judge (Family Division) 1988–95; Family Division Liaison Judge, Midland and Oxford Circuit 1990–95; Lord Justice of Appeal 1995–.

Lord Justice Thorpe (Sir Mathew Thorpe)

Born 30 July 1938; Called to the Bar (Inner Temple) 1961; QC 1980; a Recorder 1982–88; High Court judge (Family Division) 1988–95; Family Division Liaison Judge Western Circuit 1990–95; Lord Justice of Appeal 1995–.

Lord Justice Waller (Sir Mark Waller)

Born 13 October 1940; called to the Bar (Gray's Inn) 1964; QC 1979; a Recorder 1986–89; High Court judge (Queen's Bench Division) 1989–96; Presiding Judge, Northern Eastern Circuit 1992–95; Lord Justice of Appeal 1996–; Chairman, Judicial Studies Board 1999–2003; President, Council of Inns of Court and the Bar 2003–.

Lord Justice Mummery (Sir John Mummery)

Born 5 September 1938; Called to the Bar (Gray's Inn) 1964; Junior Counsel to the Treasury (Chancery) 1981–89; a Recorder 1989; High Court judge (Chancery Division) 1989–96; President, Employment Appeal Tribunal 1993–96; Lord Justice of Appeal 1996–; President, Investigatory Powers Tribunal 2000–; President, Council of Inns of Court and the Bar 2000–03; Treasurer, Gray's Inn 2005–.

Lord Justice Chadwick (Sir John Chadwick)

Born 20 January 1941; called to the Bar (Inner Temple) 1966; a Recorder 1989–91; QC 1980; Judge of the Courts of Appeal of Guernsey and Jersey 1986–93; High Court judge (Chancery Division) 1991–7; Chancery Supervising Judge (Birmingham, Bristol and Cardiff) 1995–97; Lord Justice of Appeal 1997–; Treasurer, Inner Temple 2004.

Lord Justice Buxton (Sir Richard Buxton)

Born 13 July 1938; called to the Bar (Inner Temple) 1969; a Recorder 1987–93; High Court judge (Queen's Bench Division) 1994–97; Lord Justice of Appeal 1997–.

Lord Justice May (Sir Anthony May)

Born 9 September 1940; called to the Bar (Inner Temple) 1967; a Recorder 1985–91; QC 1979; High Court judge (Queen's Bench Division) 1991–97; Lord Justice of Appeal 1997–; Deputy Head of Civil Justice 2000–3; Vice-President, Queen's Bench Division 2002–.

Lord Justice Tuckey (Sir Simon Tuckey)

Born 17 October 1941; Called to the Bar (Lincoln's Inn) 1964; QC 1981; a Recorder 1984; High Court judge (Queen's Bench Division) 1992–98; Presiding Judge (Western Circuit) 1995–97; Lord Justice of Appeal 1998–.

Lord Justice Laws (Sir John Laws)

Born 10 May 1945; called to the Bar (Inner Temple) 1970; First Junior Counsel to the Treasury, common law 1984–92; a Recorder 1985–92; High Court judge (Queen's Bench Division) 1992–98; Lord Justice of Appeal 1999–.

Lord Justice Sedley (Sir Stephen Sedley)

Born 9 October 1939; Called to the Bar (Inner Temple) 1964; QC 1983; High Court judge (Queen's Bench Division) 1992; Lord Justice of Appeal 1999–.

Lord Justice Rix (Sir Bernard Rix)

Born 8 December 1944; called to the Bar (Inner Temple) 1970; QC 1981; a Recorder 1990–93; High Court judge (Queen's Bench Division) 1993–2000; Judge in charge of the Commercial Court 1998–9; Lord Justice of Appeal 2000–.

Lord Justice Parker (Sir Jonathan Parker)

Born 8 December 1937; called to the Bar (Inner Temple) 1962; a Recorder 1989–91; QC 1979; Attorney-General of Duchy of Lancaster 1989–91; High Court judge (Chancery Division) 1991–2000; Vice-Chancellor, County Palatine of Lancaster 1994–98; Lord Justice of Appeal 2000–December 2006.

Lady Justice Arden (Dame Mary Arden DBE)

Born 23 January 1947; called to the Bar (Gray's Inn) 1971; Admitted to Lincoln's Inn ad eundem 1973; QC 1986; Attorney-General of Duchy of Lancaster 1991–3; High Court judge (Chancery Division) 1993–2000; Chairman, Law Commission 1996–99; Lady Justice of Appeal 2000–.

Lord Justice Keene (Sir David Keene)

Born 15 April 1941; called to the Bar (Inner Temple) 1964; QC 1980; a Recorder 1989–94; High Court judge (Queen's Bench Division) 1994–2000; Lord Justice of Appeal 2000–; Chairman, Judicial Studies Board 2003–.

Lord Justice Dyson (Sir John Dyson)

Born 31 July 1943; called to the Bar (Middle Temple) 1968; a Recorder 1986–93; QC 1982; High Court judge (Queen's Bench Division) 1993–2001; Presiding Judge (Technology and Construction Court) 1998–2001; Lord Justice of Appeal 2001–; Deputy Head of Civil Justice 2003–.

Lord Justice Longmore (Sir Andrew Longmore)

Born 25 August 1944; called to the Bar (Middle Temple) 1966; QC 1983; a Recorder 1992–93; High Court judge (Queen's Bench Division) 1993–2001; Lord Justice of Appeal 2001–.

Lord Justice Carnwath (Sir Robert Carnwath CVO)

Born 15 March 1945; called to the Bar (Middle Temple) 1968; Junior Counsel to Inland Revenue 1980–85; QC 1985; Attorney-General to the Prince of Wales 1988–94; High Court Judge (Chancery Division) 1994–2002; Chairman of the Law Commission 1999–2002; Lord Justice of Appeal 2002–; Senior President Designate of Tribunals 2004–.

Lord Justice Scott Baker (Sir Scott Baker)

Born 10 December 1937; called to the Bar (Middle Temple) 1961; a Recorder 1976–88; QC 1978; High Court judge (Family Division) 1988–92; (Queen's Bench Division) 1993–2002; Presiding Judge (Wales and Chester Circuit) 1991–95; Lord Justice of Appeal 2002–; Treasurer, Middle Temple 2004.

Lady Justice Smith (Dame Janet Smith DBE)

Born 29 November 1940; called to the Bar (Lincoln's Inn) 1972; QC 1986; a Recorder 1988–92; High Court judge (Queen's Bench Division) 1992–2002; Presiding Judge (North Eastern Circuit) 1995–98; Chairman, Shipman Inquiry 2001–05; Lady Justice of Appeal 2002–.

Lord Justice Thomas (Sir John Thomas)

Born 22 October 1947; called to the Bar (Gray's Inn) 1969; QC 1984; a Recorder 1987–96; High Court judge (Queen's Bench Division) 1996–2003; Presiding Judge (Wales and Chester Circuit) 1998–2001; Senior Presiding Judge for England and Wales 2003–; Lord Justice of Appeal 2003–.

Lord Justice Jacob (Sir Robin Jacob)

Born 26 April 1941; called to the Bar (Gray's Inn) 1967; Junior Counsel to the Treasury in patent matters 1976–81; QC 1981; High Court judge (Chancery Division) 1993–2003; Lord Justice of Appeal 2003–.

Lord Justice Wall (Sir Nicholas Wall)

Born 14 March 1945; Called to the Bar (Gray's Inn) 1969; QC 1988; a Recorder 1990–93; High Court judge (Family Division) 1993–2004; Family Division Liaison Judge, Northern Circuit 1996–2001; Lord Justice of Appeal 2004–.

Lord Justice Neuberger (Sir David Neuberger)

Born 10 January 1948; called to the Bar (Lincoln's Inn) 1974; QC 1987; a Recorder 1990–96; High Court judge (Chancery Division) 1996–2004; Lord Justice of Appeal 2004–; Judge in charge of modernisation 2004–.

Lord Justice Maurice Kay (Sir Maurice Kay)

Born 6 December 1942; called to the Bar (Gray's Inn) 1975; a Recorder 1988–95; QC 1988; High Court Judge (Queen's Bench Division) 1995–2004; Presiding Judge, Wales and Chester Circuit 1995–99; Lord Justice of Appeal 2004–.

Lord Justice Hooper (Sir Anthony Hooper)

Born 16 September 1937; called to the Bar (Inner Temple) 1965; a Recorder 1986–95; QC 1987; High Court judge (Queen's Bench Division) 1995–2004; Presiding Judge (North Eastern Circuit) 1997–2000; Lord Justice of Appeal 2004–.

Lord Justice Gage (Sir William Gage)

Born 22 April 1938; called to the Bar (Inner Temple) 1963; QC 1982; a Recorder 1982–93; High Court judge (Queen's Bench Division) 1993–2004; Presiding Judge, South-Eastern Circuit 1997–2000; Lord Justice of Appeal 2004–.

Lord Justice Lloyd (Sir Timothy Lloyd)

Born 30 November 1946; called to the Bar (Middle Temple) 1970; QC 1986; Attorney-General to The Duchy of Lancaster 1993–96; High Court judge (Chancery Division) 1996–2005; Vice-Chancellor of the County Palatine of Lancaster 2002–05; Lord Justice of Appeal 2005–.

Lord Justice Moore-Bick (Sir Martin Moore-Bick)

Born 6 December 1946; called to the Bar (Inner Temple) 1969; QC 1986; a Recorder 1990–95; High Court judge (Queen's Bench Division) 1995–2005; Lord Justice of Appeal 2005–.

Lord Justice Richards (Sir Stephen Richards)

Born 8 December 1950; called to the Bar (Gray's Inn) 1975; Standing Counsel to Director General of Fair Trading 1989–91; a Junior Counsel to Crown, Common Law 1990–91; First Junior Treasury Counsel, Common Law 1992–97; a Recorder 1996–97; High Court judge (Queen's Bench Division) 1997–2005; Presiding Judge, Wales and Chester Circuit 2000–3; Lord Justice of Appeal 2005–.

Lady Justice Hallett (Dame Heather Hallett)

Born 16 December 1949; called to the Bar (Inner Temple) 1972; QC 1989; a Recorder 1989–99; High Court judge (Queen's Bench Division) 1999–2005; Presiding Judge, Western Circuit 2001–05; Lady Justice of Appeal 2005–.

Lord Justice Moses (Sir Alan Moses)

Born 29 November 1945; called to the Bar (Middle Temple) 1968; Member Panel of Junior Counsel to the Crown, Common Law 1981-90; Junior Counsel to Inland Revenue, Common Law 1985–90; a Recorder 1985–96; QC 1990; High Court judge (Queen's Bench Division) 1996–2005; Presiding Judge, South Eastern Circuit 1999–2002; Lord Justice of Appeal 2005–.

Lord Justice Hughes (Sir Anthony Hughes)

Born 11 August 1948; called to the Bar, Inner Temple 1970; a Recorder 1988–97; QC 1990; High Court Judge (Family Division) 1997–2003, (Queen's Bench Division) 2004–06; Presiding Judge, Midland Circuit (formerly Midland & Oxford Circuit) 2000–03; Lord Justice of Appeal 2006–.

Lord Justice Leveson (Sir Brian Leveson)

Born 22 June 1949, called to the Bar, Middle Temple, 1970; QC 1986; a Recorder 1988–2000; Deputy High Court Judge 1998–2000; High Court Judge, Queen's Bench Division, 2000–06; Presiding Judge, Northern Circuit, 2002–06; Deputy Senior Presiding Judge 2005–06; Lord Justice of Appeal 2006–.

8

Judgments

INDIVIDUALITY AND COLLEGIALITY

IT IS THE tradition of the English common law that the appellate judge is an individual personified. By contrast, the judges in the legal systems of Western Europe opt for a system of collegiality in which benches of judges hand down synonymous, formal, collective judgments. Times change, and with the participation of the English judiciary in European tribunals so has the practice. While the European Court of Justice in Luxembourg adheres to the continental style of a composite judgment, anyone travelling forensically to Strasbourg for a hearing before the European Court of Human Rights will witness the adoption of separate assenting and dissenting judgments, although the ruling decision will reflect the composition of the majority of judges. So too in the Supreme Court of the United States, the majority vote is reflected in the style 'opinion of the court', with its author (and supporters) clearly identified. Assents and/or dissents are separately identified, to which others may join.

The individualism of the English judiciary, characterised by the intonation of formal agreement with the lead reasoned judgment, is now much less evident as a feature of the output of the Court of Appeal. Where each judge agrees with the result and the reasoning by which it is reached, there is everything to be said for a single judgment. It is absurd if the lead judgment is followed by 'I agree and have nothing to add,' and then a repeated mantra, 'I also agree and have nothing to add.' But, if a different route is taken by a Lord Justice to arrive at the same result, it is only right that the several routes should be signposted. Multiple judgments remain as due deference to judicial individualism.

It is now more common for a constitution of the Court of Appeal to deliver a single judgment to which each member has contributed. If it be thought that individualism is swamped, it has become the practice for the court to indicate specifically that each member has in fact written part of the judgment: which part may be left to the reader's speculation. Lord Phillips' annual report for 2001/02[1] (see below) supported this trend, and there is

---

[1] *The Court of Appeal, Civil Division: Review of the Legal Year 2001–2002* (www. civilappeals.gov.uk).

every indication that composite judgments will become common. Assenting or dissenting judgments have not been affected, although the former are sometimes subsumed (or is it submerged?) in the composite judgment.

The shift towards composite judgments was less a result of any European influence than of the growing proportion of reserved judgments. Unreserved judgments—which had been such a notable feature of the English judge—have become less frequent as litigation has become more complex. Appellate judges in England have traditionally displayed an astonishing talent for stating the relevant facts without significant omission or error. A few even deliver extempore judgments in a symmetrical form—an astonishing feat. It may be that the experience that many Lords Justices will have had, during service on the High Court bench, of summing up to juries in criminal cases is a distinct advantage. Others find some difficulty in giving judgment off the cuff and prefer to reserve their judgments, even if that tends to overburden the judge with homework that is antipathetic to an orderly social life. The sheer pressure of civil appellate business, on the other hand, discourages the practice of reserving judgment. Perhaps the conclusion will be that the less complex cases, where no point of law arises, will still attract the extempore judgment. If so, judicial individualism will sit comfortably alongside the collegiality of the composite judgment.

The traditional aspects of the English appellate system have clearly undergone revision under the twin pressures to overcome delays in the appeal system and to reduce the costs incurred by unnecessary time spent in the courtroom. The Court of Appeal has not so far adopted (and is unlikely to adopt) the US approach, which is to treat argument as supplementary to written material.[2] The primacy of the oral argument is enhanced by the fact that judges can assimilate the written material more effectively by reading it for themselves rather than having it read to them in court. Time spent out of court reading case papers is another aspect of change in the working habits of Lords Justices. The consequence of such preparatory and preliminary reading is that the judges will proceed to form a provisional view about the case. In the past there was a tradition of the Court of Appeal deliberately not to brief itself in advance of the oral argument. That no longer pertains. The downside is that it will be comparatively uncommon for the members of the court to change their view as a result of oral argument. This is tolerable so long as the judges keep an open mind, recognising that to have an open mind is not to have an empty mind, and that oral advocacy is about the ability to persuade the court of the litigant's case. Orality has waned in the appellate process, but is certainly not on the road to destruction: quite the contrary. The public display of advocacy, suitably refined and used to expound and

---

[2] See Delmar Karlen, 'Appeals in England and the United States' (1962) 78 LQR 371.

expand on the written submissions, themselves taking on an enhanced function, is essential to a civilised form of justice.

Court procedure has changed a good deal over the years—not least in the adversarial jurisdiction of the English legal system, which ought thereby to favour advocacy in support of opposing parties. But from time to time doubt has been cast and there has been argument as to the continuing utility and relevance of oral advocacy. With the virtual disappearance of jury trials in civil courts, the art of advocacy focuses more readily on appellate courts. The impression is easily gained that the rhetorical side of advocacy is restricted to the criminal courts, but the evidence does not provide such a clear-cut conclusion. If advocacy is the art of persuasion—choosing the powerful arguments, ordering them cogently, knowing how to cope with questioning from the Bench, and assessing on one's feet the strength and weaknesses of the case—then the oral presentation has a crucial part to play in the appellate process. In the 1950s the US Supreme Court allowed each party an hour for oral argument; now it is reduced to half an hour. If that indicated any lessening in the value attached to oral argument, the words of Justice Rehnquist (later Chief Justice) in 1986 are apt. He wrote: 'oral advocacy is probably more important in the Supreme Court of the US than in most other appellate courts [because] that court gets the most doubtful cases, and that is where both the problem and the truth best emerge through the clash of skilled and hard-fought argument: A good oral argument is in the finest tradition of our profession.'[3]

Another aspect of the contemporary Court of Appeal has been the division of labour among the trio of judges (the Court of Appeal rarely sits as a court of five judges, although one- or two-judge courts are now common for some interlocutory appeals and appeals from the county court). It is now commonplace that one of the three judges will be designated by the presiding judge to act as a kind of 'Rapporteur' and will deliver the first and only judgment of the court. This shared judicial responsibility among the Lords Justices represents a practice so different from days past. Today's Court of Appeal is hardly recognisable to practitioners at the Bar in the post-Second World War period.

First prompted by Lord Donaldson, and refined more recently, has been the reduction in the time devoted to oral argument. Whilst resistant to the imposition on advocates of short time limits, the Court of Appeal has endeavoured to curtail unnecessary prolixity on the part of counsel. The ending of the practice of reading out large chunks of judgments from decided cases, and the photocopying machine, have assisted the curtailment of dilatory procedures.

---

[3] Quoted in JA Crook, *Legal Advocacy in the Roman World* (London, Duckworth, 1995) p 28.

In our informal discussions with Lords Justices of Appeal there was no dissent from the general proposition that, while it was necessary nowadays to conserve time in oral argument and hence to curb the excesses of loquacity, there should be no time limits placed on oral arguments by counsel. There was certainly no indication of a desire to adopt the practice of the US Supreme Court. And with the more severe sieving of cases to be heard on appeal (through the system of permission to appeal) it is usually the more doubtful cases that call for resolution by high-class advocacy from the Bar. It is only the supreme cynic who would today recall the joke that advocacy by counsel is casting artificial pearls before real swine.

If brevity in oral argument is the order of the day, there is no sign of judicial reciprocity. Judgments in the electronic age seem, on the contrary, to be engendering lengthy, even prolix, judgments. Acknowledgement of this contemporary fault in judicial habit came from Schiemann LJ (now the UK judge at Luxembourg) in *HM Customs and Excise v MCA Limited* when he criticised Munby J for over-elaboration of legal issues in a case.[4] Trial judges may have no option in determining the length of their judgments. As the primary finder of facts, the judge will be bound to cover all the issues in the trial, which may require detailed consideration. Appellate judges, who are reviewers of judgments of first instance, are, however, not compelled to engage in such an exhaustive—if not exhausting—exercise. And the resolution of legal issues can often be dealt with compendiously. Footnoting and ameliorating citations can render the text more quickly and easily readable.

JUDGMENTS: SINGLE, MULTIPLE OR COMPOSITE

The composite judgment appears to have become a routine method of delivering judgments in the Court of Appeal.[5] Lord Phillips of Worth Matravers, then Master of the Rolls, in his *Review of the Legal Year 2001–2002*, said:

> It is now more convenient for a constitution of the Court [of Appeal, Civil Division] to deliver a single judgment to which all members have contributed. This is a trend which has my support. Profusion of precedent is the bain [*sic*] of judges and practitioners alike. A single judgment reduces the material that has to be read, avoids the opportunity for differences of interpretation and provides greater clarity. Providing certainty, and giving clear guidance, are among the Court's most important functions.[6]

---

[4] [2002] EWCA Civ 1039. See below.
[5] See Roderick Munday, 'All for One and One for All' [2002] *CLJ* 321; 'Judicial Configurations' [2002] *CLJ* 612.
[6] Above n 1, p 5.

At least, the shift in style of judgments would meet with the approval of Professor AWB Simpson, who wrote in 1984 that 'the undisciplined individualism of English appellate judges, and their complete lack of collegiate spirit, reduces much of their work to mere confusion ... It no longer seems possible for a single judge ... to dominate the system as once Lord Mansfield did. Law Reform seems all much better done through the more disciplined and systematic institution of the committee.'[7]

But how distinct has the shift been? And does it conform to our notions of appellate justice? It should be stated at the outset that whatever move there has been away from the individualism of the appellate judge, there is no sign that the dissenting voice has been stilled or even stifled. The question is simply the propriety in the twenty-first century of multiple, assenting judgments.

Where the judgment of the Court of Appeal turns on a different view of the facts found by the trial judge, and does not involve any question of law, other than the unquestioned application of well-established legal principles, there is little, if any, virtue in more than a single judgment, to which the other two judges subscribe without qualification, or a composite judgment to which each of the three judges contributes. (The composite judgment may be an inevitable product of a case where the facts are complex and naturally divide themselves into separate parts for which each judge takes responsibility.) Few would cavil at the disappearance of judicial individualism in such cases. The judicial incantation 'I agree' has the brand of a bookend, rather than that of a participant in the judicial process. The Master of the Rolls' reason for welcoming the departure from judicial individualism in delivering of judgments rests on the 'profusion of precedent' being the bane of judicial and practitioners' lives. Thus it is the variance in legal reasoning, rather than any review of the fact-finding process, that informs or dictates the result of the appeal, to which the Master of the Rolls is alluding. Reversal or upholding a trial judge's decision on facts does not give rise to any difficulty—other than to the losing party.

It is the function of the appellate court that should indicate the form of its decision-making. The essence of an evolving legal system, through the cases coming before the court on appeal, is that the court is primarily deciding a dispute between the parties, and to that end will be applying the relevant law. In so doing, the court will inevitably be expanding, to a greater or lesser extent, the relevant legal principles. But it is not the English tradition for appellate courts to write a treatise or exegesis on any legal topic. That function, if it applies at all, would be reserved for the House of Lords (in future, the UK Supreme Court), which does adjudicate on legal issues of public importance, although they come before the court as individual cases.

---

[7] AWB Simpson, 'Lord Denning as Jurist', in J Jowell and P McAuslan (eds), *Lord Denning: The Judge and the Law* (London, Sweet and Maxwell, 1984) p 451.

Hence, the tendency in the court of last resort for judges to indulge in legislating from the Bench. Short of the final court of appeal (and even within it) the task is more limited. There is no better exposition of the limited appellate function than the judgment of Lord Reid in *Broome v Cassell*:[8]

> The very full argument which we have had in this case has not caused me to change the views which I held when *Rookes v Barnard* was decided or to disagree with any of Lord Devlin's main conclusions, but it has convinced me that I and my colleagues made a mistake in simply concurring with Lord Devlin's speech. With the passage of time I have come more and more firmly to the conclusion that it is never wise to have only one speech in this House dealing with an important question of law. My main reason is that experience has shown that those who have to apply the decision to other cases and still more those who wish to criticise it come to find it difficult to avoid treating sentences and phrases in a single speech as if they were provisions in an Act of Parliament. They do not seem to realise that it is not the function of noble and learned Lords *or indeed of any judges to frame definitions or to lay down hard and fast rules*. It is their function to enunciate principles and much that they say is intended to be illustrative or explanatory and not to be definitive. Where there are two or more speeches *they must be read together* and often it is generally much easier to see what are *the principles involved* and *what are merely illustrations of it*. (emphasis added)

We are inclined to agree with Lord Reid's approach for all the cases before the Court of Appeal which involve expositions of legal principles and rules. Judicial individualism is a virtue in a system which, at the intermediate appellate level, calls for the legal reasoning of each of the judges. For the rest, the composite judgment is entirely appropriate.

With the increased numbers and greater spread of expertise among those promoted to the Court of Appeal it has been possible to assign cases to a panel containing a Lord Justice of Appeal with expertise in the particular field of law under direct consideration in that appeal. There are specialisms— for example intellectual property, value added tax, income tax, shipping and other complex commercial transactions—which instinctively invite the attention of a specialist judge. There is a superficial, if natural, attraction in selecting the composition of the court in a manner so as to adopt the practice of 'horses for courses'. This expression, which emanates from the world of horse racing, urges someone to stick to the topic he knows best, on the principle that some horses run better on certain courses than on others. But the deployment of specialist knowledge in the context of the collegiate decision-making of an appellate court is capable of untoward, even undesirable, results. The danger is that the Lord Justice with the specific specialist knowledge may use, unwittingly and unintentionally, his expertise in such a way as to dominate, if not drown, the views of the generalist lawyer. The

[8] [1972] AC 1027.

result is that specialist knowledge is in danger of overwhelming the non-specialist approach to the appeal. To put it crudely, the three-judge appellate court in effect becomes a hearing before the one specialist judge. There is a danger that the other two Lords Justices may take on the appearance of 'bookends'.

We are concerned that some appeals are being heard and determined by the divisions of the Court of Appeal which do not fully reflect the unalloyed attention of each of the members of the court. The imbalance between the one specialist judge and his or her two non-specialist (generalist) judicial colleagues may, and often does, create the impression of dominance by the specialist. An appeal should always fully engage the intellectual attention of all three judges, and not be in fact, or even be seen to be, the decision of the specialist. We do not think that the inclusion of a specialist judge is in any way a misuse of the proper administration of the court, but we deprecate the effect of any trumping by the specialist of the generalists—even if only in appearance. We think that the Master of the Rolls should alert his colleagues in the Court of Appeal to the potential mischief which we have observed and counsel all of them to be alive to the problem. It should be the obligation of every Appeal Court judge to guard against the possibility of being overborne by the appellate judge who possesses—and in some cases positively parades—his expertise in such a way that accords superiority over the judgments of the generalists.

It is difficult to gauge litigant satisfaction in the contemporary Court of Appeal. Our impression is that, on any objective criteria, appellants and respondents should feel content that appellate justice is well served. No appellant should nowadays do what, hypothetically, when languishing in the south of France, he did on receipt of a reserved judgment from his solicitor. The message was worded laconically: 'Justice triumphed today.' To this the client immediately replied in like manner: 'Appeal to the House of Lords immediately!'

PROLIXITY OF JUDGMENTS

Shortly before he left to become the UK judge in the European Court of Justice at Luxembourg, Schiemann LJ (a Lord Justice of Appeal from 1995) expressed judicially his concern—he employed the word 'perturbed'—about judgments becoming 'longer and longer'. His comments, in which he was joined specifically by Judge LJ in *HM Customs & Excise and Another v MCA and Another*[9] came as a result of the Court of Appeal's consideration of a judgment given by Munby J of 223 paragraphs containing a comprehensive analysis of the court's jurisdiction to assess and protect the interests of wives and former wives in matrimonial property. While commending the judge for his industry and erudition, the judgment was too long 'because it dealt at length with a number of matters which the judge held were

---

[9] [2002] EWCA Civ 1039.

not central to the decision' (the three judgments in the Court of Appeal ran to 112 paragraphs). While the instant appeal related to a particular matter of juristic interest expatiated on by a judge noted for his penchant for exiguousness, Schiemann LJ's criticism reflects a general unease about the contemporary deliverance of judicial decisions at all levels of the court hierarchy. Our own observations of the Court of Appeal in action fully support Schiemann LJ's concern.

Trial judges have a dual function: determining the facts and applying the law. The former may necessarily involve a detailed analysis of the often complex evidence; hence the length of the judgment may depend on the consideration of many highly contentious factual matters. Prolixity may not easily be avoided. As to legal issues, the trial judge is not required to do more than apply the relevant law; he can leave the resolution of any doubtful legal issues to an appellate court, although his own interpretation of what the law is may be helpful, both to the litigants deciding on their course of action and to the Court of Appeal whenever the parties exercise their desire to test the legal decision. By contrast, appellate judges are presented with the facts as found by the trial judge. In performing their function to review or rehear the case, Appeal Court judges, insofar as they need refer to factual matters, can do so summarily and, if necessary, annex the trial judge's judgment for the occasional specialist reader. Only the salient facts which identify the relevant legal principles need to be relayed to the generalist reader. If the appellate court decides to reverse conclusions of fact reached by the trial judge, it will have done so by consideration of the nature and circumstances of the case under appeal. It will necessarily have a duty to spell out its reasons for interfering with the fact-finding process. Even then, the device of annexing the judgment appealed from can be resorted to, with references made to it in the course of the appellate decision.

With regard to the main task of applying the law, there is plenty of scope for enunciating the relevant principles without overburdening the ratiocination of the decision. Citation of passages in previous decided cases should be resorted to sparingly; the temptation to quote large chunks from law reports should be resisted. Cases referred to in the course of judgment as part of the forensic process may appropriately be footnoted—a device most notably deployed in the judgments of the great justices of the US Supreme Court of the twentieth century. We have noticed that in a small number of recent decisions of the Court of Appeal this technique has also found favour.[10] Likewise, citation of statutory provisions in full is often

---

[10] In *Aerotel Ltd v Telco Holdings Ltd and others* [2006] EWCA Civ 1371 (27 October 2006), Jacob LJ, delivering the judgment of the Court of Appeal in a patent appeal, annexted to the main judgment a review of the extensive case-law on the categories of individual applications that ought not to be treated as patentable inventions. The judgment runs to 77 paragraphs, the appendix (the analysis of the case-law) to 53 paragraphs.

distracting from the thrust of the reasoned judgment and can properly be consigned to a footnote (in Schiemann LJ's own judgment in the instant case 20 per cent of his judgment contained the full text of sections 24 and 25 of the Matrimonial Causes Act 1973 and section 31 of the Drug Trafficking Act 1994).

The appellate judges' task should be to ensure clarity and conciseness in the written, reserved judgment. Less than 40 per cent of all appeal judgments are delivered extempore, and judgments are unlikely as a general rule to demand extensive treatment of law and, probably, fact. Neither of the two concepts is enhanced by extensive citation, which simply appears as padding.

The advice offered to judges by Holmes J (1841–1935) was to go for the essentials and express them in stinging brevity. He also admonished judges that there was no need to be heavy to be weighty.[11] Holmes was noted for the succinctness of his own opinions, compared with those of his brethren on the US Supreme Court,[12] and was reputed to have written them while standing up: when he got tired of standing he knew how his readers would feel when they read or listened to what he had written.

A lightness of touch will not go amiss, even in so serious a literary exercise in the courtroom. Schiemann LJ himself confessed, pithily, 'our system of full judgments has many advantages but one must also be conscious of the disadvantages.' Just so.

---

[11] See Felix Frankfurter, *Of Law and Men: Papers and Addresses of Felix Frankfurter*, edited by Philip Elman (Hamden, CN, Archon Books, 1956) p 177.

[12] For fascinating accounts of the different styles of opinion-writing in the early twentieth-century US Supreme Court see Walter F Pratt, 'Rhetorical Styles on the Fuller Court' (1980) 24(3) *American Journal of Legal History* 189–220; and Robert Post, 'The Supreme Court Opinion as Institutional Practice: Dissent, Legal Scholarship and Decisionmaking in the Taft Court', *Boalt Working Papers in Public Law* (Berkeley, CA, University of California at Berkeley, 1 June 2001) (available at http://repositories.cdlib.org/boaltwp/105/).

9

Unrepresented Applicants

I must say, as a litigant, I should dread a law suit beyond almost anything else short of sickness and death.[1]

IT IS AXIOMATIC in the English legal system that a litigant has an absolute right to present his or her case to the court of trial. The position is statutorily clear. Sections 27 and 28 of the Courts and Legal Services Act 1990 stipulate who can, and who cannot, exercise the right of audience. In *Gregory v Turner*[2] Brooke LJ stated that the statutory provision was 'a recognition of the established position before 1990 Act, which allowed an individual to appear in his own case in any court, regardless of his qualifications,' although its common law provenance is unclear. Before 1990, however, there was nothing to suggest that the right could be exercised by an agent other than someone professionally qualified: 'otherwise, there would be no purpose in the careful restrictions on those who could appear as advocates in proceedings'.

The common law position reflected the constitutional right of the citizen's unimpeded access to justice, and is linked to the litigant's right, legally represented or unrepresented, to a fair trial. This is so, however much there is an overwhelming likelihood that the respondent to the claim will be legally represented, which may or may not dissuade a litigant in person from proceeding unaided. The ensuing encounter in the courtroom process may produce an inequality of arms which cannot easily be redressed by judicial intervention. Without legal training (let alone experience of the forensic process) the litigant in person will often struggle to grasp the essential issues at stake, and lacks the capacity to present his or her claim coherently and in the best possible light. Faced with lawyers on the other side, the problems for the litigant in person are compounded, even if the court can permissibly seek to ease that inherent imbalance of opposing representation, with a view to attaining the desideratum of a fair trial.

Litigants in person are characteristically ill-equipped to handle legal material and court procedures (however much the litigant might find

---

[1] Judge Learned Hand, 'The Deficiencies of Trials to Reach the Heart of the Matter', Address to the Association of the Bar of the City of New York, 1921.
[2] [2003] EWCA Civ 183, para 75.

assistance from a user-friendly judge). They are often blinded (or, at the very most, blinkered) in appreciation and understanding of the litigation which they have embarked upon, frequently against advice from friends and legal acquaintances. They exhibit an unremitting commitment to the rightness, even self-righteousness, of their cause, often displaying an obsessive attention to peripheral, even irrelevant, detail. The result is that the litigant in person finds it impossible to apply objectivity to legal and factual reality. These personal attributes, when translated into oral advocacy, lead to rambling, unintelligible, even gibberish submissions—what Jeremy Bentham once described as 'grimgribber nonsense'. On occasions, the court is subjected to abuse or even belligerence which, were they displayed by the professional advocate, would lead to disciplinary action or even constitute contempt of court. To avoid complaints of justice not being done (or having been seen to be done) litigants are licensed to wander well beyond the limits of the orderly forensic process, to the detriment of a just and fair process, with no discernible advantage to the litigants themselves.

Patience is a judicial virtue, but the exercise of it greatly lengthens any hearing. Prolixity of the proceedings may possess some intangible, therapeutic value to the neurotic litigant, but it can hardly be a function of the civilised legal system that the court should offer a course in psychotherapy. The embarrassment to the judiciary, not to mention the inordinate burden to the administration of justice (including valuable judicial time) is acutely apparent. Yet for all the practical and severe disadvantages of unbridled licence to litigants in person, the fundamental right to conduct one's own case remains unimpaired. Much can be, and is done to mitigate the ill effects of the system by the acceptance of the McKenzie friend,[3] often an invaluable assistant and guide through the thickets of litigation.

But does the right, as an outcrop of the fundamental right of access to justice, necessarily spill over to the post-trial stage of seeking appellate review? Or is the right expended, once there is a decision of the court of trial? The questions have been asked; the answers point in the direction of a different attitude towards the status of aspiring appellants who pursue their cause without legal representation.

In 1995 the Judges' Council requested a working party under Otton LJ to review the perceptible and significant increase in the number of unrepresented parties in all judicial hearings. The report[4] identified the inadequacies of the process as they impacted upon those untrained in law, noting, as a means of mitigating the deficiencies, the enhanced role of the pro bono scheme and the availability of legal aid, now much reduced in application.

---

[3] *McKenzie v McKenzie* [1971] P 33.

[4] *Litigants in Person in the Royal Courts of Justice: An Interim Report of the Working Party Established by the Judges' Council under the Right Honourable Lord Justice Otton,* June 1995.

Finally, the report observed that 'the appellate process in particular is too complex' for litigants in person. The problem was further addressed by the review of the Court of Appeal (Civil Division). The report to the Lord Chancellor by Sir Jeffrey Bowman in 1997 (see chapters four and five) had, as its terms of reference, the task 'to carry out a full review of the Civil Division of the Court of Appeal, against the background of an increasing number of applications, appeals and consequent delays in the hearing of appeals.'

How then did this report address the concerns raised by Otton regarding the issue of complexity and the appellate process? In sum, the Otton report was revisited, with its recommendations being applied to the specific requirements of preparing and presenting an application to appeal. The Bowman Report said that litigants in person need to understand:

— the reasons for the original decision;
— what the appeal process means and what it can deliver;
— when he or she has no grounds for appeal;
— how to put in an application for leave to appeal or an appeal, if he or she chooses to go ahead;
— and the results of that application or appeal.

While litigants in person, on the one hand, were identified as partly contributing 'to the current delays faced by the appeals system [because they] consume a disproportionate amount of judicial time and the time of the Civil Appeals Office,' the report immediately identifies that: 'on the other hand, it is necessary in the interests of justice to ensure that litigants in person are provided with sufficient advice and help in order to ensure that every case is decided fairly according to its merits.'

What follows in this report is a catalogue of practical ways in which such litigants might be assisted. There is no reference in the Bowman report to the issue of complexity being relevant in the seeking of permission to appeal. Rather, the tenor of the report is that, due to the increasing numbers of litigants in person bringing such applications, the court had to reflect and produce a competent system of administration in order to accommodate such an increase.

This situation has been examined in respect of the lower courts. Whether or not litigants in person should be facilitated within the appellate structure, nothing specifically is addressed within the appellate court itself. There the matter has rested, save for remarks made in the annual reviews of the Court of Appeal,[5] wherein the Master of the Rolls and Lords Justices contribute

---

[5] These can be found on the Courts Service website (www.hmcourts-service.gov.uk/cms/1302.htm).

by way of articles. These articles are a forum for them to reflect on current and future aspects of the court processes and innovations.

In the *Review of the Legal Year 2000–2001*, Lord Phillips of Worth Matravers, then Master of the Rolls, addressed changes in the procedural arrangements for bringing appeals. He spoke of Part 52 of the Civil Procedure Rules and the accompanying Practice Directions. He said:

> Permission to appeal will only be granted where the court considers that there is a real prospect of success, or where there is a compelling reason why the appeal should be heard. This has finally closed the book on the unarguable appeal, enabling the Court to concentrate on the more important and serious appeals.

Lord Phillips did not define what constitutes an 'important appeal', nor did he expand on what he thought was an 'unarguable appeal'. He continued: 'Greater use has also been made of the lower courts in determining lesser appeals, so relieving the Court of Appeal of that additional burden.'

One can see from this that even by the year 2000—six years ago at the time of writing—the Court of Appeal in England and Wales had taken action by way of implementing the Civil Procedure Rules for what was perceived to be a real situation—the increased number of applications not only for 'lesser appeals' but also for 'unarguable appeals', without singling out litigants in person as a distinct group.

By comparison, in the *Review of the Legal Year 2002–2003*, the Master of the Rolls was more specific. Addressing the issue directly, Lord Phillips again placed the matter in the context of unarguable appeals. He said:

> There are two [challenges] to which I wish to draw attention. The first is the burden placed on the court by litigants seeking to appeal in cases which are wholly devoid of merit. There has been a significant increase of obsessive litigants determined to have no procedural stone unturned, regardless of whether they have any arguable ground of appeal. Nearly 40% of all who apply for permission to appeal are litigants in person, of whom only one tenth can demonstrate that they have arguable grounds of appeal. Yet each of them is entitled to an oral presentation hearing. Each hearing takes about half an hour. In addition to this, the two deputy Masters of the Court have to spend about two hours each day on utterly unproductive registry work: determining and dealing with appellants' notices which the Court has no jurisdiction to entertain, dealing with groundless applications which are flooding in ... and dealing with correspondence relating to defective applications. Four officers man the relevant section in the Civil Appeals Office. They handle matters, which take up an inordinate amount of the Court's time for very little advantage. Further reform of our procedure is required to ensure that our energies can be directed to providing justice for those who have a valid claim on our services.

The exasperation is clearer than it was just two years previously. Certain aspects are highlighted—the unarguability of many claims; the cost in terms of human resources; the extremely small chances of success where the litigant is in person; and the amount of time such cases take where the outcome is so often not in the applicant's favour.

Lord Phillips was not the only one who contributed to the 2002/03 Review. Brooke LJ spoke directly on this issue, saying:

> A serious worry, as the Master of the Rolls says in his foreword, relates to the extent to which litigants in person with hopeless cases are taking up the time and skills of the judges, lawyers and staff of the court on a scale which we simply lack the resources to handle. This problem can be divided into two parts: those who can be categorised as persistent vexatious litigants, and those whose proposed appeals are utterly devoid of merit, but who ... come back to the court again and again.

Brooke LJ alluded to the cost of so many appeals coming to the Court, such cost being unjustifiable. An hour of a Lord Justice's time was costed at about £200. This cost, of course, has to be added to the time taken by members of the administration in the Civil Appeal Office in preparing applications for hearing. The fee is £100, with £200 being paid where an application proceeds to an appeal hearing.

Brooke LJ concluded:

> in hopeless cases permission to appeal is invariably refused. Very many of these litigants whose appeals are hopeless are on income support, and are therefore exempt from paying any court fees at all ... Nobody wishes to deny a litigant in person the chance of pursuing an appeal in a meritorious case. The judges of the court, however, can readily distinguish the utterly hopeless cases from the cases which arguably have merit. As the Master of the Rolls has indicated, we must find a way of handling the hopeless cases that does not dig so deeply into the court's resources.

As noted in chapter five, in 2006 the Rules Committee, following a consultation exercise by the Department for Constitutional Affairs, amended the CPR so that it is now open to a Lord Justice considering a 'paper' application for permission to appeal (PTA) to designate that application as 'totally without merit'. Applications so designated are not renewable orally. This change is directed mainly at saving the judicial time that has been wasted in oral hearings of wholly unmeritorious applications, mainly from litigants in person. Such a change will no doubt have some beneficial impact, but it is less radical than our own suggestion, put forward below, that applications from unrepresented parties should be barred altogether.

Meanwhile, the figures we obtained from our sample, taken from the period 2000/01, would support the views expressed by the Master of the Rolls and Brooke LJ in every particular. While we did not delve into the cost per hour of a Lord Justice, or obtain figures for the number of litigants in person who were on income support, we did establish very firmly that the numbers of applications for PTA contained within them a very large percentage from litigants in person. In addition, when reviewing the time taken for PTA applications to be heard, we found that, very often, applicants went far beyond their allotted 30 minutes, with litigants in person again being disproportionately represented. This appeared to be because they could not make their arguments in a manner and to the degree that they felt they needed in order to get their case across to the judge. There was also the input of judicial patience, even over-indulgence, towards persistent applicants.

A LITIGANT'S VIEW

Thus far, we have examined the situation of litigants in person and their impact on the court system from the perspective of the effects on the system—as witnessed by some of those on whom they impact: the judiciary and court employees, and other represented litigants. What are their own needs? What influences are working on people who bring, often repeated, applications to an appellate court? What are their reasons, and can these be ascertained from their stories?

There is precious little literature on the subject. Jerome Frank, in his classic work *Courts on Trial*, wrote:

> There is no one type of litigant; the motivations of all litigants are not identical; nor are the motivations of any one litigant necessarily constant and unmixed. The subject of the psychology of litigants has never been properly investigated.[6]

And we know of no such psychological research. Whatever might be the results, we can see no reason why the right of personal appearance by a litigant in person, who has lost his or her case before a trial judge, should automatically remain unaltered when permission to appeal is sought.

Our researcher diligently scoured the small amount of output on the websites of the Environmental Law Centre[7] and the Civil Justice Council ADR Answer Bank[8]. In the small amount of literature discovered by this means, the prime response of litigants in person appears to be anger. At a workshop called 'DIY Litigation—Avoiding the Pitfalls', the author (who is not named) says: 'Despite the implementation of the Human Rights Act, the courts give little or no regard to the rights of litigants-in-person.' In this article, much of the anger displayed is directed at judges. They are variously described

---

[6] Jerome Frank, *Courts on Trial: Myth and Reality in American Justice* (Princeton University Press, 1950), p 374.
[7] See http://www.elc.org.uk/pages/lawlips.htm.
[8] See http://www.adr.civiljusticecouncil.gov.uk/DisplayAnswers.go?question_id=64&category_id=5&index=0.

as using technical procedures to dismiss cases, making decisions prior to a hearing, rendering the hearing a 'public relations exercise' and 'going out of their way to protect wrongdoings.' The courts, in general, are not spared criticism. They are said to 'subject litigants to unnecessary hardship in a strange environment,' one described as 'hostile, irrational and unreasonable.' None of these comments is directed specifically at aspiring appellants.

The second response seems to be confusion. Court procedures are cited as being to blame for much of the anxiety. Figures taken from the Lord Chancellor's office are given, stating that over 95 per cent of cases brought by litigants in person are dismissed, this being 'because of a lack of understanding of the court procedures.' This position would be supported by literature from other sources—indeed, it would be one reason for suggesting that people ought not to be allowed to bring cases where an appeal is being brought. If people cannot understand the procedure of court, can they really expect to understand complex legal precedent and argument?

The third response seems to be an awareness of their 'right' to be heard in their own cause, and a corresponding resolve to utilise the right. The article 'DIY Litigation—Avoiding the Pitfalls had as its subtitle: 'A one-day workshop on court procedures'. Another article is entitled: 'How to tell it to the judge'. These articles are deliberately aimed at assisting litigants in person to overcome their problems so they can feel confident in court.

In essence, litigants are angry about their perception that the system is stacked against them, with judicial attitudes that range from the dismissive through to an outright contempt that even, on occasion, manifests itself in a bias towards the other, legally represented side. Litigants in person believe that their case is just, true, and amenable to court intervention.

When one tries to analyse the anger, however, it often appears to be a result of the confusion experienced as a direct product of the individual hopelessly trying to collate material and prepare it for presentation. The idea is that, if the system were easier to access, much confusion would be avoided and anger dissipated.

Litigants in person do not expect to behave like skilled advocates, nor do they expect that they will be called upon to present their case in a manner that reflects the way a legal representative would be expected to present it. Rather, they expect the system to adapt its procedures to accommodate their lack of ability. While such accommodation might suit the principle of a right to a fair hearing, so too must it adopt the equally important principle of the court being impartial, such as not to prejudice the rights of the other, represented party.

The judges, recognising this dilemma, have accorded increasing support to the presence of the McKenzie friend; but the idea that assistance solves the problem is a topic that need not delay us. At best it can only be a palliative.

THE *TAYLOR V LAWRENCE* EFFECT

Some people need little encouragement to litigate, and sometimes they will persist in litigation and appeal long beyond the point where it has become apparent to everyone apart from themselves that they have exhausted every legitimate avenue and that their cause is hopeless. They are on the lookout for the smallest hint of encouragement, or an apparent procedural loophole, to reactivate their pursuit of that lost cause. And sometimes there is a bandwagon effect as word gets round about some apparently promising new avenue.

The decision of the Court of Appeal in 2002, in *Taylor v Lawrence*,[9] is a case in point. In this case, a five-judge Court in 2002 ruled that in exceptional circumstances, where fresh information comes to light after the determination of an appeal, the appeal might be reopened. The flood of hopeless applications generated by this case was noted by the Master of the Rolls in the *Review of the Legal Year 2002–2003*—in the context of wider concerns about the 'significant increase of obsessive litigants determined to leave no procedural stone unturned, regardless of whether they have any arguable grounds for appeal'—a high proportion being litigants in person. He went on to note that, despite, in most cases, having no demonstrable grounds for appeal, each of these applicants is entitled to an oral hearing taking about half an hour. And Lord Phillips called for further reform 'to ensure that our energies can be directed to providing justice for those who have a valid claim on our services.' This plea is strongly supported by the present authors.

THE CASE FOR ABOLITION OF THE RIGHT TO AN ORAL HEARING IN SEEKING PERMISSION TO APPEAL

The embarrassment to the appellate judiciary, not to mention the inordinate burden on judicial time and administrative costs, is not a new phenomenon. It has been fully recognised, and even partially resolved. The issue was pointedly noted in the famous case of *Rondel v Worsley*[10]—now happily consigned to the legal history books as no longer conferring immunity from suit in respect of the negligence of advocates in the courtroom.[11] In the House of Lords, Lord Pearce (undoubtedly one of the most judicious and tolerant among fellow judges of his time) observed:

> The history of this case has, in its general lines, followed a pattern which is not unfamiliar. Even in your Lordships' House [at the relevant time] many hours are

---

[9] [2002] EWCA Civ 90.
[10] [1969] 1 AC 191.
[11] See *Hall v Simmons* [1999] 3 WLR 873.

spent each year (and in the Court of Appeal the numbers are naturally larger) in listening to wholly unbalanced attempts to re-open, without justification, a case which a party has lost and which, by brooding after it, he can no longer see in an objective light. Disgruntled by a decision, he reflects on various side-issues (often quite irrelevant or at least not matters of decisive importance) of which he now considers that the judge failed to take any account or any sufficient account.[12]

The House of Lords in October 1970 remedied the transparent waste of its precious resources, by declaring that petitions for leave to appeal 'which appear to be incompetent' would thereafter be considered, without an oral hearing, by three Lords of Appeal.[13] The effect was to restrict, to the point of extinction, the petitioner for leave to the highest court.

In an address to the Thirteenth Commonwealth Law Conference in Melbourne on 7 April 2003 (the centenary year of the High Court of Australia), Murray Gleeson CJ of Australia said:

Unlike the House of Lords ... at present the High Court [of Australia], in addition to receiving written submissions from the parties, hears oral argument in all applications for special leave to appeal. Time for argument is strictly limited. Even so, the appropriateness of an inflexible requirement to hear oral argument in all applications is a matter that is presently under review. More than one-third of applications are made by self-represented litigants. Their success rate is very low—the need to balance the requirements of reasonable access to the High Court into the obligation to make the most efficient use of the court's limited resources gives rise to difficulty. It may be that, at least in the clearest cases, the court should have the capacity to dispense with the requirement of oral argument.[14]

Today, virtually all petitions for leave to appeal to the House of Lords are in written form, so that the question of oral hearings does not arise, and when, exceptionally, the Appeal Committee orders an oral hearing, only legal representatives are allowed. There is, moreover, absolutely no indication that the new UK Supreme Court, when it begins to function in 2009 (see chapter ten), will revert to the pre-1970 situation alluded to by Lord Pearce.

Australia helpfully provides a judicial authority for dispensing with the litigant in person's right of audience in seeking leave to appeal. Section 86 of the Federal Judiciary Act 1903–73 empowered the court to make rules of court, and section 78 provided that 'parties may appear personally.' Order 70, rule 2(6) of the Rules of Court stated that an application for leave or special leave to appeal should be made to a Full Court by Counsel. In *Collins (alias Hass) v The Queen*, the High Court of Australia (Barwick CJ, McTiernan, Stephen, Mason, and Jacobs JJ) held that litigants in person

---

[12] [1969] 1 AC 191, 257.
[13] *Practice Direction* [1970] 1 WLR 1218.
[14] 'State of the Judicature' (2003) 77 *Australian Law Journal* 505, 507.

could be excluded from representing themselves. Barwick CJ, giving the main judgment, said:

> In the ordinary course of litigation, criminal or civil, it is considered that a party to proceedings should have the right to present his own case. But an application for leave or special leave (to the High Court) is not in the ordinary course of litigation[15]

He gave two reasons. First, under the grant of leave or special leave, there are no proceedings inter partes before the Court. This is so even in a case where the application is in fact opposed by the respondent who chooses to appear on the ex parte application. Secondly, the application must exhibit features which attract the court's discretion in granting leave. There is no right to leave: which, of course, is the position in England under Part 52 of the CPR.

Is it time to extend a similar restriction to the Court of Appeal in England? We examined the question, and concluded that the time is ripe to inflict this limited constraint on the unrepresented litigant who has lost his or her case at trial and is no more than an aspiring appellant. There is no reason, jurisprudentially or in practicality, why the Court of Appeal should not now introduce a practice direction disallowing an unrepresented party seeking permission to appeal to appear without counsel.

Such loss to the unrepresented litigant might seem to be publicly unpopular, but it will be a corollary of the change in the nature of the appellate process, post-1999. It is time to grasp this nettle of reform and leave the appellate system to be conducted forensically by legal representatives, even if they have to be supplied by the Court in the manner of *amici curiae*.

We categorically do not advocate any greater impingement on the litigant in person's access to justice. Our main reason for this change is not just the desideratum of reducing the judicial workload and costly effects of the current practice, important though those considerations are, but recognises that access to justice is fully deployed by the trial process. Convention rights under the Human Rights Act 1998 or otherwise under the Convention[16] do not explicitly confer any human right to challenge a verdict of a trial court. At most, it would accord an appellate right only where the trial at first instance was arguably unfair, in the case of a wrong decision or some perceptible procedural irregularity sufficient to warrant a review or a retrial. Such cases would qualify as 'competent permissions to appeal' for which there would be no bar to the litigant in person.

---

[15] (1975) 133 CLR 120, 122.

[16] It is interesting to observe that Art 2 of Protocol 7 to the ECHR provides for a right of appeal to everyone convicted of a criminal offence; the Protocol has not been ratified by the United Kingdom.

10

Who has the Last Word? The Court of Appeal and the House of Lords[1]

The people may be taught to believe in one court of appeal; but where there are two they cannot be blamed if they believe in neither. When a man keeps two clocks which tell the time differently, his fellows will receive with suspicion his weightiest pronouncements upon the hour of the day, even if one of them happens to be right.[2]

NOTWITHSTANDING THE APPELLATE functions of the House of Lords, the Court of Appeal has long been, in practice, the final port of call for civil cases that are litigated and then appealed—constituting a tiny fraction of the total number of civil proceedings that are initiated. In relation to the volume of legal disputes, fully fledged litigation is something of a rarity. An overwhelmingly large proportion of civil proceedings are withdrawn or settled out of court at an early stage, sometimes (metaphorically) at the courtroom door; only a minuscule proportion of cases actually go to trial. And appeals are very much rarer. Very few decisions at the trial stage are appealed even one rung up the judicial ladder, let alone two. Most cases go no further than the court or tribunal of first instance. Of those that are appealed, many are covered by special appellate arrangements, for example involving a higher appellate tribunal. Other decisions, of county courts and of the High Court, may proceed, by leave, to the Court of Appeal.

But, to a litigant who has been unsuccessful in the Court of Appeal there still remains the tantalising possibility of going one step higher, to the House of Lords—and then perhaps higher still, beyond the finality of the 'final appeal' in the domestic court hierarchy to the European Court of Human Rights in Strasbourg; or to the European Court of Justice in

---

[1] Some parts of this chapter draw upon material in Louis Blom-Cooper and Gavin Drewry, *Final Appeal. A Study of the House of Lords in its Judicial Capacity* (Oxford, Clarendon Press, 1972), and from Charles Blake and Gavin Drewry, 'The Role of the Court of Appeal in England and Wales as an Intermediate Court' in Andrew Le Sueur (ed), *Building the UK's New Supreme Court* (Oxford, Oxford University Press, 2004) pp 221–35. The authors have also made grateful use of the House of Lords Library Note, *The Appellate Jurisdiction of the House of Lords*, LLN 2003/007.

[2] AP Herbert, *Wigs at Work* (Harmondsworth, Penguin, 1966) p 94.

Luxembourg, in the event of a reference to that Court of a point of EU law by the House of Lords or by another UK court.

The post-Bowman restriction on second appeals (see chapter five), and the introduction of a strict requirement of obtaining permission to appeal has reduced the number of substantive appeals heard by the Court of Appeal. But the fact remains that the Court of Appeal, normally constituted of ten benches of three Lords Justices when hearing full appeals, disposes annually of about a dozen times as many appeals as the House of Lords, whose appellate committees normally consist of five Lords of Appeal, usually sitting in just one division at any one time.[3] Thus the annually published *Judicial Statistics* indicate that in 2004 the Court of Appeal (Civil Division) disposed of 1,059 appeals,[4] while the House of Lords disposed of 77 (52 of them from the Court of Appeal).[5] In the same year, the Court of Appeal disposed of 2,402 applications for permission to appeal;[6] the House of Lords disposed of 271 petitions for leave to appeal (202 of them from the Court of Appeal (Civil Division)).[7] On the face of it, there might appear to be some pertinent questions to be asked in this context about the relative cost-effectiveness of the two institutions in terms of their respective deployment of expensive judicial manpower.

However, we must not, of course, proceed from the assumption that both courts are performing exactly the same role: if they were, then even more pertinent questions about apparent duplication of effort would arise. The House of Lords (with its own strict requirement of leave to appeal—see below) nowadays reverses the Court of Appeal in about half of the appeals heard[8] (we discuss some recent notable instances of this in

---

[3] With a current establishment, since 1994, of 12 Lords of Appeal (plus the possibility of calling upon the services of retired Law Lords under the age of 75) it is sometimes possible to have two five-judge Appellate Committees (or one Appellate Committee and one Appeal Committee) sitting at the same time. In practice, however, Law Lords are often busy elsewhere-sitting in the Judicial Committee of the Privy Council, presiding over official inquiries, or undertaking judicial engagements overseas (eg in Hong Kong)-so parallel sittings, although by no means unknown, are not common. The appointment of Lord Saville of Newdigate to chair the Bloody Sunday inquiry has meant that, from January 2000 when he last sat on an appeal, the House has in practice only 11 full-time Law Lords to call upon.

[4] *Judicial Statistics 2004*, Cm 6565, table 1.9.

[5] *Ibid*, table 1.4. The House of Lords also has a criminal jurisdiction, and hears cases from Scotland (civil appeals only) and Northern Ireland.

[6] *Ibid*, table 1.11.

[7] *Ibid*, table 1.3.

[8] Of the 45 appeals from the Court of Appeal that proceeded to full judgments in the House of Lords in 2004, 23 were allowed (one in part): *Judicial Statistics 2004*, table 1.4. *Judicial Statistics 2005*, table 1.4 shows 68 appeals proceeding to judgment, of which 40 were allowed (59 per cent). The corresponding figure for 2003 was 26 out of 50: *Judicial Statistics 2003*, Cm 6521, table 1.4. In the period covered by *Final Appeal* (1952–70) (above n 1, table 48), 144 out of 405 appeals from the Court of Appeal (Civil Division) were allowed wholly or in part by the House of Lords-a reversal rate of 35.6 per cent. The apparent increase in the reversal rate should be interpreted with caution, not least because of some idiosyncracies in the *Judicial Statistics* (particularly in their treatment of consolidated and conjoined appeals, which are multiple-counted). However, other factors may be relevant: for instance, the fact that the House of Lords now takes almost exclusive responsibility for the granting of leave to appeal—see below.

the next chapter). It must surely follow, particularly given that the number of opportunities to appeal has been severely restricted, that the continued existence of the House of Lords—and of its prospective successor, a Supreme Court, separate from Parliament—can be justified only if it can be shown to be performing an appellate function that is both *important* in its own right, and *different* from that of the Court of Appeal. And, given that appeals reaching the House of Lords will already (other than in a tiny number of 'leapfrog' cases—see below) have been subject to at least one dose of appellate scrutiny, then the work of the House of Lords must also derive some benefit from the spadework done in the court below. In the brave 'new public management' world of efficiency, effectiveness, and value for money that characterises official policy towards the delivery and funding of public services, including the administration of justice, duplication of functions is not an affordable luxury.

This chapter examines the relationship between the respective functions of the Court of Appeal (Civil Division) and the House of Lords. In so doing, it revisits some of the ground covered, more than three decades ago, by two of the present authors in *Final Appeal*.

REVIEW AND SUPERVISION

The Bowman Report identified the purpose of an appeals system as not merely correcting wrong decisions as far as they concern the parties to a dispute. There is also a wider public purpose in ensuring confidence in the administration of justice and, where appropriate, in clarifying the law, and rules of practice and procedure, and helping to maintain the standards of performance of first instance courts and tribunals.

This corresponds closely to the argument that we put forward in *Final Appeal* to explain the rationale of a two-level appellate process.[9] There, we argued that appeals serve two separate but related purposes. The first is best termed *review*. This is the means of correcting mistakes at first instance and of creating some kind of continuity, consistency, and certainty in the administration of justice. To use the kind of managerial vocabulary that has become familiar in the discussion of public services, review is about both *quality control* in the administration of justice and providing a mechanism of *accountability* in respect of those exercising judicial functions in the lower courts. The second function is termed *supervision*. This is the process of laying down fresh precedents and statutory interpretations and updating old ones for the guidance of lower courts in the hierarchy. It also consists in resolving legal problems of a particularly high order both of difficulty and of public importance that arise in that important minority of 'hard'

---

[9] See also ch 2.

cases that require judicial attention of the highest order. In managerial vocabulary, this has to do with top-down leadership and the formulation and refining of policy.

We also pointed out that, although the two functions are closely interconnected, there is an important difference of emphasis between them. Review is principally to do with achieving justice for individual litigants in the instant case while supervision has primarily to do with addressing legal problems in the wider public interest. This highlights the most important distinction—or, at least, a major difference of emphasis—between the respective functions of the Court of Appeal and of the House of Lords. As Lord Bingham observed in *R v Secretary of State for Trade and Industry ex p Eastaway* (a decision of the House of Lords that reaffirmed the rule in *Lane v Esdaile*,[10] discussed below):

> In its role as a supreme court the House must necessarily concentrate its attention on a relatively small number of cases recognised as raising legal questions of general public importance. It cannot seek to correct errors in the application of settled law, even where such are shown to exist.[11]

We discuss the numerous ramifications of the concept and rationale of the appellate process more fully elsewhere in the present study, particularly in chapter two.

At the time of our work on *Final Appeal*, most appeals ending up in the House of Lords had obtained leave from the Court of Appeal. Of the 366 civil appeals heard by the House of Lords in the period 1952–68 that required leave,[12] 286 (78.1 per cent) had obtained leave from the court below.[13] But nowadays the position is strikingly different. Since the Court of Appeal nowadays very rarely grants leave to take a case further, it falls to the House of Lords, in effect, to cherry-pick the cases it wishes to hear—to control its own docket, as Americans might say. 'Justice à la carte' is a term that is sometimes used. The role of the Court of Appeal is mainly one of review, although if a case stops there, as most do, the Court inevitably acts also as a supervisory body in many instances. This is particularly so in relation to important points of practice and procedure, an area where the House of Lords very seldom seeks to intrude.

One other major change since the days of *Final Appeal* is the sharp diminution in the proportion of Revenue appeals in the caseload of the House of Lords. In the period 1952–68, such appeals constituted more than 30 per cent of all Lords appeals.[14] The torrent of Revenue business (even including

---

[10] [1891] AC 210.

[11] [2001] 1 All ER 27, 33.

[12] The main exception was, and still is, appeals from the Inner House of the Scottish Court of Session, that lie, in general, as of right, subject to the petition being signed by two counsel certifying that the appeal is reasonable.

[13] See *Final Appeal*, above n 1, table 5.

[14] *Final Appeal*, above n 1, p 145, table 11.

post–1972 VAT cases) has since dwindled to little more than a mere trickle: the annual *Judicial Statistics* for the five years 2000–2005 suggest that the current proportion is about eight per cent.

However, the shrinkage of the House's engagement in tax-related matters has been offset by a substantial growth in the number of judicial review and (since 2000) human rights appeals. *Final Appeal* identified just 14 appeals in the subject-categories of administrative and constitutional law, out of 349 appeals heard by the House in the period 1952–68—just 4 per cent. The *Judicial Statistics* for the three years 2003–2005 (by which time the first human rights appeals under the 1998 Act were beginning to reach the House) show that, of the 175 appeals determined, 31 were in the field of administrative law and 38 involved human rights—a figure, adding the two categories together, of 38.4 per cent.[15]

And the growing volume of such business tells only part of the story. Many of the cases in these subject categories have been very high profile events that have brought the House of Lords into an unaccustomed media spotlight, and have sometimes given rise to interesting tensions between the judiciary and the executive. The landmark decision of a nine-judge Appellate Committee in December 2004, in a human rights case involving the detention of suspected Al-Qa'ida terrorists on the orders of the Home Secretary, exercising powers conferred by the Crime and Security Act 2001, is one of many instances that could be cited in this context.[16] And the judgments delivered by the members of another nine-judge Appellate Committee in October 2005, concerning the constitutionality of the Parliament Act 1949, which had been used to enact the Hunting Act 2004, are major landmarks in contemporary constitutional law.[17]

If it was only a slight exaggeration to suggest that the House of Lords in the 1950s and 1960s functioned substantially as a specialist tax tribunal, it is surely no more of an exaggeration to suggest that it has now become a court specialising substantially in public law. And this has interesting implications for the role and public perception of the final appellate court when it moves from the House of Lords and is rebadged with the evocative title of Supreme Court.

APPEALS IN THE ABSTRACT

Because English law has no universal means of resolving points of law in the abstract, functions of supervision and review cannot strictly be separated. However, since we first identified these two functions, limited

---

[15] As noted elsewhere, some caution must be exercised in comparing statistics in *Final Appeal* with those in the *Judicial Statistics*, because they are compiled and presented somewhat differently.

[16] *A v Secretary of State for the Home Department* [2005] 3 All ER 169.

[17] *R (on the application of Jackson and others) v Attorney General* [2005] 4 All ER 1253.

but significant means of resolving abstract issues have been developed. These take two forms. First, there is the possibility of any court referring an issue of interpretation or legality in EU law to the European Court of Justice (ECJ) in Luxembourg. This is significant in a case that would otherwise give rise to European points of complexity or principle or ones which would otherwise be likely to go as far as the House of Lords. By obtaining an authoritative ruling on the applicable point of EU law, the Court of Appeal or even a lower court may be able to dispose of the case itself. A court from which there is no appeal must, if a decision on the point is necessary to resolve the case, refer the issue to the ECJ but the case may never be taken that far. (We will leave aside the arcane debate about whether the Court of Appeal is to be classified as such a court where it or the House of Lords refuses to allow a case to proceed from the Court of Appeal to the House of Lords.)

Secondly, there is the possibility of the Administrative Court (the specialist public law limb of the High Court) deciding an abstract point of public law by means of a declaration, as part of an application for judicial review. This development of such a jurisdiction is proceeding very slowly and is, at present, limited to public law, including human rights.

APPEALING TO THE LORDS

We have already noted, in chapter three, that the Administration of Justice (Appeals) Act 1934, implementing a recommendation of the Business of the Courts Committee, chaired by Lord Hanworth MR,[18] imposed a requirement of leave to appeal to the House of Lords in place of the absolute right of appeal that had existed hitherto. Leave was to be granted either by the Court of Appeal, to which application had first to be made, or by the House of Lords itself. So, if both bodies refused leave, the Court of Appeal would become the final court for the parties in that case. This procedure remains in place. The origin of the leave requirement seems to have lain more in concerns about the workload of the Judicial Committee of the Privy Council than in concerns about that of the House of Lords,[19] remembering that the membership of both bodies was, broadly speaking, the same—although the Judicial Committee also contained some Lords Justices and retired judges, along with members from the dominions and what were then British colonies.

Those who supported the 1934 Act apparently did so more out of concern to protect poor litigants who had won their cases in the lower courts from any further challenge than being actuated by arguments about the

[18] Second Interim Report, Cmd 4471 (HMSO, 1934).
[19] See Robert Stevens, *Law and Politics* (London, Weidenfeld and Nicolson, 1979) p 189.

desired nature and form of the appellate process. A multiplicity of appeals was seen as a source of delay and as a device that enabled one party, usually the stronger one, to force a settlement on the other. In particular, it was felt that an unlimited right of appeal placed great power in the hands of large corporations and government departments. Concerns about the powerful litigious leverage of the latter were becoming evident even though public law still remained undeveloped and the Crown Proceedings Act 1947 (removing many anomalous and outdated procedural and substantive privileges and immunities of the state) had yet to be enacted. (More recent reforms to enhance the accessibility of judicial review, including the establishment of an Administrative Court, would still have been seen in the 1930s as a heresy against Diceyan orthodoxy.)

The requirement of leave to appeal has remained firmly—statutorily—in place since its first introduction. Losing parties in the Court of Appeal do, fairly routinely, ask for leave to go to the Lords—on the principle, perhaps, that making such an application takes little time or trouble, and that there is surely no harm in asking, even if, in the overwhelming majority of cases, the answer is bound to be 'no'. Moreover, any party who intends to petition the House of Lords for leave (or wishes to keep open the possibility of doing so) must first have applied for and been refused leave in the Court of Appeal. An examination of 398 Court of Appeal transcripts in the first six months of 2001 found that applications for leave to petition the Lords were made in 147 cases (36.3 per cent of the total). But only two of these applications were granted. The policy is clear. The Appeal Committee of the House of Lords now decides which cases are to reach the House, rather than the court below.

The strict requirement of leave to appeal, now applied almost exclusively by the House of Lords itself, goes to the heart of the 'review' function. If the job of a final appeal court is to pay in-depth attention to the small proportion of difficult cases that raise important issues of principle, then it must have control of both the quantity and quality of its caseload. Lord Bingham of Cornhill, delivering a lecture to the Constitution Unit at University College London, in May 2002, on the prospective establishment of the new Supreme Court, was in no doubt on the matter:

> I am very clearly of the opinion that since the House can, under existing arrangements, hear only some 60–80 full appeals a year, there must be a power to decide which those cases should be. If, as in many countries in Europe and elsewhere there existed an unfettered right of appeal, the inevitable consequence would be the summary dismissal of the overwhelming majority of those appeals, probably on paper without a hearing. I doubt whether such a process would be very satisfying to litigants brought up on our tradition.[20]

[20] http://www.ucl.ac.uk/constitution-unit/files/90.pdf

In *Final Appeal*, two of the present authors quoted Frankfurter J's words concerning the right of appeal to the US Supreme Court that bear upon this point (always remembering, of course, that there are important procedural differences between that court and the House of Lords):

> [T]he judgments of this court are collective judgments. Such judgments pre-suppose ample time and freshness of mind for private study and reflection in preparation for discussion at conference. Without adequate study there cannot be adequate reflection; without adequate reflection there cannot be adequate discussion; without adequate discussion there cannot be that fruitful interchange of minds which is indispensable to thoughtful unhurried decision and its formula-tion in learned and impressive decisions. It is therefore imperative that the docket [ie list of cases for hearing] be kept down so that its volume does not preclude wide adjudication. This can be avoided only if the Court rigorously excludes any case from coming here that does not rise to the significance of inevitability in meeting the responsibilities vested in this Court.[21]

In this respect, the Court of Appeal's growing reluctance to grant leave to appeal to the House of Lords may be seen as inevitable, and perhaps over-due. Lord Bingham of Cornhill was certainly of that mind, in his lecture to the Constitution Unit, cited above:

> I would not, for my part, echo the criticism, sometimes heard, that the Court of Appeal is nowadays too reluctant to grant leave: no division of that court can know what cases are competing for the attention of the House, and the decision is usually best left to the House unless considerations of time weigh in favour of immediate leave. If the Court of Appeal considers the case to be one which probably does merit consideration by the House, it can helpfully give its reasons for holding that opinion when refusing leave and the House will then have the benefit of its view.

By the same token, it can be argued that the introduction of a PTA require-ment in the Court of Appeal has been conducive to the exercise of a more effective review function by that Court, particularly in those cases that are not destined to proceed to the Lords.

THE NEAR-EXTINCTION OF ORALLY ARGUED PETITIONS FOR LEAVE

So far as petitioning the House of Lords is concerned, a major change in the operation of the means of turning an intermediate appeal into a final

---

[21] *Dick v New York Life Insurance Co*, 359 US 437, 458–59 (1959), quoted in *Final Appeal*, above n 1, p 119. As was pointed out in a footnote, the 'collective' character of Supreme Court judgments is not exactly replicated in the House of Lords, or indeed in the Court of Appeal, where separate assenting (and dissenting) judgments are common.

one, dating back to the 1970s, has been effectively to remove an oral hearing from the process. If the Court of Appeal refuses leave to appeal to the Lords (which it almost invariably does today, even if the broad, unstated but generally recognised criterion of general public importance is met), a renewed application to the House of Lords will normally be dealt with on the papers without a hearing before a three-judge Appeals Committee. Only if the committee is divided will there be an oral hearing of such an application.

This move away from orality in disposing of such applications prefigures similar moves in the Court of Appeal, under discussion at the time of writing (see chapter five).

The Rule in *Lane v Esdaile*

In *Final Appeal*[22] we noted the significance in this context of a decision of the House of Lords in 1891, in *Lane v Esdaile*.[23]. Here it was held that no appeal can lie to the House of Lords from the Court of Appeal's refusal of leave to appeal *to itself*,[24] since such a refusal does not constitute a 'judgment or order' within the meaning of the Appellate Jurisdiction Act 1876.

The rule was subsequently restated in section 54 of the Access to Justice Act 1999, which provides, in line with *Lane v Esdaile*, that 'no appeal may be made against a decision of a court under this section to give or refuse permission.' Direction 1.14 of the House of Lords *Practice Directions and Standing Orders Applicable to Civil Appeals* provides that the categories of petition that are not admissible include 'petitions for leave to appeal to the House of Lords from a refusal by the Court of Appeal to grant leave to appeal to that court from a judgment or order of a lower court, or from any other preliminary decision of the Court of Appeal in respect of a case in which leave to appeal to the Court of Appeal was not granted.'

We noted in *Final Appeal* that the rediscovery of this useful precedent in the 1950s enabled the Appeal Committee of the House of Lords to dispose summarily of a high proportion of unmeritorious petitions for leave (which in those days were considered in oral hearings before the Appeal Committee). Our own research has found, however, that a significant number of petitions covered by the *Lane v Esdaile* rule are still lodged by hopeful would-be appellants, often in the face of well-intended informal advice from the staff of the Judicial Office that they stand no chance of

---

[22] Above n 1, pp 128–29.

[23] [1891] AC 210.

[24] At the time of *Lane v Esdaile* there was of course no general requirement to obtain permission to appeal. However, leave was required, for instance, in order to appeal from the interlocutory ruling of a judge in chambers or, as in *Lane v Esdaile* itself, where an appeal was out of time.

success because they are clearly inadmissible. The potential deterrent effect of having to pay a substantial fee (£570 at the time of writing) is much blunted by the availability of fairly liberal provisions for the waiver of fees for petitioners in receipt of state benefits—a modern version of what used to be called the *in forma pauperis* procedure. And, although Article 6 of the European Convention on Human Rights certainly does not confer an unlimited right of appeal, the House of Lords has tended in recent years to err on the side of caution in its approach to even the most unmeritorious and incompetent petitions.

This major change, more than 70 years ago, abolishing the unrestricted right of appeal to the Lords, more recently replicated by the introduction of a permission requirement for the Court of Appeal, did not give rise to any serious discussion about abolishing either the Court of Appeal or the House of Lords. Indeed, the judicial role of the Lords hardly featured at all in recent discussions of the future of the second chamber, although the issue was on the table, at least by implication, in the debates about the establishment of the Supreme Court and the enactment of the Constitutional Reform Act 2005. Still less has there been any examination of the relationship between the two courts. The fundamental reforms of civil justice brought about by the interim and final reports of Lord Woolf on Access to Justice did not touch on appeals in their initial implementation.

'Leapfrog' Appeals

A development that was first recommended by the Evershed Committee in 1953,[25] the leapfrog appeal, enjoyed some popularity when it was first introduced in 1970.[26] However, perhaps for reasons given by Megarry J in *IRC v Church Commissioners for England*,[27] which gave a restricted interpretation of the requirement that a leapfrog case must relate 'wholly or mainly to the construction of an enactment,'[28] the procedure fell out of favour and is seldom used today. Professor Brice Dickson has noted that, in the 30-year period from 1967 to 1996, there were only 54 such appeals. He concluded from this that 'clearly this fast-track facility for appeals has not done much to alleviate the burden on the Court of Appeal, since [in the period under review] leapfrog appeals represent[ed] less than five percent of the combined total of these civil appeals.'[29]

---

[25] *Final Report of the Committee on Supreme Court Practice and Procedure*, Cmnd 8878, 1953, paras 483-530.

[26] Administration of Justice Act 1969, Part II. See Gavin Drewry, 'Leapfrogging-and a Lords Justices' Eye View of the Final Appeal' (1973) 89 *LQR* 260.

[27] [1975] 1 WLR 251.

[28] Administration of Justice Act 1969, s 12(3)(a).

[29] Brice Dickson, 'The Lords of Appeal and their Work 1967-96' in Brice Dickson and Paul Carmichael (eds), *The House of Lords. Its Parliamentary and Judicial Roles* (Oxford, Hart Publishing, 1999) pp 127-54 at p 146.

The low take-up rate of the procedure may be explained in part by its being little known (or its having been forgotten) by advocates and those who instruct them. The first-instance court must certify that such an appeal is appropriate and that the criteria specified in the legislation are met (a point of law of general importance arises from the construction of legislation or a binding precedent in the Court of Appeal or the House of Lords, and the House agrees to take the case). It seems unlikely that such an issue would be actively canvassed before the first-instance court has given judgment.

It is probable, moreover, that the Law Lords themselves are reluctant to be deprived of the benefit of the preliminary spadework done by the Court of Appeal on a difficult case—even in those instances where, in the event, their Lordships prove all too willing to trample over that spadework by allowing the appeal. In this respect, the leapfrog procedure, while serving the cause of expedition, conflates the review and supervision functions, and risks starving the former of some of the raw material that is needed to do the job properly. And this is probably why, in the very rare instances (on average, no more than one a year) where a certified leapfrog application comes before the Appeal Committee, leave is usually refused.

However, there still are occasional reminders that the leapfrog procedure is not quite defunct. Thus in July 2005, in *Jones and Others v Ceredigion County Council (No 2)*,[30] the Court of Appeal was called upon to consider a rather curious jurisdictional point relating to the procedure. The substance of the case had to do with the interpretation of a statutory provision requiring local education authorities to provide free school transport. The judge at first instance, having decided against the county council, granted it a leapfrog certificate, allowing it to apply to the House of Lords for leave to appeal in respect of two points at issue in his decision. He also gave permission to appeal to the Court of Appeal in the event of the House of Lords refusing leave. The House of Lords then granted leave in respect of one of the issues, but refused it in respect of the other. The 1969 Act says that if, in a leapfrog case, the House of Lords grants leave, 'no appeal from the decision of the judge to which the [leapfrog] certificate relates shall lie to the Court of Appeal.' So did the Court of Appeal now have jurisdiction to hear the appeal in respect of the issue in which the Lords had refused leave? By a majority, the Court decided that it did have jurisdiction in these circumstances.

THE FINAL COURT OF APPEAL IN PARLIAMENT

We have already noted, in chapter three, that in its very early days, before the Royal Courts of Justice in the Strand were opened in 1882, the Court of Appeal conducted much of its business in Westminster Hall. But the Court, although a statutory body, is not a parliamentary one.

---

[30] [2005] 1 WLR 3626

The status of the House of Lords is quite different. One very striking feature of the judicial functions of the House is that, since feudal times and until now, they have been part and parcel of the second chamber of the legislature. As Robert Stevens has observed:

> By the thirteenth century, the development of the common law had led to the delegation of judicial work at the trial level (and by the Tudor period even to the establishment of a hierarchy of judicial appeals), but the idea that a final appeal from the regular courts lay to Parliament was not seriously questioned after the fourteenth century. Parliament recognised no subtle distinction among its judicial, executive, and legislative functions. As the laws and customs of Parliament had developed, the appellate function was seen as no more and no less a part of the work of the political sovereign [the King in Parliament] than those original (trial) aspects of its judicial work—impeachment and the hearing of felony charges against peers.[31]

Walter Bagehot, writing in 1867, criticised the splitting of appellate responsibility between the House of Lords and the Judicial Committee of the Privy Council and opined that 'the supreme court of the English people ought to be a great conspicuous tribunal, ought to rule all other courts, ought to have no competitor, ought to bring our law into unity, ought not to be hidden beneath the robes of a legislative assembly.'[32] However, even in Bagehot's day, this historically interesting but constitutionally anachronistic aspect of the work of the House had increasingly been separated from the mainstream of political and legislative activity. This process was carried substantially forward, nine years later, by the passing of the Appellate Jurisdiction Act 1876, which put the judicial function onto a proper statutory footing and created the first life peers—judicially qualified Lords of Appeal in Ordinary—to hear appeals.

In 2000, the Wakeham Commission on Reform of the House of Lords quoted Bagehot's observation that 'no one, indeed, would venture *really* to place the judicial function in the chance majorities of a fluctuating assembly: it is so by a sleepy theory; it is not so in living fact.' But the Commission went on to note that the doctrine of separation of powers has never strictly applied in the United Kingdom, and concluded that 'there is no reason why the second chamber should not continue to exercise the judicial functions of the present House of Lords.'[33] In its White Paper responding to the Wakeham Report, the government declared itself to be 'committed to maintaining judicial membership within the House of Lords.'[34]

---

[31] Robert Stevens, *Law and Politics. The House of Lords as a Judicial Body, 1800-1976* (London, Weidenfeld and Nicolson, 1979) p 6.

[32] Walter Bagehot, *The English Constitution* (London, Fontana Library, 1963) p 147.

[33] Report of the Royal Commission on the Reform of the House of Lords, *A House for the Future*, Cm 4534, 2000, para 9.5.

[34] *The House of Lords—Completing the Reform*, Cm 5291, 2001, para 81.

But the Blair Government's commitment to retaining the status quo proved to be short-lived. On 12 June 2003 a press release from Downing Street (coinciding with Lord Irvine of Lairg's resignation as Lord Chancellor) announced that the office of Lord Chancellor was to be abolished and replaced by a new office of Secretary of State for Constitutional Affairs; that there was to be a new judicial appointments commission for England and Wales; and that the judicial functions of the House of Lords would be transferred to a new UK supreme court.

The announcement came out of the blue—not least to Mr Blair's cabinet colleagues and to the judiciary, who, it transpired, had not been consulted.[35] Consultation papers on the government's proposals were published by the new Department for Constitutional Affairs.[36] The document concerning the proposed Supreme Court indicated one reason for the government's change of mind, when it referred to the Human Rights Act 1998 and Article 6(1) of the European Convention on Human Rights, which

> now requires a stricter view to be taken not only of anything which might under-
> mine the independence or impartiality of a judicial tribunal, but even of anything
> which might appear to do so. So the fact that the Law Lords are a Committee of
> the House of Lords can raise issues about the appearance of independence from
> the legislature.[37]

In the background of this concern were recent decisions of the Strasbourg court in *Procola v Luxembourg*[38] and, closer to home, *McGonnell v United Kingdom*,[39] which had strongly affirmed the need for 'objective impartiality' in judicial proceedings.

There was much subsequent debate, and not a little controversy. In Parliament, there were two divergent select committee reports on the subject. In a report published in February 2002, the House of Commons Select Committee on Public Administration, responding to the government's White Paper on reform, supported the establishment of an independent Supreme Court.[40] However, in December 2002, the Joint (ie Lords and

---

[35] See Andrew le Sueur, 'New Labour's Next (surprisingly quick) Steps in Constitutional Reform' [2003] *Public Law* 368-77.

[36] *Constitutional Reform: A Supreme Court for the United Kingdom*, July 2003. There were separate consultation documents relating to the proposed independent judicial appointments commission and to the future of Queen's Counsel.

[37] *Ibid*, para 3. See Roger Masterman, 'A Supreme Court for the United Kingdom: Two Steps Forward, But One Step Back on Judicial Independence' [2004] *Public Law* 48–58.

[38] (1995) 22 EHRR 193: the case concerned members of the Judicial Committee of Luxembourg's Conseil d'Etat, who had previously given a pre-legislative opinion on a legislative instrument that was at issue in an administrative law case.

[39] (2000) 30 EHRR 289: the case concerned the Bailiff of Guernsey, who presided over the hearing of a planning appeal, having previously presided over the passage of the development plan on which the decision in question was based.

[40] *The Second Chamber: Continuing the Reform*, HC 494, 2001-02.

Commons) Committee on House of Lords Reform noted that opinion, including judicial opinion, was divided on the issue, and called for an independent inquiry into the judicial function of the Lords.[41]

Continuing discussion and negotiation culminated in the enactment of the Constitutional Reform Act 2005. The new Supreme Court will come into operation in 2009. It will be located in refurbished Crown Court accommodation across Parliament Square, in the old Middlesex Guildhall. The Law Lords in post at the time of the changeover will retain their life peerages and their seats in the House of Lords, but subsequent appointees to the Supreme Court will not hold peerages by virtue of their membership of the Court.[42]

In the meantime, all the parliamentary trappings remain in place: occasional judicial sittings in the chamber of the House rather than in a separate committee room; appeals presented, and leave to appeal sought, by petition; judgments, although nowadays delivered in printed form, referred to as 'speeches'; and the possibility (tightly circumscribed in recent years by self-restraining convention)[43] of serving Law Lords contributing to legislative debate or chairing parliamentary committees such as those on consolidation Bills and on EU legal questions.

The status of the Appellate and Appeal Committees and the conduct of judicial business are regulated by the Standing Orders of the House of Lords, as explained in the bible of parliamentary practice, *Erskine May*.[44] The officials in the Judicial Office are staff of Parliament, not civil servants in the Courts Service Agency of the Department for Constitutional Affairs, like those in the Civil Appeals Office which supports the work of the Court of Appeal. All this will change with the advent of the Supreme Court and the exodus of the Law Lords from the Palace of Westminster. The reviews conducted by Lord Woolf and Sir Jeffery Bowman that had such a major impact on the Court of Appeal, were not directly concerned with the House of Lords. However, they have certainly impacted on the judicial work of the House, which has, in reviewing its procedures, taken on board some of the recommendations, such as simplification of language and employing some of the new terminology used in the courts below.

One significant aspect of this is that the relationship between a major intermediate appellate court and the top court has straddled an interface between the main body of the legal system and a function that originated and developed within Parliament. Appeals flow out of one world into

---

[41] Joint Committee on the House of Lords Reform, *First Report*, HL 17, HC 171, 2002-03; this view was reiterated in the Committee's *Second Report*, HL 97, HC 668, 2002-03.

[42] But see the concerns expressed by Masterman, above n 37.

[43] See *Hansard*, HL Deb, 22 June 2000, cols 419-20.

[44] See Sir William McKay *et al* (eds), *Erskine May's Treatise on the Law, Privileges, Proceedings and Usage of Parliament*, 23rd edn (London, LexisNexis, 2004) pp 69-73.

another, with its own culture and its own conventions. At the level of the judiciary this hardly matters. Lords Justices and Law Lords are part of the same professional fraternity (and, to a small extent in recent years, sorority[45]) of the Inns of Court, where the wheels of justice are routinely, and often convivially, oiled. Appointment as a Law Lord is, to all intents and purposes, a straightforward promotion from one level of the judicial hierarchy to the next (although such appointments are, for the time being, outside the remit of the Commission for Judicial Appointments). Masters of the Rolls, who preside over the Civil Division of the Court of Appeal, sit from time to time as Law Lords, in the House of Lords. Very occasionally, a Law Lord (usually a retired Lord of Appeal) may venture across to the Strand to sit in the Court of Appeal. And, of course, as a matter of professional practice, the judges in the Court of Appeal routinely read the judgments handed down in the House of Lords, and vice versa. So, the cross-flow of legal ideas between judges at all levels happens formally and informally, and as a matter of course.

But the administration of the Court of Appeal and that of the House of Lords—in part because of the physical distance involved, in part because of the constitutional separation already mentioned—takes place, for the most part, in separate compartments. However, every so often, dialogue takes place. If, for instance, a large backlog of cases has built up in the Court of Appeal, pending the outcome of a crucial appeal in the House of Lords, then there may be a polite enquiry from the former to the latter about the possibility of expediting the hearing in the Lords. But such contact is neither frequent nor routine. This is one of many features of the relationship between the two courts that may be expected to change with the transfer of the judicial functions of the House of Lords to the new Supreme Court. The latter will be embedded in the mainstream of the judicial system, under the auspices of the Department for Constitutional Affairs. Eventually, all memories of the parliamentary status and trappings of the final appeal will fade into the footnotes of constitutional history.

But still the big question remains unasked—and unanswered. Whether the final appeal lies to the House of Lords or to a Supreme Court, is it really necessary to retain it at all? And if there are to be two appeals, why not three, or even more? In *Final Appeal*, we argued strongly for retention of the judicial functions of the House of Lords, and we remain of that opinion—perhaps more firmly so, given that the House of Lords has become the predominant final court of appeal in the crucial field of public law—a role that will be an important part of the jurisprudential inheritance of the

---

[45] This is a very recent phenomenon. At the time of writing, the 12 Lords of Appeal in Ordinary include one woman, Lady Hale of Richmond (appointed in 2004); the 37 Lords Justices include three women, Dame Mary Arden (appointed in 2000), Dame Janet Smith (2002), and Dame Heather Hallett (2005).

new Supreme Court. However, these questions deserve to be asked from time to time—and further research needs to be done to address them.

Meanwhile, if our assessment is correct, the Court of Appeal is now, even more firmly, the final court for the resolution of disputes in the field of civil litigation. In short, there are, to all intents and purposes, two final courts of appeal—finality in two streams of dispute resolution.

11

Reversal by the Lords: Polanski, Porter, Roma, and Begum

I am startled, even a little dismayed, at the suggestion and the acceptance by the Court of Appeal majority that the deeply-rooted tradition [against the use of torture] and an international obligation solemnly and explicitly undertaken can be overridden by a statute and a procedural rule which makes no mention of torture at all.[1]

THIS CHAPTER OFFERS critiques of four important, high profile cases, in each of which a decision of the Court of Appeal was reversed by the House of Lords. They are each, in their own way, instructive in assisting an evaluation of the purpose and need for a two-tier appellate system of courts. Not only can the Appellate Committee of the House of Lords (soon to be the UK Supreme Court) pay more detailed attention to the arguments presented by the parties before them and provide expansive treatment in five separate judgments, it can also usefully develop the law in a manner that enhances legal and social policy, as well as incidentally correcting the errors of the intermediate appeal court. Had these cases stopped at the Court of Appeal level, the consequences would have been a stultification, even ossification, in important segments of the law.

It is significant, moreover, that all these landmark cases were in the field of public law—a point to which we will return in our final chapter.

POLANSKI V VANITY FAIR

The late Professor Sir Rupert Cross in his classic work on *Evidence* wrote that 'perhaps the most important feature of an English trial, civil or criminal, is its "orality",'[2] meaning that the process of eliciting evidence from a witness was through the spoken form of language. Verbal communication could be effected, until modern times, only by the physical presence of the

---

[1] Lord Bingham of Cornhill, in *A and others v Secretary of State for the Home Department* [2005] UKHL 71, para 51.

[2] Sir Rupert Cross, *Evidence*, 4th edn (London, Butterworths, 1974) p 202.

witness giving his or her testimony in the face of the court. But modern technology has rendered it feasible for the witness to give oral testimony without being physically present in the courtroom—that is, through remote control by video conference link (VCF). Rule 32.3 of the Civil Procedure Rules—probably in declaration of the common law—now provides that 'the court may allow a witness to give evidence through a video link or by other means.'

In *Polanski v Condé Nast Publications Ltd*,[3] the Court of Appeal reversed the judge's order directing that Mr Polanski could give his evidence from a hotel in Paris (where he has lived since 1978, after leaving the United States to avoid incarceration for conviction in a Californian court for unlawful sexual intercourse with a girl of 13). The Court of Appeal considered that Mr Polanski's flight from justice disentitled him to the alternative procedure allowed under the law. If he wished to litigate a libel suit in England against the publisher of *Vanity Fair*, he had to present himself in the court of trial in accordance with the normal rule, and the publisher could take advantage of the claimant failing to give evidence to protect his reputation.

By a majority of three to two, the House of Lords allowed Mr Polanski's appeal. In the lead judgment, Lord Nicholls of Birkenhead emphatically ruled that 'seeking a VCF order is not seeking an indulgence.' Although extradition treaties were to be treated with mutuality, and therefore akin to a crime committed in the requested country (which England could be, if Mr Polanski came to this country), nevertheless fugitives from justice are not precluded from enforcing their rights through the courts of this country. The fugitive from justice is no outlaw; our law knows of no principle of fugitive disentitlement. While use of the VCF is a departure from the norm, it is positively sanctioned by the Civil Procedure Rules without any indication of primacy for the physical presence of the witness. Perhaps the most compelling norm for acceding to Mr Polanski's desire not to expose himself to extradition proceedings in England is that it would not affect one iota his evasion of US justice. French law has effectively protected him for nearly 30 years.

The flaw in the Court of Appeal's approach was to feel bound, on the ground of public policy, to intervene in litigation in the area of private law. As between the parties to the action, the court was perfectly entitled to make the VCF order as being a sensible alternative method of deciding the mode of communication between the parties. So long as the applicant for VCF was not achieving a forensic advantage over his opponent, there should be no bar to a procedure which provides a convenient, cost-saving device. So long as equality of arms is maintained, and the technical equipment of the VCF is up to standard, no conceivable reason can be advanced for denying the advance of modern technology.

[3] [2005] UKHL 10.

Both the Court of Appeal and the minority in the Lords—in particular, Lord Carswell—placed some reliance on paragraph 2 of the VCF guidance set out in Annex 3 to CPR Practice Direction 32, *Written Evidence*. After setting out the advantages of VCF, it is stated:

> It is, however, inevitably not as ideal as having the witness physically present in court. Its convenience should not therefore be allowed to dictate its use ... In particular, it needs to be recognised that the degree of control a court can exercise over a witness at the remote site is or may be more limited than it can exercise over a witness physically before it.

Such a view was endorsed by Simon Brown LJ (now Lord Brown of Eaton-under-Heywood) in the Court of Appeal, that 'VCF evidence is less ideal even than usual in a case like this'—inferring, one supposes, that a libel action is more conducive to the physical appearance of the claimant seeking to maintain his or her good reputation.

What evidence is there for preferring a testimony given in the face of the court to one which is relayed via a television screen? No doubt, as a result of experience of the dominant mode of taking evidence, the legal profession vastly adheres to what is familiar. But, putting aside such traditional attitudes, one should question the whole notion of 'orality' to which English law is historically committed.

Orality is the quality of language spoken or verbally communicated. It does not necessarily involve the speaker's presence. In the litigious process, the audience is the judge and the legal representatives of the parties. The latter may or may not see an advantage in the physical presence of the witness, but as between the rival disputants there should be no disturbance of equal treatment of the witnesses; they will speak their words and be tested in cross-examination. Assessment of the credibility of the witness, which may flow from the manner in which he or she comports himself or herself, is more relevant to the task of the decision-maker than to that of the advocates.

There is much loose talk about the judge's need to 'see the whites of the witness's eyes' in order to gain the best picture of the testimony. If that is true (and, as we have remarked in chapter 2, it is questionable whether the sight of the witness enhances or distracts from the spoken words) the judge is often subjected to submissions which depend on how the witness gave his or her evidence, often referred to as 'demeanour'. But justice is truly blind, in the sense that it is not to be deflected from judging on the written or spoken word. How else could it be tolerated that a blind person should sit in the seat of justice? Sir John Fielding (the half-brother of Henry Fielding), a stipendiary magistrate at Bow Street, administered justice in that court without sight of accused or witnesses. It is claimed that he knew all of the 2,000 or so rogues who plagued the citizens of eighteenth-century London. In recent times, the Lord Chancellor sanctioned the appointment of lay magistrates who are blind.

Whatever may be the virtues of witnesses appearing in person in the courtroom, VFC replicates the existing procedure, enhanced by modern technology. And the new code of civil procedure acknowledges as much. The annex to the practice direction is not a part of the new rule; it merely expresses an unsubstantiated opinion of a method of procedure. The courts would do well to validate such an opinion, or at least treat it with suitable caution.

Neither the intermediate nor the final court of appeal can be an ideal forum for putting assertions of practice and procedure to the test. But if we are to make advances in court procedures, the civil procedure code needs to be informed of the values of alternative procedures. In any event, evidence from witnesses in the witness box does not provide an 'ideal' form of procedure; it merely reflects a long-standing practice in English courts, although increasingly resort is had to written materials. Judicial review itself is conducted almost exclusively by written statements.

The House of Lords in Polanski's case undoubtedly provided the right answer to an issue that was less problematical than the Court of Appeal judges foresaw. It is only to be regretted that the existence of modern technology was not given a more emphatic welcome to improve and assist the process of litigation in a world ever more conscious of cost and efficiency in ensuring justice.

APPEAL AND AUDIT—THE DAME SHIRLEY PORTER CASE[4]

The second in our survey of four high profile cases is one in which members of a local authority in London were found to have perverted the authority's housing policies to secure an electoral advantage for the majority party. The story was dubbed the 'homes for votes' scandal by the newspapers. The central figures in it were the wealthy and flamboyant Thatcherite politician, Dame Shirley Porter, Conservative leader of Westminster City Council, and a local government auditor, John Magill. Of particular relevance to the present study is the divergence of views between the majority of the Court of Appeal and a unanimous House of Lords. The case also illustrates some wider characteristics of the appellate process itself.

The story began in the early part of 1986, the high summer of the Thatcher era, at which time Westminster City Council consisted of 60 elected councillors representing 23 wards, with the Conservative Party holding an overall majority of 26 seats. Shirley Porter had been leader of

---

[4] Much of the following account is adapted from an article by Gavin Drewry, 'The Complementarity of Audit and Judicial Review: the "Homes for Votes" scandal in the UK', published in (2005) 71(3) *International Review of Administrative Sciences* 375–89. For the general background, see A Hosken, *Nothing Like a Dame: The Scandals of Shirley Porter* (London, Granta, 2006).

the council since 1983, and was chair of several council committees. Local elections held in May 1986 had reduced the majority of 26 to four seats, and the discomfited leaders of the Conservative majority group set about devising a strategy to ensure that the party improved its position in the next elections, scheduled for 1990.

The council had already adopted a policy of 'designated sales', designed to reduce the authority's tenanted housing stock, whereby in selected blocks of council flats, when a flat fell vacant it would be offered for sale at a discount to an approved applicant, with the intention that, in due course, the block concerned would become fully owner-occupied. The Conservative leadership of the local authority now decided to adapt this policy so as to increase the party's support in eight 'key wards' with marginal majorities. This policy of targeted gentrification for party political advantage was euphemistically known as 'building stable communities'. An unkind observer might have been forgiven for preferring the more pejorative US term, 'gerrymandering'.

It was not long before warnings about the legality of the new policy, suggesting that it might conflict with the authority's statutory obligations to find accommodation for homeless people, and that the political motives behind it might be open to challenge, began to be heard. The council's own in-house legal adviser, a city solicitor, warned Dame Shirley that 'it is fundamental that the arguments in favour of selling be soundly based and properly argued. Anything which smacks of political machinations will be viewed with great suspicion by the courts.' He confirmed that careful arguments in support of the policy would be needed to avoid the risk of successful judicial review and/or surcharge.[5] The director of housing also warned that the scale of designation proposed might prevent the council from meeting its statutory obligations to homeless households. But Dame Shirley made it quite clear that the policy was already decided and that the only advice she required was on how it was to be achieved, not alternative options. She took the same pre-emptively dismissive line with consultants who had been appointed by the council to examine the designated sales policy, but whose findings offered no support for it.

Counsel's opinion confirmed that designated sales could not legally be confined to marginal wards. On the basis of this advice, the council decided to extend the designated sales across the whole of the City of Westminster, on a scale that would produce the desired number of sales in the eight marginal wards. This meant designating 500 sales in total per annum from 9,360 designated properties, 40 per cent of its total housing stock. The original, pre-1987 version of the scheme, not tainted by electoral

---

[5] The surcharge—requiring local councillors and officers to reimburse their council for expenditure unlawfully incurred—was subsequently abolished by s 90 of the Local Government Act 2000.

manipulation, had yielded just 10–20 sales per annum from 300 designated properties. The magnitude of this development would inevitably have a significant impact upon the council's capacity to meet its statutory obligations towards the homeless, and would surely need a lot of explaining if challenged by an auditor or made subject to judicial review. And the fact that in the 'key' wards 74 per cent of eligible properties were designated, compared with only 28 per cent in the other wards, would also be hard to explain.

Dame Shirley Porter and her Conservative colleagues, assisted by senior officers, took steps to monitor the progress of their policy in the eight key wards, but the reports presented to other members of the council and its committees, and information released into the public domain, sought to conceal the selectivity of the designations and the underlying political motives involved. Suspicious Opposition councillors sought explanations for the selective monitoring of key wards, but received no answers. Attempts were made to find a rationale—other than their political marginality—for the focus on the eight wards. But none could be found.

In October 1989, following representations from leading Opposition councillors and local electors, the independent local auditor, John Magill—working under the auspices of the Audit Commission, and subject to the Commission's professional guidelines—began his painstaking investigation into allegations of bad faith and financial malpractice. In January 1994, Mr Magill issued notices of his provisional findings to 10 individuals, to the objectors, and to the Council. He also, controversially and probably unwisely, held a televised press conference to announce his findings, using language later described by the Divisional Court as 'florid'. This featured prominently on TV news bulletins and attracted huge journalistic attention, prompting Dame Shirley and others to complain to the Audit Commission, questioning the auditor's impartiality (having given so much publicity to his provisional findings, would he not now find it difficult to depart from those findings in the light of subsequent evidence?) and requesting his replacement. The Commission refused this request and, after further meetings and hearings, Mr Magill rejected applications that he should disqualify himself.

Eventually, in May 1996, after nearly seven years of sifting through the voluminous records (his task was not made easier by the fact that some significant papers had apparently been shredded) the auditor finally came to his decision. His task was to issue a certificate under section 20 of the Local Government Finance Act 1982, quantifying the loss caused by the 'wilful misconduct' of Shirley Porter (now Dame Shirley) and those of her colleagues who were implicated in the 'homes for votes' policy.

He issued surcharge certificates in the sum of £31.677 million against Dame Shirley, against the deputy leader of the council, and against four others (including two non-elected officers, the director of housing and the managing director of the council). The bulk of the sum certified was the amount adjudged to have been lost by the council as a result of the decision of the Housing Committee in July 1987 to extend the programme of designated sales, including the losses arising from the sale of properties at a discount on their true market value. The auditor's final report ran to some 2,000 pages. He had conducted 135 interviews and a hearing lasting 32 days. The notes and transcripts of his interviews filled 14 lever-arch files containing 10,000 pages. This material was to be both the raw material and the substantive basis for the appeals that followed.

The court hearings in this case were by way of a *statutory appeal* from the auditor's decision, as provided by section 20(3) of the Local Government Finance Act 1982. So this was not a *judicial review*, which is the more familiar route by which an administrative law dispute reaches the courts. There were some important procedural differences between a judicial review and an appeal under the 1982 Act: in particular, the former required the leave of the court while an appeal of the latter kind did not. Moreover, in this case the form of appeal provided for a complete rehearing of the *merits* of the auditor's adjudication and for the courts, if they saw fit, to substitute their own decision for that of the auditor. This illustrates another important distinction between this type of appeal and a judicial review, since the latter—much more in keeping with the English appellate tradition—is concerned entirely with issues of law.

The case went on appeal against the auditor's certificate to a three-judge Queen's Bench Divisional Court (the predecessor of what is now the Administrative Court). This was a rehearing in the full sense of that word: the court sat for 23 days, received a huge volume of written evidence and submissions, and heard evidence from Dame Shirley Porter and the deputy leader—before unanimously dismissing their appeals on 19 December 1997. However, it did reduce the sum certified slightly, and it allowed the appeals by the other respondents, who in consequence played no part in the subsequent proceedings. (The favourable treatment of these other appellants gave rise to claims by Dame Shirley and her deputy that the Divisional Court had been inconsistent, but although this contention troubled the judges of the Court of Appeal it was eventually dismissed by the House of Lords.)

Dame Shirley and her deputy now appealed to the Court of Appeal, where they were successful, but with one judge dissenting. One important issue on which the two judges who formed the majority in the Court of Appeal disagreed with the auditor and with the court below concerned the issue of electoral advantage. Kennedy LJ thought it 'unreal' to suggest that any councillor who allows the possibility of electoral advantage to cross his mind before he decides upon a course of action is guilty of misconduct, given that most decisions in local and in national government 'carry an electoral price tag.' Schiemann LJ said:

> It is legitimate for councillors to desire that their party should win the next election. Our political system works on the basis that that they desire that because they think that the policies to which their party is wedded are in the public interest and will require years to be achieved. There is nothing disgraceful or unlawful in councillors having that desire. For this court to hold otherwise would be to depart from our theory of democracy and current reality.

However, the dissenting judge, Walker LJ (now Lord Walker of Gestingthorpe), found that 'the most influential members of the Conservative group on the city council, led by Dame Shirley and Mr Weeks, had electoral advantage as the overriding objective in formulating their housing policy, securing its adoption by the council, and implementing it with high priority given to the marginal wards.' He also took a strong line in asserting a presumption, surely central to any appellate system, that the decision of a court *a quo* should stand unless there are substantial grounds for holding to the contrary. In this case he could see no reason why the Court of Appeal, which had not heard witnesses, should depart from the Divisional Court's findings, which were confirmed by ample documentary evidence.

The Court of Appeal then gave leave to the auditor to appeal to the House of Lords, which agreed with Walker LJ, unanimously reversed the Court of Appeal, and restored the judgment of the Divisional Court in favour of the auditor. The respondents, relying on the majority judgments below, argued that councillors could not be expected to be oblivious to party political advantage and that their actions could not be deemed unlawful provided that they were not taken purely for partisan reasons. They also argued that Mr Magill's media statements in January 1994 had infringed the councillors' right to an unbiased judge. In addition, the basis on which the quantum of surcharge had been calculated was contested.

The composite conclusions of the House of Lords (four of the five Law Lords gave substantive judgments) on these main points were, in summary, as follows:

(1) Although the council did have statutory authority to dispose of property for proper housing objectives, it could not use that power to promote the advantage of a political party on the council. The latter had been the motive behind the designation policy. The respondents had both known that they were acting unlawfully and there had been (in the words of Lord Bingham) 'a deliberate, blatant and dishonest abuse of public power.' Lord Scott of Foscote called it 'corruption'—see below.

(2) The auditor had made an error of judgment in deciding to hold a press conference—it was an 'exercise in self promotion' in which he

should not have indulged. However, there was nothing in the words
he used to indicate any real possibility that he was biased.

(3) The basis on which the auditor had calculated the quantum had been correct.
A surcharge was not a punishment; it was intended to put the body that had
suffered loss or deficiency through wilful misconduct in the same position that it
would have been in had the misconduct not taken place.

As Lord Scott of Foscote pointed out, a case like this is essentially about a
special kind of political corruption:

> The corruption was not money corruption. No one took a bribe. No one sought
> or received money for political favours. But there are other forms of corruption,
> often less easily detectable and therefore more insidious. Gerrymandering, the
> manipulation of constituency boundaries for party political advantage, is a clear
> form of political corruption. So, too, would be any misuse of political powers,
> intended for use in the general public interest but used instead for party political
> advantage. Who can doubt that the selective use of municipal powers in order
> to obtain party political advantage represents political corruption? Political cor-
> ruption, if unchecked, engenders cynicism about elections, about politicians and
> their motives and damages the reputation of democratic government ... When
> detected and exposed it must be expected, or at least it must be hoped, that
> political corruption will receive its just deserts at the polls. Detection and expo-
> sure is, however, often difficult and, where it happens, is usually attributable to
> determined efforts by political opponents or by investigative journalists or by
> both in tandem.

Lord Scott went on to highlight the special role of the auditor, who was,
of course, the appellant at the House of Lords stage of the proceedings.
But the political element was crucial. The auditor's investigation gained
impetus from the concerns of members of the minority group in the local
authority (and indeed from some members of the majority group, who
wanted to distance themselves from the damaging actions of their leaders);
transparency, which is a prerequisite of political accountability, counts for
little if public meetings are pre-empted by the machinations of party cabals
meeting behind closed doors, and if documentation intended for public
consumption is inaccurate or misleading. The case gave rise to inter-party
sniping at a national level. And everyone concerned—accusers and accused,
auditors and judges—operated under the constant spotlight of media and
parliamentary attention.

The House of Lords considered the (retrospective) implications of the
Human Rights Act 1998, incorporating the European Convention on
Human Rights into UK domestic law—which had come into effect only as
recently as October 2000. It concluded that the respondents' Convention
rights had not been breached; in particular, the fairness of the audit process,
under Article 6, was protected by the fact that there was a statutory right
to an appellate rehearing by the Divisional Court. A subsequent attempt by

Dame Shirley to bring the case before the European Court of Human Rights was summarily rejected in April 2003, as 'manifestly ill-founded'. The surcharge was 'not disproportionate to losses sustained by local taxpayers'; the audit process satisfied the ECHR's requirements of independence and impartiality; and the decision of the UK courts did not interfere with Dame Shirley's right to hold political opinions.

The subject-matter of this case is as much of interest to political commentators as its public law content is interesting to observers of the legal process. And there are particular points of interest to analysts of the numerous ramifications of the appellate process. Apart from the substantive legal disagreements among the judges—reversal of a unanimous Divisional Court by a divided Court of Appeal, which was reversed in turn by a unanimous House of Lords—one important aspect is the juxtaposition of an audit with an appellate process that is firmly grounded in the inquisitorial traditions of the common law.

The Porter saga highlights both the complementarity and the duplication involved in proceeding from an essentially *inquisitorial* audit process that has the capacity to investigate a complex set of events in very great depth to a judicial process that is essentially *adversarial* in character. The judicial process, set within a political culture that attaches great importance to judicial independence and the rule of law, offers an accountability mechanism of the highest constitutional authority. The iterative and hierarchical nature of appeal can take an important case to even higher levels of judicial authority, refining the legal issues along the way—albeit with mounting costs in time and money.

In 2004, Westminster City Council, having managed (with great difficulty and at great expense) to locate and freeze substantial overseas financial holdings controlled by Dame Shirley and her family, negotiated a settlement with her in the sum of £12.3 million. This was far less than the final sum owed, estimated at about £42 million including interest, but it was apparently felt by the council that the risks and high costs of overseas litigation outweighed the speculative benefits of continuing to pursue the entire outstanding sum. Reaching this conclusion had taken the best part of 15 years since the auditor began his investigations.

On its own, an adversarial judicial process has serious limitations: it is activated by an inter-party dispute, and tends therefore to treat multidimensional problems in a two-dimensional or 'bi-polar' way.[6] Despite the concentration of public law litigation in a Divisional Court (now the Administrative Court), judges cannot possibly have the technical expertise of a specialist auditor. And—even when, as was the case here, they are empowered to requisition documents and summon witnesses to a full appeal

---

[6] See Gavin Drewry, 'Public–Private Partnerships: Rethinking the Boundary between Public and Private Law' in Stephen P Osborne (ed), *Public–Private Partnerships: Theory and Practice in International Perspective* (London, Routledge, 2000) p 66.

rehearing (something that is not permitted in judicial review proceedings)—
they simply do not have the time to do the kind of digging that an auditor
can do. Many cases that involve malpractice and fraud are exceedingly
complex, and are often beyond the capacity of a court to handle effectively
on its own.

THE ROMA AT PRAGUE AIRPORT

This test case of major jurisprudential significance came before the Court of
Appeal in May 2003. In form, it was an application for judicial review of an
unusual and controversial scheme to extend the scope and place of operation of UK immigration officers to Prague Airport in the Czech Republic.
As is well known, the flow of asylum seekers to the United Kingdom has
increased in recent years, although more recently the trend has gone into
reverse.

The paradox at the heart of the Refugee Convention of 1951 is that the
signatory states are bound not to return to their home states those who would
face a real risk of persecution for a ground specified in that Convention.
But there is no obligation on such states to admit those who wish to claim
the protection of the Convention in order that they might pursue a claim
to asylum. Successive governments have sought to control what is seen as
a problem (by the public, if not by politicians) by imposing a visa regime
upon those states whence most asylum seekers originate. An admission by
an individual that he or she wishes to seek asylum would be met by a refusal
of a visa. Those satisfying the visa officer at a British post abroad that they
wished to enter for a visit would be granted a visa, so long as that officer
was persuaded that the real object of travelling to the United Kingdom was
not for asylum purposes. Carriers transporting people who required a visa,
but who did not possess one, would be fined. In short, asylum seekers who
gain entry to the United Kingdom may pursue their asylum claims. Those
who do not succeed in gaining entry cannot pursue such claims.

There are political difficulties in imposing a visa regime on friendly governments. The states of Eastern Europe fell into this category shortly after
communism in the former Soviet Union and elsewhere in Europe collapsed.
In 1999 the UK Parliament authorised the executive to implement a scheme
enabling the Immigration Rules to operate extra-territorially, in addition to
authorising ports of entry. In this manner, intending asylum seekers would
be refused entry by immigration officers working at overseas ports of
embarkation. They would not be able to travel to the United Kingdom and
would not be able to claim asylum on, or after, entry.

One such scheme was introduced in the Czech Republic in 2001. Pre-
entry immigration controls were set up at Prague Airport. The object was to
stem the flow of asylum seekers from that country. It was common ground

that the vast majority, if not the entirety, of asylum seekers from the Czech Republic were of Romani ethnic origin (Roma). As part of the negotiations for the entry of Eastern European states to the European Union, applicant governments were urged, encouraged, and even required to take serious steps to improve the social and economic circumstances of their Roma citizens. There is no doubt that they faced discrimination (and often worse) throughout Eastern Europe.

The scheme was successful. In the three weeks before the scheme began, the number of asylum claims made at UK ports of entry from the Czech Republic fell from over 200 to 20. Over 110 intending travellers (the number was probably higher if dependants are included) presented themselves. The pre-clearance procedure at Prague Airport operated unpredictably, but sufficiently often to deter intending asylum seekers.

The challenge to the scheme was made on two grounds. First, it was said that it was a breach of the obligations of the United Kingdom under the 1951 Convention. The argument was that states party to the Convention are not permitted to take active steps to impede would-be claimants to asylum from leaving their home state. Secondly, it was said to constitute direct racial discrimination against Czech Roma, should they wish to come to the United Kingdom for a purpose permitted under the Immigration Rules. A variation or development of this argument was that claiming asylum is a purpose recognised and permitted under the Immigration Rules, so Czech Roma could not be excluded on the grounds that they intended to seek asylum. The claim was brought by the European Roma Rights Centre and by six Roma who were refused entry at Prague Airport. Five of the Roma intended to claim asylum in the United Kingdom, one claimed entry for another purpose.

The application failed before Burton J (a judge greatly experienced in employment law by virtue of his presidency of the Employment Appeal Tribunal), who gave permission to appeal to the Court of Appeal on grounds other than discrimination; the Court itself gave permission to appeal on the discrimination ground. The claim on the Convention ground was supported by the UNHCR, which conceded that there was no explicit requirement in the Convention to this effect, but that it was implicit in the scheme and within customary international law. Simon Brown LJ reasoned that the right claimed by the appellants was not recognised in customary international law and was not implicit in the Convention. A refugee and a person seeking asylum had to be outside his or her home state. A number of domestic and foreign cases were cited in support of this proposition. In short, the government was entitled to take steps to prevent the arrival of asylum seekers. Moreover, there was no obligation to admit such persons so as to facilitate a claim to asylum. The Prague operation was as lawful as the imposition of visa requirements. This ground of decision was supported by Mantell and Laws LJJ, as was the argument based on the

Immigration Rules. This failed because the Court unanimously held that the rules gave no right of entry for the purposes of claiming asylum.

The Court was, however, sharply divided on the discrimination issue. The relevant legislation was intended to make a firm public statement after the Macpherson report on the death of Stephen Lawrence, that discrimination by public bodies will be as unlawful as that by private employers. After setting out the complex statutory framework, Simon Brown LJ explained that the argument advanced was that Roma seeking entry to the United Kingdom for a purpose other than claiming asylum, for example as visitors, were subjected to longer and more intrusive questioning than non-Roma. But, as discrimination between individuals on the grounds of ethnicity and nationality is inherent in the operation of immigration control, certain exceptions were incorporated in the legislation. The Home Secretary contended that the scheme was not discriminatory, and that, as was accepted, any exception that might have covered the Prague scheme was not in fact relied upon in the proceedings.

The applicants argued that, very starkly, Roma applicants for entry for reasons other than to claim asylum were discriminated against in two ways. First, they were subjected to longer and more intrusive questioning than were other non-Roma individuals. Secondly, the decision-making was such that Roma were refused whereas non-Roma were not. The evidence was that the refusal figures for non-Roma were very low (0.2 per cent) yet those for persons apparently Roma (Roma being for the most part identifiable as such) the figure was 87 per cent.

The existing English jurisprudence about discrimination had mostly been built up in employment cases, where it is unusual to find direct evidence of discrimination. Inferences have to be drawn from the facts. If an individual can show that he or she has been less favourably treated than comparable individuals from a different racial group, the onus shifts to the employer to demonstrate that no discrimination has occurred. It is clearly established that, if discrimination has occurred, motive is irrelevant. It is likewise true that unconscious attitudes and stereotypical assumptions are as objectionable as deliberate discrimination.

At first instance, Burton J found that the Prague scheme was not discriminatory. His findings of fact, and the attack upon them in the Court of Appeal, raised issues of great statistical importance. The conclusion on the evidence, both below and before the Court of Appeal, needs to be read with a close eye to statistical probabilities and it need not be given further attention here. The issue that must be examined is the one identified as central in the Court of Appeal. Given that the overwhelming majority of applicants for asylum from the Czech Republic were Roma, were immigration officers working at Prague Airport acting unlawfully in bringing a greater degree of scepticism to bear on Roma applicants than on other Czech nationals? The Court of Appeal did not make separate findings of fact about the way in which immigration officers in Prague carried out their work. It acted on the findings of the judge at first instance, that the officers had treated all would-be passengers fairly and had done their best not to discriminate. But the immigration officers tended to subject Roma to more extensive questioning than any other passengers, because the Roma had a much greater incentive to claim asylum in the United Kingdom. Was this unlawful racial discrimination?

Simon Brown LJ justifiably found this issue very difficult. At first he thought that, as the policy of excluding prospective asylum seekers from travelling was lawful, it was logical to say that the very group most likely to claim asylum, if admitted, had to be questioned more intrusively than others not of that group. But the applicants had an answer to this point. First, if the scheme had to depend on differential questioning of one group from another, it involved unlawful discrimination. In brief, the established principles of not stereotyping and the irrelevance of motive had been infringed.

After reviewing some applicable case law, Simon Brown LJ accepted that the impermissibility of stereotyping and the irrelevance of motive were powerfully raised by the facts. If asked whether the applicants had been treated less favourably on racial grounds, his initial view was that they had made out their case. But on reflection he moved away from that conclusion. Individuals had to be treated individually. If necessary, that might mean they had to face long questioning. A policy of extending immigration controls to an extra-territorial base in Prague must necessarily focus on those most likely to seek entry for a permitted purpose, but then make an application for asylum. Roma were not refused at Prague Airport because they were Roma, but because an immigration officer, acting in accordance with a mandate, did not accept that they would not claim asylum on arrival in the UK. No assumptions were being made about the characteristics of individual Roma. Questioning would reveal the true reason for travelling.

The process of questioning did not involve stereotyping. Roma were undoubtedly disadvantaged citizens in the Czech Republic. Because of such disadvantage they might be more likely to claim asylum than if they were Czech nationals who were not Roma. A requirement was applied to them which was similarly applied to non-Roma—would they be likely to claim asylum in the United Kingdom? Fewer Roma would be able to comply with that requirement. But the requirement was not thereby impermissible.

Laws LJ took a very different view. (On the issues under the Refugee Convention he agreed with Simon Brown LJ.) On the discrimination issue, he had no difficulty in holding that the different treatment of Roma (longer and more intensive questioning) constituted less favourable treatment. Was it a policy carried out on racial grounds? He gave the example of an immigration officer at Prague Airport being approached by Czech nationals wishing to visit London for a short period. The officer identifies one by appearance as an ethnic Roma, and the other as not. He questions the Roma more intensively. Because Roma are known to have a greater propensity for claiming asylum than the other, this is racial discrimination, even though it is carried out for the purpose of avoiding the admittance of those more likely to claim asylum than those not in that category. The wrong made unlawful by the legislation was thus made out.

How was it that the two Lords Justices, having had the same experience as Treasury Counsel when practising at the Bar, were able to come to such mutually opposing views? Laws LJ founded his judgment on the application of the statute to the facts as found by the judge at first instance. Discrimination is impermissible and unlawful. There was discrimination because one group of passengers were treated less favourably than another. Simon Brown LJ, on the other hand, thought that the Roma were not treated less favourably on racial grounds. They merely found it more difficult to satisfy the questioner that they were not likely to make claims to asylum.

The difference between these two approaches is that Laws LJ concludes that the statutory test is satisfied. Simon Brown LJ concludes that it is not. Put more bluntly, the former thinks that the reality is that Roma cannot be separated from their likely propensity to claim asylum, a Roma attribute; the latter thinks that Roma can be divided into those who meet the test (unlikely to claim asylum) and those who cannot. Laws LJ applies the law as he interprets it, irrespective of the consequences. Simon Brown LJ interprets it so as to facilitate the scheme for pre-travel vetting of passengers overseas. Both conclusions were reasonable even if they were in conflict. The House of Lords were thus given two clearly and powerfully reasoned views. (Mantell LJ agreed with Simon Brown LJ; he thought that the differential questioning was justified by not being founded on racial or ethnic grounds.)

The case then passed to the House of Lords,[7] the Court of Appeal having given leave to appeal. Where there has been a powerful dissent, such a course may be taken; otherwise, as noted in the previous chapter, leave to take the case to the House of Lords is normally left to the Appeal Committee of the latter to decide. The senior Law Lord, Lord Bingham of Cornhill, gave the lead judgment. He agreed with all of the judgments in the Court of Appeal on the Refugee Convention grounds. He did not enter into the debate between Lords Justices Simon Brown and Laws. On the matters on which those two judges differed, he agreed with the speech of Lord Hope of Craighead, to which we will come shortly.

Lord Steyn identified the essential issue as why the immigration officers had treated the Roma as they did. He had no doubt that they did so because they were Roma. He referred to an academic article by Rabinder Singh QC, a specialist in human rights law.[8] He argued, rather as we have done, that Laws LJ had applied the statute as it stood and read, whereas Simon Brown

---

[7] [2004] UKHL 55.

LJ had effectively taken from, or added to both as possibilities, the words of the statute to legitimise the operation of the scheme.

Lady Hale of Richmond, the most recent appointee to the House, a former academic lawyer and a Law Commissioner, whose Harry Street Lecture in October 2004 anticipated her approach,[9] dealt with the discrimination issue at length. She identified the issue as whether Roma were treated differently because of their ethnicity or group membership, or whether it was because of their propensity to claim asylum. Given that the immigration officer identified those who had to be subjected to more intensive questioning as being Roma, that was an end of the matter.

Lord Hope agreed with both Lord Bingham and Lady Hale. He focused on some minor aspects of the argument in the House that were not central to the discrimination issue. The first was a contention that it was unlawful to refuse to grant entry clearance to anyone (for present purposes, Roma from the Czech Republic). The point is central to the manner in which the Refugee Convention is interpreted by successive UK governments. The Convention does not provide for anyone, however compelling the claim to asylum, to be admitted to the country for the purpose of making a claim to asylum. But paragraph 320 of the Immigration Rules (the detailed content of immigration control for, for example, students, family members, and visitors) provides for those individuals who seek admission for a purpose not covered by such Rules. The argument was that the Rules give primacy to the Refugee Convention and acknowledged that asylum applicants would be determined by the Secretary of State, and would not be summarily decided by an Immigration Officer at a port of entry. Therefore, the entry clearance officers stationed at Prague Airport should have permitted Roma passengers to travel to the United Kingdom where their claims to asylum would have to be determined. For that purpose, those passengers would be given temporary leave to enter.

The answer given by Lord Hope was that there is no specific provision in the Rules stating that leave to enter is to be given to persons who seek asylum. To be sure, persons in the United Kingdom are to be given asylum if they meet the criteria set out in the Refugee Convention. Passengers at Prague Airport were, necessarily, not in the United Kingdom. The appellants recognised this difficulty. They said that a provision in the Rules, stating that 'normally' entry is to be refused to those who do not qualify under a specific Rule meant that, as an immigration officer is not bound to refuse entry to passengers arriving from Prague who intended to claim asylum,

---

[8] 'Equality; the neglected virtue' [2004] EHRLR 142.

[9] The lecture, which was prepared at the time of the hearing of the *Roma* appeal, was subsequently published: Baroness Hale of Richmond, 'The Quest for Equal Treatment', *Public Law*, Autumn 2005, pp 571–85.

such passengers had to be allowed to proceed to London where they could present their asylum claims. This argument failed. There is no obligation on an immigration officer to give leave to enter to a person who wishes to claim asylum, even less any obligation on an officer stationed abroad to permit a passenger to proceed to London.

The second argument dealt with by Lord Hope was that by denying certain Roma permission to travel the Home Secretary was in breach of the obligation of good faith not to frustrate or thwart the purposes of the Refugee Convention. It was certainly a general principle of public international law but, Lord Hope said, it was not a free-standing obligation operating outside the scope and provisions expressed in an international legal instrument so as to enlarge those obligations beyond the agreement the parties to the Convention had reached. He then considered the theory of the principle of good faith. In an erudite and cogent discussion, with ample reference to academic texts, he concluded that good faith is a principle of public international law which always relates to specific behaviour; it is not itself an autonomous source of rights and obligations. It could not be understood as imposing new obligations on states party to international conventions. The Convention did not itself extend the obligation of member states beyond the generally understood scope of its provisions. None of the judgments in the Court of Appeal entered into the type of theoretical discussion that Lord Hope found essential to deal with the arguments raised by the appellants concerning internationally-founded arguments as to the legality of the acts of the Home Secretary in placing immigration officers at Prague Airport.

Lord Hope went on to consider another aspect of the international law issues that arose in the appeal. This involved considering a decision of the Supreme Court of the United States,[10] and criticism made of it by the Inter-American Commission for Human Rights. The Supreme Court had been asked to review the legality of an executive order to the US Coastguard to intercept ships in the Caribbean Sea which transported passengers from Haiti to the United States with a view to returning those ships to Haiti so that the passengers would not be able to present an asylum claim to the US authorities. The specific question which the Court had to resolve was whether it was unlawful under the Refugee Convention for the US authorities to return the passengers to Haiti without inquiring whether they were refugees under the terms of the Convention. As explained above, the principal mandatory provision in the Convention is one which prohibits the return of established refugees to the frontiers of the state in which they have a well-founded fear of persecution.

---

[10] The US Supreme Court case in question was *Sale, Acting Comr, Immigration and Naturalisation Service v Haitian Centers Council Inc* (1993) 509 US 155, and the criticism of it can be found in Report No 51/96 by the Inter-American Commission for Human Rights.

The majority in the Supreme Court had held that such an order was not unlawful. Quite simply, the prohibition in the Convention did not apply to those who were intercepted on the high seas. In the Court of Appeal, Simon Brown LJ thought that the majority decision of the Supreme Court of the United States was wrong. The argument by the appellants used in the House of Lords in this regard was, as with the argument based on 'good faith', that to intercept passengers, either on the high seas or at an airport, was to breach the Refugee Convention by forcing refugees to return to, or to remain in, the Czech Republic. As he reasoned, concerning the good faith argument, Lord Hope thought that the Refugee Convention did not bear the weight contended for by the appellants. He did not consider that the Supreme Court of the United States had erred. The Convention did not have extra-territorial effect. Its provisions could not apply to persons seeking entry, but who had not yet succeeded in doing so. Moral arguments could not prevail over the clear meaning of the text of the Convention. It did not apply to those outside the territory of a signatory state.

The approach of the House of Lords was more receptive to arguments based on broad intellectual concepts than was that of the Court of Appeal. This may be explained as a decision taken by the appellants' advocates in the Court of Appeal to limit argument to points that the Court wished to hear, or to which it appeared receptive. By the same token, the House of Lords may have indicated a willingness to receive such submissions. In any event, the Law Lords brought clarity to the law on discrimination that can only be welcomed.

BEGUM: ANOTHER APPROACH TO DISCRIMINATION AND HUMAN RIGHTS

By the time the Human Rights Act 1998 came into force in October 2000, one might have safely assumed that every member of the higher judiciary had imbibed (or should it be ingested?) the indisputable fact that incorporation into English law of the European Convention on Human Rights was designed to 'bring rights home'—in short, UK citizens could assert and enforce their fundamental rights under the Convention through the ordinary courts and tribunals of this country. No one would have expected that this new judicial tool, to give effect to established civil liberties, would be misunderstood or misapplied by the Court of Appeal, let alone appear to be heresy. Yet, surprisingly, that has been the case in at least one notable instance. The Denbigh High School case, *R (on the application of Begum by her litigation friend, Rahman) v Head Teacher and Governors of Denbigh High School, the Secretary of State for Education and Skills intervening*[11] concerned the dress prescribed for female pupils of the Muslim faith attending secondary education.

The case was brought by a Muslim female pupil at a maintained second-ary community school in Luton, Bedfordshire, which took pupils of both sexes aged 11–16. The applicant, Shabina Begum, was now 17. The school is multicultural in its student population. There were 21 different ethnic groups and 10 religious groupings represented. About 80 per cent of its pupils were Muslim, the number having fallen from 90 per cent in 1993. The school was open to children of all religious faiths and of none. The high percentage of Muslims meant that the school was exempt from the ordi-nary duty of maintained schools to secure an act of daily worship, wholly or mainly of a broadly Christian character. The head teacher of the school was herself a Bengali Muslim. It was acknowledged that she had converted an under-performing school into one that was performing well above the local and national average.

The issue was the wearing of the school uniform by female pupils. In addition to the regulation jumper, skirt, tie, socks, and shoes—none of which was in issue in the case—girls were permitted to wear a skirt, trou-sers or a shalwar kameeze (trousers and tunic). Girls were also allowed to wear headscarves, so long as they met specific requirements. The policy was painstakingly formulated by the school to satisfy the religious requirement for Muslim girls to wear modest dress. Shabina Begum, having complied with the dress code for two years, asserted (mainly through her brother, the litigation friend) that, as soon as she started to menstruate, the shal-war kameeze no longer complied with the requirement of her religion. She insisted that she should be allowed to wear the even more modest garb of a full-length dress which effectively conceals the shape of a woman's arms and legs. She believed that the Islamic Sharia required women over the age of 13 to cover their bodies completely, apart from their face and hands. Nothing other than the jilbab would meet the dress requirements for a Muslim woman.

In September 2002 she presented herself at school for the first time wearing a jilbab. She was told that she should comply with the policy that did not allow the wearing of the jilbab. She declined to do so; hence she failed to attend the school until an alternative school in the area (less geo-graphically convenient) was found. She persisted nonetheless in seeking a declaration that her Convention rights had been violated. Bennett J rejected her challenge; the Court of Appeal reversed the judge, whose decision was reinstated by the House of Lords. On agreed facts, the Law Lords considered that the school was fully justified in framing and insisting upon its policy about school uniform. As Lord Bingham put it, the school governors 'had taken immense pains to devise a uniform policy which respected Muslim beliefs but did so in an inclusive, non-threatening and uncompetitive way.

[11] [2006] UKHL 1.

The rules laid down were as far from being mindless or uniform rules could ever be.' He added, for good measure, that it would be 'irresponsible of any court, lacking the experience, background and detailed knowledge of the head teacher, staff and governors to overrule their judgement in a matter as sensitive as this [the qualified right of the individual to manifest his or her religion or belief under Article 9 of the European Convention on Human Rights].' What then prompted the Court of Appeal to contemplate overruling the school's decision?

Brooke LJ, while disavowing any suggestion that it would be impossible for the school to justify its stance over its uniform policy, had indicated that Denbigh High School had gone about its decision in an impermissible way. It should have asked itself primarily a series of questions—what Lord Hoffmann described as an examination paper with questions, for example about whether the pupil had established an infringement of her Article 9 right or whether the school could establish any justification for its policy. (Lord Hoffmann offered the opinion that the Court of Appeal would have failed the examination in giving the wrong answer, at least to the alternative question.) Since the school had distinctly not approached its decision-making in that way, it had wrongfully excluded her from school, although the majority of the Law Lords considered that there had been no 'exclusion' since that was an educational term of art, referable to the school's disciplinary powers.

How did it come about that the intermediate appellate court got a basic question of Convention law so wrong? The answer simply is that the Court of Appeal failed to appreciate that 'the focus of Strasbourg is not and never has been whether a challenged decision or action is the product of a defective decision making process [a procedural question only for the domestic law of a member state] but on whether in a case under consideration, the applicant's Convention rights had been violated.' The Human Rights Act 1998 has amply catered for that pragmatic approach by providing that unlawfulness arises from a public authority acting in a manner incompatible with a Convention right; there was no requirement to search for a defective process of reasoning by the public authority.

Lord Bingham of Cornhill noted that the Court of Appeal—Lords Justices Brooke, Mummery, and Scott-Baker—had mistakenly approached the legal challenge before them: '[But] the House has been referred to no case in which the Strasbourg Court has found the violation of a Convention right on the strength of failure by a national authority to follow the sort of reasoning process [the questions] laid down by the Court of Appeal.' As one academic critic of the Court of Appeal's decision put it: that approach injected a 'new formalism' into human rights cases that would be a 'recipe for judicialisation on an unprecedented scale.' Public administrators would not only have to observe 'the Judge over Your Shoulder' but also become 'the Judge in Your Head'.[12]

The Secretary of State for Education and Skills, who intervened in the final appeal, was amply justified in describing the Court of Appeal's decision as 'a fundamental misunderstanding of the Human Rights Act.' Judicial orthodoxy in human rights has been restored—even to an atheist commentator. Thank God for the House of Lords.

---

[12] See Thomas Poole, 'Of headscarves and heresies: the Denbigh High School case and public authority decision-making under the Human Rights Act' [2005] *Public Law* 685, at 691–95.

12

The Court in the Twenty-first Century—Some Reflections

S INCE THE 1980s, if not before, the machinery of justice in Britain has been undergoing a period of near-revolutionary change and the Court of Appeal has been at the vortex of that change. The purpose of this book has been to take stock of the changing role and operation of the Court in the years spanning the turn of the century. We have not made—nor did we expect to make—startling discoveries that might have enabled us to round off this book with a dramatic denouement in the last few pages, in the manner of detective fiction. But although we do not seek to offer a definitive 'conclusion' it seems appropriate to end this study with an overview, rather in the nature of an executive summary, of some of our findings, along with some reflections and suggestions.

One major aspect of 'change' has been the 'new public management' reforms that began in the Thatcher era and have now embraced courts and tribunals at every level of the judicial system. The Thatcherite watchwords of efficiency, effectiveness, and economy, monitored through increasingly extensive and rigorous measurement of performance, have become an established feature of the judicial landscape. The courts have been required to pay much more attention to tests of customer satisfaction, user-friendliness and transparency than their predecessors ever did. Information and communication technology has come to play an increasingly important part in the management of court business and, to some extent, in the judicial process itself. The spectacle of judges using laptops inside and outside the courtroom is, if not yet quite universal, no longer a matter worthy of surprise or comment.

The most notable landmark in the extension of the management revolution to the courts was the review of civil justice conducted in the 1990s by Lord Woolf, complemented by Sir Jeffrey Bowman's subsequent review of the Court of Appeal. The manifest significance of these important exercises, discussed extensively in earlier chapters of this book, played a significant part in prompting us to undertake the present study. One change that they have brought about has been to require judges to become proactive case managers, no longer leaving it to litigants and their legal representatives to dictate the pace at which business flows through the courts. As we have noted in chapter six and elsewhere, this change, along with improved bureaucratic and technical support, has resulted in a marked improvement in throughput times and a sharp reduction in the worrying and growing backlog of cases that prompted the Woolf-Bowman inquiries.

But perhaps the most significant development in this context has been the introduction of the requirement of permission to appeal (PTA) to the Court of Appeal, as described in chapter five and whose impact and significance is discussed in several other chapters. For the first time, access to the main appeal court in the United Kingdom in substantive[1] civil appeals has been made subject to a rigorous judicial filter. This has had the important positive effect of excluding unmeritorious and time-wasting appeals and of giving the Court some real control over its own docket. The downside is that a lot of judicial time is now spent considering applications for permission—some of them unmeritorious and time-wasting. There is, moreover, a significant qualitative difference between deploying senior judges to act as gatekeepers and deploying them in their mainstream judicial roles of hearing full appeals or writing judgments.

The time-wasting factor is particularly relevant with regard to many of the applications submitted by unrepresented applicants, some of whom are very reluctant to take no for an answer. As noted in chapter five, the Court has moved towards quicker and tougher procedures for disposing of applications that are 'totally without merit'—and in chapter nine we have suggested the more radical possibility of requiring all PTA applicants to be legally represented.

Some of the increased expedition and time-saving achieved by the introduction of the PTA filter, coupled with the new judicial case management arrangements, must be offset against the consumption of judicial time needed to discharge these functions. And the logistics of managing the deployment of 37 Lords Justices (and, in some appellate contexts, puisne judges too), not just in the Civil Division but also in the Criminal Division and the Administrative Court, present considerable challenges. One important proposed administrative change that was announced while this book in preparation was the merger of the top administrative posts of Head of the Civil Appeals Office and Registrar of Criminal Appeals.[2] The present study has been concerned, first and foremost, with civil appeals, but we have taken sidelong glances along the way at the criminal jurisdiction—not least because the same Lords Justices sit in both divisions of the Court of Appeal. We have wondered, in the course of conducting this study, whether the time might be ripe—and the administrative rationalisation just mentioned might provide a focus for considering

---

[1] Interlocutory appeals were already subject to a leave to appeal requirement.
[2] See ch 4, n 15,

this—for achieving a greater convergence between the working practices of the two divisions.

We believe, in particular, that the statutory provision in the Criminal Division providing for only a single judgment (except on a point of law and with permission of the presiding judge)[3] seems an oddity in the twenty-first century. Other than in appeals against sentence, there is no more compelling reason for a unified judicial voice in criminal as in civil law, particularly now that the Court of Appeal in its Civil Division is resorting more frequently to composite judgments (in which all the sitting Lords Justices contribute to the reasoned decision) but contemplating separate assenting and dissenting judgments, where appropriate. It may be noted that no distinction is made between the treatment of criminal and civil appeals at the highest level of the House of Lords (where composite judgments are rare).

Nowadays, the 'rights' of appeal of convicted persons and aspiring appellants in the civil jurisdiction have in effect been assimilated: both require permission (or leave, in Anglo-Saxon terminology) to appeal. Certification of a point of law of public importance as a prerequisite for leave to appeal to the House of Lords in criminal cases is comparable to the Civil Division's practice of rarely exercising its discretion to grant leave at all, leaving it to the Law Lords themselves to decide on their judicial menu (see chapter ten). Moving towards a more uniform system of appeals seems sensible.

While 'new public management' reforms have been an important ingredient in the present study, so too have the extensive but piecemeal constitutional reforms that have been taking place since the late 1990s, under the Blair administration. Two aspects of this agenda have been of particular relevance to our present work: first, the cluster of reforms culminating in the enactment of the Constitutional Reform Act 2005—the transfer of many of the Lord Chancellor's former judicial functions to the senior judiciary, the transformation of his department into a new Department for Constitutional Affairs, and the decision to transfer the judicial functions of the House of Lords to a new Supreme Court, scheduled (at the time of writing) to come into operation in 2009; and secondly, the enactment of the Human Rights Act 1998, which, from October 2000, rendered the provisions of the European Convention on Human Rights directly applicable in trials and appeals by the UK courts.

The latter development has had a significant impact on the work of all UK courts and tribunals, including the Court of Appeal, although not quite the transformative effect that some commentators—in some cases optimistically, in others pessimistically—predicted. All aspects of the administration of justice are nowadays conducted in the shadow of the European Convention (particularly Article 6); the judges have acquired an additional

---

[3] Supreme Court Act 1981, s 59.

string to their jurisprudential bows, particularly in judicial review proceedings. But the 1998 Act has also led to some interesting tensions in the relationship between Parliament, the executive, and the judiciary, particularly in the context of adjudications relating to—and often striking down—various of the government's anti-terrorist measures, brought in after the 9/11 atrocities. At the time of writing, there has been a spate of parliamentary and ministerial sniping at the Act—much of it tabloid-driven, ill-informed, and/or disingenuous. The fact is that the substantive law relating to human rights has not been changed significantly by the statutory incorporation into domestic law of an international convention to which the United Kingdom was already fully committed.

One intriguing phenomenon, related to this, and highlighted in chapter ten, concerns the relationship between the Court of Appeal and the House of Lords. Back in the 1950s and 1960s—before the major recent changes in the procedures and remedies of judicial review, and long before the Human Rights Act—the House of Lords dealt with very few cases in the fields of administrative and constitutional law. Now such cases (including human rights appeals) constitute nearly 40 per cent of its appellate caseload. What is more, it has frequently and regularly overturned the Court of Appeal in such cases, and has often deployed panels larger than the customary five Law Lords to do so: we have discussed some particularly graphic and high-profile examples of this in chapter eleven. The political sniping, mentioned above, has been directed very largely (although by no means exclusively) at the House of Lords—soon to be transformed into the Supreme Court.

We have noted, incidentally, that the Court of Appeal hardly ever grants leave to appeal to the House of Lords, deferring to their Lordships' prerogative in controlling their own docket. It may be that, with the establishment of the Supreme Court now (barring accidents) imminent, the time is ripe to remove the theoretical possibility of obtaining leave from the Court of Appeal and explicitly transfer the entire responsibility to the Appeal Committees of the House of Lords, and its successor.

At various points in this book (see, in particular, chapter two) we have revisited the conceptual distinction—which lay at the heart of our previous work in *Final Appeal*—between the different but complementary appellate functions of 'supervision' and 'review'. We still consider the distinction to be important and heuristically useful—but in practical terms it cannot be used to draw a clear distinction between the respective functions of the Court of Appeal and the House of Lords. Both courts exercise a mixture of these functions—and if the House of Lords still exercises the lion's share of 'supervision' it certainly does not enjoy the monopoly.

Given that the caseload of the Civil Division of the Court of Appeal is so much greater than that of the House of Lords, and that very few appeals are allowed to progress from the Court to the Appellate Committee, the former has become, to all intents and purposes, the final appellate court for non-public law cases. It would be only a slight exaggeration to say that, whatever the formal organisation chart of the courts hierarchy may suggest, there are now, in effect, two 'final' courts of appeal. (Indeed, given the post-Woolf restrictions on second appeals, there may be more than two, given that a lot of appeals from inferior tribunals go no further than the High Court.)

In the 1870s, while the fate of the judicial functions of the House of Lords hung in the balance, the Court of Appeal was established at the top tier of a 'Supreme Court'. Now the same terminology has been adopted again, as the title of the successor body to the House of Lords in its judicial capacity. The new Supreme Court of the United Kingdom can never, under present constitutional circumstances, replicate the functions of its US namesake. However, the very use of the term 'Supreme Court' has a powerful constitutional resonance, and the recent development of such a strong public law and human rights jurisprudence in the House of Lords promises to get the new Court off to an interesting start. But the Court of Appeal will remain firmly in place, occupying its crucial position as, to all intents and purposes, the court of last resort—indeed, a supreme court—for most civil appellants.

Bibliography

ALLEN, C (Sir), *Law in the Making,* 7th edn (Oxford, Oxford University Press, 1964).

ANDREWS, N, *Principles of Civil Procedure* (London, Sweet & Maxwell, 1994).

ASQUITH, Lord Justice, 'Some Aspects of the Work of the Court of Appeal' [1950] *Journal of the Society of Public Teachers of Law* 350.

BAGEHOT, W, *The English Constitution* (London, Fontana Library, 1963).

BINGHAM, T, 'The Judge as Juror: The Judicial Determination of Factual Issues' (1985) 38 *Current Legal Problems* 1.

BIRKENHEAD, Lord, *Points of View,* vol 1 (London, Hodder and Stoughton, 1922).

BLAKE, C, 'Modernising Civil Justice in England and Wales' in M FABRI and P LANGBROEK (eds), *The Challenge of Change for Judicial Systems* (Amsterdam, IOS Press, 2000).

BLAKE, C and Drewry, G, 'The Role of the Court of Appeal in England and Wales as an Intermediate Court' in A Le Sueur (ed), *Building the UK's New Supreme Court* (Oxford, Oxford University Press, 2004).

BLOM-COOPER, L, 'Judges Among the Literati', Howard Lecture, 2002.

BLOM-COOPER, L and DREWRY, G, *Final Appeal. A Study of the House of Lords in its Judicial Capacity* (Oxford, Clarendon Press, 1972).

BLOM-COOPER, L and DREWRY, G, 'The Appellate Function' in B DICKSON and P CARMICHAEL (eds), *The House of Lords: Its Parliamentary and Judicial Roles* (Oxford, Hart Publishing, 1998).

BOWEN, Lord Justice, 'The Law Courts under the Judicature Acts' (1886) 5 *LQR* 1.

BRADNEY, A, 'The Changing Face of the House of Lords' [1958] *Juridical Review* 178.

BROOKE, Lord Justice, 'Behind the Times? IT in the Court of Appeal' [2004] *NLJ,* 5 March, pp 331–32.

BROWNE-WILKINSON, N, 'The Independence of the Judiciary in the 1980s' [1988] *Public Law* 44.

COHEN, Lord Justice, 'Jurisdiction, Practice and Procedure of the Court of Appeal' (1951) 11 *CLJ* 3.

Court of Appeal, Civil Division, The: Review of the Legal Year, annual publication, available at www.hmcourts-service.gov.uk/cms/1302.htm.

Crook, JA, *Legal Advocacy in the Roman World* (London, Duckworth, 1995).

Cross, R (Sir), *Evidence,* 4th edn (London, Butterworths, 1974).

Denning, Lord, *The Security Service and Mr Profumo,* Cmnd 2152 (1963).

Department for Constitutional Affairs, *Constitutional Reform: A Supreme Court for the United Kingdom,* Consultation paper (London, Department for Constitutional Affairs, July 2003).

DICKSON, B, 'The Lords of Appeal and their Work 1967–96' in B DICKSON and P CARMICHAEL (eds), *The House of Lords: Its Parliamentary and Judicial Roles* (Oxford, Hart Publishing, 1999).

DREWRY, G, 'Leapfrogging—and a Lords Justices' Eye View of the Final Appeal' (1973) 89 *LQR* 260.

DREWRY, G, 'Public–Private Partnerships: Rethinking the Boundary between Public and Private Law' in SP OSBORNE (ed), *Public–Private Partnerships: Theory and Practice in International Perspective* (London, Routledge, 2000).

DREWRY, G, 'The Complementarity of Audit and Judicial Review: The "Homes for Votes" Scandal in the UK' (2005) 71(3) *International Review of Administrative Sciences* 375–89.

ENSOR, RCK, *Courts and Judges in France, Germany and England* (London, Oxford University Press, 1933).

EVERSHED, Lord, *The Court of Appeal in England* (London, Athlone Press, 1950).

EVERSHED Committee, *Final report of the Committee on Supreme Court Practice and Procedure*, Cmd 8878 (1953).

FLYNN, N, *Public Sector Management*, 4th edn (Harlow, Financial Times/Prentice Hall, 2002).

FRANKFURTER, F, *Of Law and Men: Papers and Addresses of Felix Frankfurter*, edited by P ELMAN (Hamden, CN, Archon Books, 1956).

GENN, H and GRAY, LA, *Court of Appeal Permission to Appeal Shadow Exercise* (London, University College London, March 2005), available at http://www.hmcourts-service.gov.uk/cms/files/PTAFinalReportMarch20051.pdf.

GLADWELL, D, 'Alternative Dispute Resolution and the Courts' [2004] *Civil Court News* 27.

GLEESON, MURRAY, CJ (Australia), 'State of the Judicature' (2003) 77 *Australian Law Journal* 505.

HALE of RICHMOND, BARONESS, 'The Quest for Equal Treatment' [2005] *Public Law* 571–85.

HANWORTH Committee, *Second Interim Report of the Business of Courts Committee*, Cmd 4471 (HMSO, 1934).

HERBERT, AP, *Wigs at Work* (Harmondsworth, Penguin, 1966).

HOOD, C, 'A Public Management for All Seasons' (1991) 69(1) *Public Administration* 3–20.

HORTON, S and FARNHAM, D (eds), *Public Management in Britain* (Basingstoke, Palgrave Macmillan, 1999).

HOSKEN, A, *Nothing Like a Dame: The Scandals of Shirley Porter* (London, Granta, 2006).

House of Commons Select Committee on Public Administration, *The Second Chamber: Continuing the Reform*, HC 494 (February 2002).

House of Lords Library Note, *The Appellate Jurisdiction of the House of Lords*, LLN 2003/007.

HUGHES, O, *Public Management and Administration*, 3rd edn (Basingstoke, Palgrave Macmillan, 2003).

JACOB, J (Sir), *The Fabric of English Civil Justice* (London, Stevens, 1987).

JACOB, JM, 'The Bowman Review of the Court of Appeal' (1998) 61 *MLR* 390.

Joint Committee on the House of Lords Reform, *First Report*, HL 17, HC 171, 2002–03.

Joint Committee on the House of Lords Reform, *Second Report*, , HL 97, HC 668, 2002–03.

JOLOWICZ, JA, *On Civil Procedure* (Cambridge, Cambridge University Press, 2000).

JOWELL, JL and McAuslan, PWB (eds), *Lord Denning: The Judge and the Law* (London, Sweet & Maxwell, 1984).

Judicature Commission, *Second Report* (HMSO, 1871), C 631.

Judicial Statistics, annual publication (Directorate of Judicial Offices for England and Wales), available at http://judiciary.gov.uk.

JUSTICE, *The Administration of the Courts* (London, JUSTICE, 1986).

KARLEN, D, 'Appeals in England and the United States' (1962) 78 *LQR* 371.

KARLEN, D, *Appellate Courts in the United States and in England* (New York, New York University Press, 1963).

KERR, M, *As Far as I Remember* (Oxford, Hart Publishing, 2006).

LE SUEUR, A, 'New Labour's Next (surprisingly quick) Steps in Constitutional Reform' [2003] *Public Law* 368–77.

MCKAY, W (Sir) *et al* (eds), *Erskine May's Treatise on the Law, Privileges, Proceedings and Usage of Parliament*, 23rd edn (London, LexisNexis, 2004).

MCLEAN, I, *The House of Lords—Completing the Reform*, Cm 5291 (2001).

MASTERMAN, R, 'A Supreme Court for the United Kingdom: Two Steps Forward, But One Step Back on Judicial Independence' [2004] *Public Law* 48–58.

MEAGHER, R and FIELDHOUSE, S, *Portraits on Yellow Paper* (Rockhampton, Australia, Central Queensland University Press, 2004).

MUNDAY, R, 'All for One and One for All' [2002] *CLJ* 321.

MUNDAY, R, 'Judicial Configurations' [2002] *CLJ* 612.

MURPHY, WT and RAWLINGS, R, 'After the Ancien Regime: The Writing of Judgments in the House of Lords, 1979–80' (1981) 44 *MLR* 617 and (1982) 45 *MLR* 34.

OLIVER, D and DREWRY, G, *Public Service Reforms: Issues of Accountability and Public Law* (London, Pinter, 1996).

OTTON, LORD, *Interim Report of the Working Party Established by the Judges' Council into Litigants in Person in the Royal Courts of Justice* (June 1995).

PATERSON, A, *The Law Lords* (Basingstoke, Macmillan, 1982).

PATTENDEN, R, *English Criminal Appeals 1844–1994* (Oxford, Oxford University Press, 1996).

PETERS, BG and SAVOIE, DJ (eds), *Taking Stock: Assessing Public Sector Reforms* (Montreal, Canadian Centre for Management Development and the McGill-Queen's University Press, 1998).

PLOTNIKOFF, J and WOOLFSON, R, *Evaluation of the Impact of the Reforms in the Court of Appeal (Civil Division),* for the Lord Chancellor's Department, November 2002 (www.dca.gov.uk).

POLLITT, C, *Managerialism and the Public Services*, 2nd edn (Oxford, Blackwell, 1993).

POOLE, T, 'Of Headscarves and Heresies: The Denbeigh High School Case and Public Authority Decision-making under the Human Rights Act' [2005] *Public Law* 685.

POST, R, 'The Supreme Court Opinion as Institutional Practice: Dissent, Legal Scholarship and Decisionmaking in the Taft Court', *Boalt Working Papers in Public Law*, University of California at Berkeley, Berkeley, CA, 1 June 2001 (http://repositories.cdlib.org/boaltwp/105).

PRATT, WF, 'Rhetorical Styles on the Fuller Court' (1980) 24(3) *American Journal of Legal History* 189–220.

ROBERTSON, D, *Judicial Discretion in the House of Lords* (Oxford, Clarendon Press, 1999).

RYAN, D and BRIDEN, J, *Review of the Administrative Functions at the Royal Courts of Justice*, May 2006 (unpublished).

SALZBERGER, E, 'A Positive Analysis of the Doctrine of Separation of Powers, or: Why do we have an Independent Judiciary?' (1993) 13 *International Review of Law and Economics* 349–79.

SALZBERGER, E and FENN, P, 'Judicial Independence: Some Evidence from the English Court of Appeal' (1999) xlii(2) *Journal of Law and Economics* 831–47.

SHETREET, S, *Judges on Trial* (Amsterdam, North-Holland Publishing Company, 1996).

SIMPSON, AWB, 'Lord Denning as Jurist' in J Jowell and P McAuslan (eds), *Lord Denning: The Judge and the Law* (London, Sweet & Maxwell, 1984).

STEVENS, R, *Law and Politics. The House of Lords as a Judicial Body, 1800–1976* (London, Weidenfeld and Nicolson, 1979).

STEWART, J and WALSH, K, 'Change in the Management of Public Services' (1992) 70(4) *Public Administration* 499–518.

VENNE, R, DI MAMBRO, D, SANDS, P, DI MAMBRO, L and JOSEPH, I, *Manual of Civil Appeals* (London, Butterworths, 2000).

Wakeham Commission, *A House for the Future*, Report of the Royal Commission on the Reform of the House of Lords, Cm 4534 (London, The Stationery Office, 2000)

WOOLF, LORD, *Access to Justice: Interim Report to the Lord Chancellor on the Civil Justice System in England and Wales* (London, Lord Chancellor's Department, July 1995)

WOOLF, LORD, *Access to Justice: Final Report* (London, Lord Chancellor's Department, September 1996)

ZIFCAK, S, *New Managerialism: Administrative Reform in Whitehall and Canberra* (Buckingham, Open University Press, 1994).

1832 Tract: *Some Observations on the Necessity of Reforming the Judicial House of Lords, considered as the Court of Ultimate Appeal in the Administration of Civil Justice.*

Index

Administrative and constitutional law
  increased caseload 184
Alternative dispute resolution 76–8
Appeal
  civil
  rationale 20–22
  differing expectations 14
  feudal system, and 15
  hearing of. *See* Hearing of appeals
  historical perspective 15–16
    limited procedure 16
    supervisory role 16
  justifications for 21–22
  King, and 15
  meaning 13–14
  'rehearing' 22
  'review' 22
  review and supervision
    distinguished 21
  species 16–20
  three basic elements 13–14
  trial process, and 22–30
Appeals in the abstract 147–8
Appellate approach
  Tanfern direction 60–61
Arden, Lady Justice 118
Asquith, Lord 41–2
  extempore judgments, on 42
  general theory of appellate
    process 41
  law reports, on 42
  overseas jurisdictions, on 42
Auld, Lord Justice 115–16

Bench memorandum access to 93
Blake, Charles
  judges as case managers, on 61–2
Bowen, Lord Justice comments on
  Court of Appeal 45–6
Bowman Report 4, 5, 8, 47, 55–7, 65,
  67, 76, 135, 145, 156, 181

conclusions 56–7
implementation 58–61
recommendations 56–7
summary 56–7
terms of reference 56
Brooke, Lord Justice 115
Browne–Wilkinson, Lord
  judicial independence, on 52
Buxton, Lord Justice 117

Carnwath, Lord Justice 119
Case management
  appeals about, restrictions on 73
Case stated 17–18
Cassation 19–20
  appeal, relationship to 19
  Jolowicz on 19–20
  role of 19–20
CEDR Solve 77–8
Certiorari 18
Chadwick, Lord Justice 117
Civil Appeals Office 100–04
  appeals pack 101
  bundles 102
  lodging of application 100–01
  separation of cases by subject
    matter 102–4
Civil Justice Review *see* Woolf Reforms
Clarke, Sir Anthony 114
Cohen, Lord Justice 43
  written arguments, on 43
Constitutional reforms 183
Costs
  mediation, and 76–7
Court of Appeal
  academic investigation 2–3
  Civil Procedure Rules, and 4–5
  collegiality 29–30
  creation 31
  development 31–46
    academic lawyers, and 37–8

Administration of Justice
(Appeals) Act 1934 35
Bowen, Lord Justice on 45–6
Cohen, Lord Justice on 43
Evershed Committee 35–6
Hansworth Committee 35
House of Lords, and 32
Imperial Court of Appeal
32–3
Lord Asquith 41–2
Lord Evershed on 39–41
moves towards modernisation
37–9
position before 1875 31–4
pre-reading 38
premises 34
RCK Ensor on 33–4
Registrar 38–9
reorganisation in nineteenth
century 33
rights of appeal 34–7
'Supreme Court' 31–2
Woolf Reforms 43–5. *See also*
Woolf Reforms
Lord Denning, and 3
management reforms 4–5
manpower 1
nature of 3–4
origins 31–46
pinnacle of hierarchy of judicial
bodies, as 1
recent membership 6

Denning, Lord 106–8
influence of 3
selection of appeals 108
Department for Constitutional Affairs
6, 53–4, 63–4, 102, 137,155
Determination on papers
statistics, of 96–7
Directorate of Judicial Offices 54
Donaldson, Lord 108–9
Dyson, Lord Justice 118

Ensor, RCK
Court of Appeal, on 33–4
Error of law
scope of jurisdiction 81–2

European Convention on Human
Rights
influence of 183–4
Evershed Committee 35–6
Bar, and 37
cost of litigation, on 35–6
county courts, on 37
'leapfrog' appeal, on 36–7
reduction of multiplicity of appeals,
on 36
Evershed, Lord 107
lecture 1950 39–41
further reform, need for 40
leapfrog system, on 40–41
modernisation, need for 39
nature of rehearing, on 40
reserved judgments, on 40
two or three appeals, need
for 40

Gage, Lord Justice 120
Greene, Lord 107

Hailsham, Lord
judicial independence, and 50
Hallett, Lady Justice 121
Hanworth Committee 35
Hearing of appeals 23–30
adjudication, art of 24
blind persons, and 26
conclusions of trial judge,
and 26–7, 28
function of trial judge, and 29
inference-drawing 27–8
Lord Hoffman, on 28
orality, system of 24–5
'rehearing' 23
'review' 23–4, 26–7
witnesses, demeanour of 25–6
Hoffman, Lord
hearing of appeals, on 28
Hooper, Lord Justice 120
House of Lords 143–58
academic investigations 2–3
appealing to 148–150
appeals in abstract 147–8
argument for retention of judicial
functions 157–8

dialogue with Court of Appeal 157
Erskine May 156–7
final Court of Appeal in Parliament
    153–8
Lane v Esdaile, rule in 151–2
'leapfrog' appeals 152–3
leave to appeal to 148–50
media spotlight 147
petitions for leave
    orally argued, near-extinction of
        150–53
proposed Supreme Court, and 155–6
Revenue appeals 146–7
reversal by. *See* Reversal by Lords
review 145–7
statistics 144–5
status of 154
supervision 145–7
treatment of cases passing to 6
Wakeham Commission 154
Hughes, Lord Justice 121
Human Rights Act 1998 5, 7, 142,
    167–8, 176–7, 183, 184
statistics 90

Jacob, Lord Justice 119
Jolowicz, JA
    cassation, on 19–20
Judge, Lord Justice 114
Judges 105–21
    appointment 111–13
    current judicial strength 109–11
    promotion, absence of 112
    remuneration 112
Judges as case managers 61–6
    Charles Blake on 61–2
    Civil Appeals Office, and 64
    DCA Public Service Agreement
        2004 63
    impact of Woolf-Bowman reforms 65
    Moses, Lord Justice on 62
    potential tensions between judicial
        and managerial priorities 65
    supervising Lords Justices
        relationship with Civil Appeals
            Office 64
    Woolf-Bowman reforms, impact
        of 63

Judgments 123–31
    application of law 130–31
    clarity, need for 131
    collegiality 123–6
    composite 126–9
    shift towards 124
    conciseness, need for 131
    court procedure, and 125
    division of labour, and 125
    function of appellate court, and
        127–8
    functions of trial judges, and 130
    individuality 123–6
    multiple 126–9
    primacy of oral argument 124–5, 126
    prolixity 129–31
    single 126–9
    specialist judges 128–9

Kay, Lord Justice Maurice 120
Keene, Lord Justice 118

Latham, Lord Justice 115
Laws, Lord Justice 117
Leveson, Lord Justice 121
Litigants in person 133–42
    abolition of right to oral hearing
        in seeking permission to appeal
        140–142
        Australia 141–2
        case for 140–42
    awareness of rights 139
    Bowman Report 135
    common law 133
    confusion 139
    cost 136–7
    disadvantages 133–4
    litigant's view 138–9
    McKenzie friend 134, 139
    Otton Report 1995 134–5
    paper application for PTA 137
    psychology of 138
    statistics 93, 137–8
    statutory provision 133
    Taylor v Lawrence effect 140
Lloyd, Lord Justice 120
Longmore, Lord Justice 118
Lord Chancellor's Department 53

Mandamus 18
Master of the Rolls 105–9, 113
   Lord Denning 106–8
   Lord Donaldson 108–9
   Lord Evershed 107
   Lord Greene 107
   role of 105–6
May, Lord Justice 117
McKay, Lord
   consultation papers 51
Mediation 76–8
   Court of Appeal, in 77–8
   CEDR Solve 77–8
   costs, and 76–7
Methodology 6–8
Moore-Bick, Lord Justice 120
Morritt, Lord Justice 114–15
Moses, Lord Justice 121
   judges as case managers, on 62
Mummery, Lord Justice 116

Nature of appellate process 13–30
   factors affecting 14
New public management 48–52
   courts, and 52–54
   Department for Constitutional
      Affairs 53–4
   Directorate of Judicial Offices 54
   influence of 181
   Lord Chancellor, and 54
   Lord Chancellor's Department 53
   Next Steps 49
   radical nature and extent of 48
   Registrar of Civil Appeals 52–3
Neuberger, Lord Justice 120
Next Steps 49

Oral hearings
   statistics 96–7
   time taken at 98
Outcome of appeal 81–2

Parker, Lord Justice 118
Permission to appeal 69–71, 182–3
   consumption of judicial time,
      and 182
   DCA consultation paper 2005 74–6
   dealing with application 69–71

discretion, and 73
filter 5
initial application to lower court 69
introduction of requirement 182
oral hearing 70
procedure in practice 84–90
'real prospect of success' 70–71
reform of 74–6
refusal on paper 70
requirement for 69
research exercise 75
review or rehearing after grant,
   whether 78–81
     CPR rule 52.11 79–80
     distinction between review and
       appeal 79
     form of rehearing 80–81
   'some other compelling reason'
     70–71
statistics. *See* Statistics
Tanfern direction 58–9
time-saving 182
Phillips of Worth Maltravers, Lord 114
Pill, Lord Justice 116
Potter, Lord Justice 114
Prerogative orders 18–19
   feudal system, and 18–19
Privy Council 15
Prohibition 18

Registrar of Civil Appeals 52–3
Rehearing 17
Research agenda 5–6
Researchers' aide-memoire 10–11
   full listing 10–11
   general function of Court 10
   leave to appeal to House of Lords 11
   permission stage 10
Reversal by Lords 159–79
   Begum 176–79
     Article 9, European Convention
       on Human Rights 178–9
     facts 177
   Dame Shirley Porter case 162–9
     adversarial process, and 168–9
     auditor, role of 167
     conclusions of House of Lords
      166–9

facts 162–5
Human Rights Act 1998 167–8
political corruption 167
Polanski v Vanity Fair 159–62
VCF order 160–62
Roma at Prague Airport 169–76
arguments based on broad
intellectual concepts 176
asylum seekers, and 169–70
discrimination 170–73
immigration controls 169–70
international law issues 174–6
judgments of Lords 173–6
Richards, Sir Stephen 121
Right of appeal 67–82. *See also*
Permission to appeal
case management 73
new procedure in outline 67–9
procedure 67–9
second appeals. *See* Second appeals
specialist tribunals 74
Tanfield 68–9
Rix, Lord Justice 118
Rose, Lord Justice 115

Scott Baker, Lord Justice 119
Second appeals 71–3
measures limiting 71
reasons for 71–2
security for costs 72–3
Tanfern direction 59–60
Sedley, Lord Justice 117
Single judgment
provision for 183
Smith, Lady Justice 119
Specialist tribunals
permission to appeal from 74
Statistics 83–104
appeals set down for year ending
September 2001/02 to 2004/05 85
applications for permission to
appeal 2000/01 to 2004/05 87
applications set down for year
ending September 2001/02 to
2004/05 86
determination on paper 96–7
final appeals set down and disposed
of 1999–2004 84
Human Rights Act 1998 90
method of disposal of permission to
appeal applications
1999/2000 to 2004/05 87
oral hearings 96–7
outcome of application 99–100
permission to appeal applications
county courts 89
court where application made
91–2
courts below 88–90
judicial time taken to hear 97–9
jurisdiction 92
litigants in person 93
procedural errors, and 91
represented clients 93
subject areas 89–90
tribunals 89
progression of applications 88
progression of permission to appeal
applications 88
success rate 99–100
throughput of appeals 1997/98 to
2004/05 87
time for applications to be processed 94–5
alternative dispute resolution,
and 95
delay 94–5
dismissal of application, and 94–5
Supervising Lords Justice
role of 64–5
Supreme Court
prospective establishment of 4
significance of use of term 185

Tanfern direction 58–61
appellate approach 60–61
permission to appeal 58–9
second appeals 59–60
Thatcherism 48–52
judiciary, and 49–52
Civil Justice Review 50–51
Justice, and 49–50
Lord Browne-Wilkinson 52
Lord Hailsham 50
Lord McKay 51
new public management, and 48–52

Thomas, Lord Justice 119
Thorpe, Lord Justice 116
Time for applications to be processed
    statistics. *See* Statistics
Tuckey, Lord Justice 117

Unrepresented applicants 133–42. *See
    also* Litigants in person

Wall, Lord Justice 119
Waller, Lord Justice 116
Ward, Lord Justice 116
Witnesses
    demeanour 25–6

Woolf Reforms 43–5, 54–5
    Access to Justice 43
    case management 44–5
        procedural decisions 44
        substantive decisions 44
    hearing of appeals 45
    implementation 58–61
    judges as proactive case
        managers 55
    object of 55
    problems of civil litigation 43
    right of appeal 44
    significance of 181–2
Writ of error 16–17